Greek Tragedy and the Middle East

Classical Diaspora

Series editors: Sarah Annes Brown & Katherine Harloe

This series enriches classical reception studies both by examining the ways in which different nations and peoples relate to classical antiquity and also by studying how classics as a discipline is a product of diaspora. Classical Diaspora addresses issues of national and ethnic identity within classical studies, reflecting the classical world's complex and diverse legacy in fields such as education, government, technology, literature, painting, cinema, philosophy and empire building. By examining classical receptions, often as one among a range of cultural engagements, the series engages with the ways in which classical antiquity has functioned as a point of inspiration, contestation or provocation for framing of community identities. Focusing on reception within specific cultural or geographic modes, individual volumes interrogate scholarly notions of how the classical canon was formed and modified within these contexts, framing classical antiquity as an idea developed through diasporic reception.

Greek Tragedy and the Middle East

Chasing the Myth

Edited by Pauline Donizeau,
Yassaman Khajehi and Daniela Potenza

BLOOMSBURY ACADEMIC
LONDON • NEW YORK • OXFORD • NEW DELHI • SYDNEY

BLOOMSBURY ACADEMIC
Bloomsbury Publishing Plc, 50 Bedford Square, London, WC1B 3DP, UK
Bloomsbury Publishing Inc, 1359 Broadway, 12th Floor, New York, NY 10018, USA
Bloomsbury Publishing Ireland, 29 Earlsfort Terrace, Dublin 2, D02 AY28, Ireland

BLOOMSBURY, BLOOMSBURY ACADEMIC and the Diana logo
are trademarks of Bloomsbury Publishing Plc

First published in Great Britain 2024
This paperback edition published 2025

Cover image: *Medea*, Fanous Art & Culture House (2016), directed by Neda Shahrokhi &
Yassaman Khajehi, photo by Mona Moghadam

A catalogue record for this book is available from the British Library.

Library of Congress Cataloging-in-Publication Data
Names: Donizeau, Pauline, editor, author. | Khajehi, Yassaman, editor, author. |
Potenza, Daniela, editor, author.
Title: Greek tragedy and the Middle East : chasing the myth / [edited by] Pauline Donizeau,
Yassaman Khajehi, and Daniela Potenza.
Description: London ; New York : Bloomsbury Academic, 2024. |
Series: Classical diaspora; vol. 4 | Includes bibliographical references and index.
Identifiers: LCCN 2023052721 (print) | LCCN 2023052722 (ebook) |
ISBN 9781350355699 (hardback) | ISBN 9781350355736 (paperback) |
ISBN 9781350355705 (pdf) | ISBN 9781350355712 (ebook)
Subjects: LCSH: Greek drama (Tragedy)–Appreciation–Middle East. | Greek drama
(Tragedy–Adaptations. | Greek drama–Modern presentation. | Theater–Middle East–History–
20th century. | Theater–Middle East–History–21st century.
Classification: LCC PA3238 .G747 2024 (print) | LCC PA3238 (ebook) |
DDC 882.009/56—dc23/eng/20240108
LC record available at https://lccn.loc.gov/2023052721
LC ebook record available at https://lccn.loc.gov/2023052722

ISBN: HB: 978-1-3503-5569-9
PB: 978-1-3503-5573-6
ePDF: 978-1-3503-5570-5
eBook: 978-1-3503-5571-2

Series: Classical Diaspora

Typeset by RefineCatch Limited, Bungay, Suffolk

For product safety related questions contact productsafety@bloomsbury.com.

To find out more about our authors and books visit www.bloomsbury.com
and sign up for our newsletters.

Contents

Illustrations

Contributors

Marvin Carlson is Professor Emeritus from the Graduate Center of the City University of New York, has been awarded the ATHE Career Achievement Award, the George Jean Nathan Prize, the Bernard Hewitt prize, the George Freedley Award and a Guggenheim Fellowship. He has been a Walker-Ames Professor at the University of Washington, a fellow of the Institute for Advanced Studies at Indiana University, a visiting professor at the Freie Universität of Berlin, and a fellow of the American Theatre. In 2005 he was awarded an honorary doctorate by the University of Athens and in 2022 was named a fellow of the American Academy of Arts and Sciences. His best-known book, *Theories of the Theatre* (1993), has been translated into nine languages. His 2001 book, *The Haunted Stage*, won the Calloway Prize. His most recent book is *Theatre and Islam* (2019).

Astrid Chabrat-Kajdan is a PhD candidate in performing arts at the University of Lyon 2. Her research areas and teachings focus on international collaborations, extra-European production contexts, Arab theatre, cultural policies and the representation of war and conflicts in theatre. She is writing a thesis directed by Bérénice Hamidi on theatrical collaborations between European and Palestinian artists since the Oslo Accords of 1993. She mainly studies co-productions of plays including a mixed Euro-Palestinian team, at all stages of their realization-production, creative process, performance up to their circulation and reception. She uses fieldwork and participant observation in Europe and Palestine. Since 2019, her research has led her to integrate creations as a dramaturge.

Pauline Donizeau is a lecturer at the University Lumière-Lyon 2 (France) where she teaches Theatre Studies. She completed a PhD in 2019; her thesis was investigating the transformations of the Egyptian theatrical contemporary stage, especially during and in the aftermath of the 2011 revolts. Her current researches deal with Arab contemporary theatre, the cultural exchanges between Europe and the MENA since the Independences and the representations of the Middle Eastern topics on the European contemporary stages. Between 2018 and 2020, she co-organized a cycle of researches focusing on the MENA theatres since the turn of the twenty-first century. Among her publications, she is the author of a monograph entitled *La scène égyptienne en révolutions* (2023).

Omar Fertat is a lecturer at the University of Bordeaux-Montaigne where he teaches Arab literature, theatre and cinema in the Department of Arab Studies. He is also director of the international review *Horizons/Théâtres* and of the collection 'Monde arabe et Monde musulmans'. His research focuses on the performing arts in the Arab world in general and more specifically on the issues of translation and adaptation, to which he has devoted several studies and books (*Le Théâtre marocain à l'épreuve du texte étranger: traduction, adaptation, nouvelles dramaturgies* (2018), *L'adaptation au Maroc des débuts à nos jours* (2021)). He is also the director of the event 'Arab Scenes: University Meetings on the Performing Arts in the Arab World', a space for exchange and work which every two years brings together researchers and artists from both sides of the Mediterranean.

Yassaman Khajehi is Associate Professor of Theatre Studies in the Department of Cultural Studies and in the Management of Cultural Projects and Institutions at the University of Clermont Auvergne. She also teaches Persian studies at the National Institute for Oriental Languages and Civilizations (Inalco) in Paris. After studying the socio-political functioning of the Iranian puppet and its power of diversion, she is currently working on ultra-contemporary socio-political theatre in the Middle East, particularly in Iran and Lebanon. She is currently conducting a research project in France on the revival of popular and religious *ta'zieh* performances in Iran.

Erica Letailleur has been Doctor of Performing Arts, Associate Researcher at the CTEL, Université Nice Côte d'Azur since 2019. From 2004 to 2016, she was in charge of the international development of the French-Turkish company 'Ideogram Theatre'. She then taught at the National Conservatory of Dramatic Arts in Ankara (Hacettepe University), Turkey, before returning to France where she has been researching, translating, creating and teaching since 2020. She is a specialist in Turkish theatre and the author of several articles and books on the subject, including *L'Humain face à lui-même dans les arts vivants* (2018).

Antonio Pacifico is a PhD candidate at the Jean Moulin University of Lyon 3. He obtained his Master's in Comparative Literature from the University of Naples 'L'Orientale'. With his project, which he conducts under the joint supervision of

Prof. Elizabeth Vauthier and Prof. Monica Ruocco, he explores the main cleavages and symbolic struggles that have emerged in the Iraqi literary field since the 1990s. His academic interests include contemporary Iraqi literature and theatre, the relationship between literary and historical narratives, and Arab intellectual history. He has also published several articles in *Alif: Journal of Comparative Poetics*, *La rivista di Arablit* and *LiCArC*. He is currently a member of the Bureau des jeunes chercheur·e·s of the Groupement d'Intérêt Scientifique Moyen-Orient et mondes musulmans (GIS MOMM).

Daniela Potenza is a researcher of Arabic Language and Literature at Università degli Studi di Messina (Italy) at the Department of Ancient and Modern Civilisations, where she also teaches Arabic Language and Literature. Her research investigates modern and contemporary Arabic theatre, modern Egyptian literature and popular Arabic literature, with a particular interest in intertextuality. She holds a PhD in Arabic Literature from INALCO (Institut National des Langues et Civilisations Orientales, Paris) and UniOr (Università degli Studi di Napoli 'L'Orientale'). She is the author of *The Kaleidoscope Effect: Rewriting in Alfred Farag's Plays as a Multifunctional Strategy for a Multi-layered Creation* (2020). She has recently translated Muhammad Taymur's collection of short stories (2022) and has co-authored a manual of Arabic language (2022). She is currently a member of the directory board of SeSaMO, the Italian Society for Middle Eastern Studies.

Roberto Salazar is a researcher in comparative literature, specializing in ancient literature and its reception in the contemporary world, particularly in Europe, the Arab world and Latin America. He studied classics at the École Normale Supérieure de Paris (2010–15). He also obtained two undergraduate degrees in Philosophy and classics and a Master's degree in classics (Comparative Literature) at the University of Paris IV. He is currently preparing a PhD in comparative literature at the University of Versailles-Saint-Quentin-en-Yvelines, entitled: 'Under the Empire of Translation: Greek Tragedy in Egypt, Greece and Latin America since 1850'.

Emmanuelle Thiébot completed a PhD in Theatre Studies in 2019 and is currently a secondary school teacher. Her research entitled 'Theater Performances of the Israeli-Palestinian Conflict in France, from 1991 to Today' focuses on the processes of (de)legitimization of dramatic works based on the circulation of Israeli and Palestinian works to France. This work articulates the historiography of theatre, the history of theatrical representatiors and the study of the field of cultural production. The reversibility of the political dimension of theatre and the notion of cultural hegemony are at the heart of her research. She edited the seventeenth issue of *Double Jeu* entitled: 'The Artwork and the Institutions: International Approaches'.

Rezvan Zandieh works as a teacher and researcher at the University of Caen Normandie in France. Her educational background began with Drama Studies at the College of Fine Arts – University of Tehran. She obtained a Doctorate in Theatre Studies from Sorbonne Nouvelle, Pars III University, where she completed her PhD thesis on the 'Aesthetic of Injured Body in Performative Practices today'. Her research interests centre on exploring the expression of the aesthetic and the political in the study of performance and theatre, and analysing the relationship between the body and power. Her research primarily focuses on the intersection of contemporary theatre, performance and gender studies, theatre and performance in Iran. In addition to her academic pursuits, Rezvan is also an actress, performance artist, and video artist, actively engaging in artistic practices.

Foreword

Classical Reception Studies emerged in the anglophone academy in the early 1990s and was initially sited very much on the margins of classics. Indeed, it was in those early years very much a second cousin struggling to establish itself as a sub-discipline within the much hallowed and largely elitist discipline of classics.[1] Classical Reception's focus in the early days was broadly Euro-centric, although unlike other modern literary studies, it was apparent from the outset that Reception could never be confined to the nation state; nor would it be delimited by vernacular constraints. But reception of the classics in Europe – given the status of Latin in the early modern period and in the *Respublica literaria/*Republic of Letters from the late seventeenth century until late in the eighteenth century – provided more than enough material for scholarly research in those early years. And it is important to remember that Latin was not simply the *lingua franca* of Europe in the early modern period; it also remained the language of government in the Austro-Hungarian Empire well into the early nineteenth century.

However, since Reception Studies hailed from the periphery rather than the centre, its interests, perhaps not surprisingly, from an early stage included the non-canonical in all its guises. By the 1990s, it proved impossible for scholars working in classical performance reception, in particular, to ignore the fact that Greek tragedy was often enjoying a far more vigorous life outside of Europe – in Africa, in Latin America and Asia – than it was in the European metropolitan centres.[2] Studies delineating the vibrant performance cultures of former British colonies, where plays often inspired by Greek tragedies began to enjoy international prominence, began to appear in print.[3] The extraordinary flowering of theatre from the late 1950s to the 1960s around the newly established Department of Theatre at the University of Ibadan, though well documented by theatre specialists and modern literary scholars alike, now came to the attention of those in classics. It was in Ibadan, for example, that landmark plays by the Nobel Laureate, Wole Soyinka and the award-winning playwrights, Ola Rotimi and Femi Osofisan received their premieres – many of which are now canonical texts within Classical Reception Studies.[4]

Theatre specialists had much earlier begun to work on the affinities between South Asian performance traditions and Greek tragedies, between Japanese Noh and Kabuki, the Beijing Opera and Aeschylus, Sophocles and Euripides.[5] Again, it was productions of Greek tragedies by well-known Japanese directors such as Ninagawa and Suzuki that brought this area of research within classics. More recently, there has been an exciting wave of interest in the reception of Greek theatre in the Americas – both in Canada and the United States and, above all, in Latin America.[6] But considerably later to come into focus – and most oddly given the well-documented role of the Arabic and Syriac scholarly traditions in the transmission of the Graeco-Roman texts in later antiquity – is the subject of this volume: the reception of Greek theatre in the Middle East.

In July 2019, the Archive of Performances of Greek and Roman Drama (APGRD) was very proud to host a conference entitled 'Classical Theatre and the Middle East' at St Hilda's College, Oxford.[7] At the end of the conference, the APGRD was honoured to host a performance of *Jogging*, by the Lebanese actor and director, Hanane Hajj Ali, a brilliantly moving and uplifting solo-show inspired by Euripides' *Medea*. With specialists from Arabic Studies, classics and Theatre Studies, we were fully aware during the course of our discussions that we were participating in the very early stages of a much bigger conversation that was both timely and necessary.

This research owes much to the introduction and generosity of the much-lamented Professor of Theatre, Christian Biet, who tragically died in 2020. By the time of the Oxford conference in 2019, the APGRD had already enjoyed a ten-year partnership with Christian's research group at Paris-Nanterre, 'Histoire des arts et des représentations' (HAR), which continues to this day, now expanded and retitled 'Chorus'. In many ways it is the spirit of Christian that has led to the invitation from Pauline Donizeau, Yassaman Khajehi and Daniela Potenza to write this Foreword, since we too originally met through the HAR/APGRD network.

This volume *Greek Tragedy and the Middle East: Chasing the Myth* is the first to bring together research that is being conducted in many different parts of the world on this major new area of research for Classical Performance Reception. The editors need to be applauded for making this possible.

Fiona Macintosh

Professor of Classical Reception, Director of the Archive of Performances of Greek and Roman Drama, Curator of the Ioannou Centre, Fellow, St Hilda's College, Oxford University

Notes

1 See the essays in the Special Issue of *Classical Reception Studies Journal* 5 (2013) for an overview of the first twenty years of anglophone Classical Reception studies.

2 E. Hall, F. Macintosh and A. Wrigley (eds), *Dionysus since 69: Greek Tragedy at the Dawn of the Millennium* (Oxford 2005).

3 Notable studies include K. J. Wetmore, *Black Dionysus: Greek Tragedy and African American Theatre* (Jefferson, N.Carolina 2003); B. Goff (ed.), *Classical and Colonialism* (London 2005); L. Hardwick and C. Gillespie (eds), *Classics in Post-colonial Worlds* (Oxford 2007); B. Goff and M. Simpson, *Crossroads in the Black Aegean* (Oxford 2007); E. Mee and H. Foley (eds), *Antigone on the Contemporary World Stage* (Oxford 2011).

4 For Soyinka, see F. Macintosh, 'From the Court to the National: The Theatrical Legacy of Gilbert Murray', in C. A. Stray (ed.), *Gilbert Murray Reassessed* (Oxford 2007), 145–66 and J. McConnell, 'Postcolonial Sparagmos: Toni Morrison's *Sula* and Wole Soyinka's *The Bacchae of Euripides: A Communion Rite*' in *Classical Reception Studies Journal*, 8 (2016), 133–54. For Rotimi, see Goff and Simpson (2007). For Osofisan, see F. Budelmann, 'Trojan Women in Yorubaland: Femi Osofisan's *Women of Owu*', in Hardwick and Gillespie (eds, 2007), 15–39.

5 For Japanese traditions, see M. Smethurst, *The Artistry of Aeschylus and Zeami: A Comparative Study of Greek Tragedy and Noh* (Princeton 1989).

6 K. Bosher, F. Macintosh, J. McConnell and P. Rankine (eds), *The Oxford Handbook of Greek Drama in the Americas* (Oxford 2015).

7 For the conference, see www.apgrd.ox.ac.uk.

Introduction

The adaptation and updating of myths and their fables seems as old as their appearances. The number of theatrical writings in which myths are told demonstrates this fact.

> Such celebration of (re)writing, (re)imagining, updating or whatever terminology is employed in order to foreground artistic agency, is not necessarily a modern phenomenon, as similar creative strategies were also employed by the Greek playwrights.
>
> Krebs 2021: 69

In the modern era, we observe an effervescence of the ancient myths in the creations of the nations where socio-political current events are quite active. Also, we frequently observe Western theatre directors who approach Middle Eastern concerns from the perspective of Greek tragedy. For instance, consider the two American adaptations of *The Persians* by Aeschylus. The play was staged in 1990 during the Gulf War by Peter Sellars, who focused on the effects of US imperialism on the Iraqi people. After that, in 2007, Calixto Bieito's version of *The Persians* (subtitled 'Requiem for a Soldier') offered 'an extreme reformulation of the politics of the play as a musical interpretation of the US war in Afghanistan in 2003' (Sidiropoulou 2021: 147). This is probably linked to the fact that the contemporary situation of MENA countries (i.e. the war contexts, social transformations, questions of migration and imperialism, ethno-confessional conflicts, the importance of belief, religions and old traditions as cultural elements, etc.) directly refers to Greek tragedy as a theatrical narrative model. The ancient characters, conflicts and events are still there and in a tangible way, while in the West these elements seem rather symbolic or historical. In The Contemporary Performance of Ancient Greek and Roman Drama meeting, organized by the Department of Antiquities at the Paul Getty Museum in June 2003, Peter Hall, English theatre and film director, discussed the adaptation of Greek myths, the current belief in Greek gods and his desire to 'find equivalents for our audience'. A member of the audience reacted to this observation and pointed out 'The fact [is] that we are living in the Middle East, day by day, a Greek tragedy' (Hart 2003: 141–2). Indeed, this observation built the initial idea of this book and was explored during a research cycle between 2017 and 2020 entitled 'Revolts, revolutions and performance in the Near and Middle East in the 21st century'.[1] We found that adaptations of ancient plays are very present in contemporary MENA theatre. These texts often become a safe place to criticize social and political current events and especially the place of power. When artists adapt these texts, they directly target their societies, but censorship seems less applicable. A form of paradoxical protection is created, since these pieces speak finally about an old time and a 'foreign' country. Then, the expressive capacity of these plays and their potential for detour are created. From this observation and thanks to a research programme financed by the Maison des sciences de l'Homme de Clermont-Ferrand (MSH), CHEC laboratory, the University of Lyon 2 and Inalco, we worked between 2020 and 2023 on adaptations of ancient tragedy in the Middle East.

The Greek classics: questioning a hegemonic and imperialist model

The Middle East has always been interested in Greek culture in both Arabic and Persian areas. In light of interactions between the Persians and the Greeks, it is hard to believe that the Greek theatrical tradition did not circulate in ancient Persia. We know, for example, that according to Greek authors such as Xenophon, the Persians possessed performative events based on music and narration (Malekzadeh 2022: 40). In *The Theater and Dance in Iran*, Majid Rezvani (1962: 25) supports this hypothesis:

> If one studies carefully the religious history of Iran one realizes that its people adored this typically Aryan god since before the Alexander conquest and one can deduce that the festivities given in his honor must have influenced the Greek theatre.

As early as the reign of Alexander (334–323 BC), Greek troupes performed for Persian princes. This theatre of Greek origin is still attested under the Parthians (from 247 to 225 BC), then disappears completely before the Arab conquest. There are even some architectural elements, like mosaics, representing masks of the Roman theatre (Floor 2005: 21–5). But this theatrical circulation seems to have been non-existent for several centuries. It is only at the turn of the twentieth century that the first translations of ancient theatrical texts were made in Iran. A 1900 manuscript translation of Sophocles' *Electra* – probably from French – by Prince Hossein Qoli Mirza Salour, also known as Emad Al-Saltaneh, is preserved in the Iranian National Library in Tehran.

Regarding the Arab countries, a large body of philosophical, scientific, and medical literature from ancient Greece was translated into Arabic during the Abbasid dynasty, before many of these texts were translated into Latin or other European languages, even if the Arabic translations of Aristotle's *Poetics* by the four mediaeval philosophers al-Kindi (al-Kindī), Farabi (Fārābī), Avicenna (Ibn Sīnā), and Averroes (Ibn Rushd) were merely synoptic epitomes of this work.[2] Moreover, ancient Greek literature – and drama in particular – was not translated until the nineteenth century. The categories of theatre were not covered in this most well-known translation, *Middle Commentary on Aristotle's Poetics* (*Talkhīṣ Kitāb Arisṭūṭālīs fī'l-shi'r, c.* 1174), which was twice translated into Latin. Only at the tail end of the nineteenth century, during the so-called Nahda (*nahḍa*, 'awakening'), the cultural and intellectual revival that took place in Egypt and other Arab nations between 1870 and 1950, did the concept of tragedy make its way into Arabic theatre through the lens of Europe. The Arab public sphere in Egypt and the Levant was increasingly assimilated into the European-dominated world order of states and national cultures, particularly during the late nineteenth century. Alongside this development, a conflict over the applicability of European literary canons to Arabic literary practice emerged (Noorani 2019: 236). Political movements promoting social reforms occurred at the same time as this cultural resurgence. Arabic literary modernizers, such as the Lebanese dramatist Najib al-Haddad (Najīb al-Ḥaddād, 1867–99), therefore, sought to justify the adoption of European literary genres and 'rectify the perceived deficiencies of the Arabic literary heritage by aligning Arabic and European literatures in a manner that gives Arabic a position of primacy' (ibid.: 237).

In this setting, the effort to remake the Arabic literary heritage in simultaneously national and global terms relied heavily on the translation of ancient 'classics' into Arabic (ibid.: 236). Sulayman al-Boustani's translation of the *Iliad*,[3] which was published by Maṭba'at al-Hilāl of Cairo in 1904 and was accompanied by extensive introduction and commentary, carries this strategy much further through its sustained effort to universalize the concept of the *jāhiliyya* (the pre-Islamic period of Arabian history) 'as the basis of a linkage between Arabic and Homeric poetry that is more profound than any enjoyed by modern European literatures' (ibid.: 237). Al-Boustani's monumental translation was praised as the most important literary work in the era of the modern Arab renaissance; it inspired interest and enjoyed popularity in the Arabic-speaking world, and was reprinted several times (Pormann 2006: 9). Aiming at homogenization of literary tastes and practices, Boustani's translation of the *Iliad* 'performs the hegemonic function of establishing a specific set of universal values and a specific version of nationality through the articulation of the cultural heritage to this universality' (Noorani 2019: 240). With his work, he not only rendered a great service to the Arabic language, but he laid the foundations for the construction of a renewed Arab identity which was rooted in its own heritage (literary, cultural and mythological) and which at the same time did not fear confronting the great works of world literature (Monaco 2022: 1). The message he wanted to convey was that the *Iliad* was an essential text for the development of national literatures. Therefore, if Arabic literature wanted to develop, it would necessarily have to assimilate it (Monaco 2022: xli).

The first translations of Aristotle from Greek to Persian are in fact very recent. In 1948 Soheil Muhsin Afnan translated *The Poetics* from Greek into Persian, and in 1952 he translated *The Persians* as well. Newspapers report performances of Sophocles' *Oedipus* and Aeschylus' *Prometheus Bound*, but the translations and adaptations are not based on the original Greek version (see Anvar, Kheradman: 1972). This kind of research is quite hard since a system of archiving theatrical performances in Iran does not exist.

From the 1960s onwards, as part of the decolonization movements, the so-called 'encounter' between Western cultural heritage and Middle Eastern societies within the framework of the Nahda was largely reconsidered. In 1959, during the Second Congress of Black Artists and Writers in Rome, directly addressing to the Arab experience, Frantz Fanon (1963) underlined the anxiety and sense of devaluation that prevailed in the context of these encounters. Fanon considers Pan-Arabism as an answer to European colonization and, from the same perspective, the Nahda can be considered as 'the need for Arab intellectuals to proclaim the values of Arab-Islamic civilization in turn' (Sibley 2019: 34). With a similar decolonial and critical gaze, Edward Said (1978) some years later also highlights the link between cultural domination and political imperialism in his famous book *Orientalism*. Greek tragedy does not escape criticism since Europeans are accustomed to seeing it as a part of their own literary and dramatic legacy. It automatically becomes a symbol of cultural hegemony when it is imported into the MENA regions in the nineteenth century and portrayed as high culture. And thus, in his text 'Towards an Egyptian Theatre', the Egyptian playwright and novelist Yusuf Idris (Yūsuf Idrīs, 1927–91) considers Greek theatre a cultural fact that is part of European heritage. He clearly differentiates it from 'other theatrical forms', among which are the traditional forms of Egyptian theatre (Idris 2019 [1974]: 7). His aim is to get rid of European culture in order to develop a truly Egyptian theatre.

The permanence of classical materials in the MENA theatre and the 'paradoxical situation of classical texts'

The following is how Patrice Pavis summarizes the problem of cultural interactions in a postcolonial world:

> Here it is difficult to avoid the dichotomy between dominant and dominated, between majority and minority, between ethnocentric and decentred culture. From there it is only a small step to seeing interculturalism as an ethnocentric strategy of Western culture to reconquer alien symbolic goods by submitting them to a dominant codification, an exploitation of the poorer by the richer.
>
> 1996: 4

Nevertheless, it seems to us necessary to go beyond the binary opposition between Eastern and Western heritage and rather approach the relationship of non-European works to Greek materials in an intercultural or transcultural continuum.

Indeed, even during the colonial period, the Greek heritage was questioned and adapted and this desired conjunction of Greek heritage with the local literature has not always been considered a success. In 1912, the brilliant Lebanese actor George Abyad (Jūrj Abyaḍ, 1880–1959) produced the first translation of *Oedipus Tyrannos* into Arabic.[4] It was a landmark event in the history of Egyptian theatre. Concerns about the genre and debates about the place of singing in Egyptian theatre and its relationship to 'serious' acting dominated theatre criticism (Cormack 2017: 74). Despite that, the influence of Abyad's play on subsequent versions of the story of Oedipus in Egypt was huge: the 1912 production was performed for over thirty-five years and it was seen by many of the most important Egyptian theatre practitioners of the twentieth century (ibid.: 66).

Taha Hussein (Ṭāhā Ḥusayn, 1889–1973), perhaps the most influential twentieth-century Egyptian intellectual, has still another point of view on the Greek heritage: he claims Greek heritage as part of Egyptian culture. His approach to translation is radically different from that adopted by al-Boustani.

Whilst the latter used Arabic verse to express the meaning of the original, and supplied copious notes explaining both historical and literary problems, Taha Hussein opts for 'letting the text speak for it' (Pormann 2022: 10). Taha Hussein was a fine connoisseur of Greek tragedy. He had studied Greek and Latin while in Paris and translated most of Sophocles' extant plays, namely *Electra*, *Ajax*, *Antigone*, *Oedipus the King*, *Oedipus at Colonus* and *Philoctetes*. He wanted to add Latin and Greek to the curriculum of secondary and tertiary education in Egypt and aspired to the merging of the local heritage with the classics of world literature in Modern Arabic literature.[5] However, the 'Greek' history that was coming to Taha Hussein 'was mediated by European sources and European education and so, via the Greeks, European ways of thinking came into Arabic writing, through the back door' (Cormack 2017: 109). As portrayed in Taha Hussein, the ancient Greeks and their historical relationship to Egypt, are at once colonial and cosmopolitan (ibid.: 109).

During the intense political debate and quest for independence in Egypt, which was ultimately successful in 1952, the renowned Egyptian playwright Tawfiq al-Hakim (Tawfīq al-Ḥakīm, 1898–1987) championed the viewpoint of integrating the ancient Egyptian and Arab legacy with the Greek one (Denooz 2022, 2003, 2004 and 2015; Pormann 2016). Tawfiq al-Hakim believed that a return to Greek sources was necessary to revitalize Arabic literature. However, he believed that this literary manumission could not be accomplished simply by translating Greek texts; rather, it required critical and creative interaction with them in order to incorporate them into the Arabic tradition (Pormann 2006).

Moreover, even at the time of the Independences, and while intellectuals criticized the use of European heritage, Greek tragedy remained a cultural reference. Dominique Combe (1996) shows that the Algerian playwright Kateb Yacine was inspired by the form of tragedy to compose his trilogy *Le Cercle des représailles* (*The Circle of Retaliation*, 1959), which he actually defines as a tragedy.

The Iranian relationship to Greek heritage in the twentieth century is quite different from the Arab one, as the colonial/postcolonial issue does not present itself in the same way in the country, since Iran has not been concerned with Western colonialism like other MENA countries. The Iranian nationalist movement was not primarily based on a reaction to colonialism. From the Islamic Revolution of 1979 in Iran, we see a great interest in the staging of Greek plays with a political connotation. For example, in 1987, we had two versions of *Ajax* by Sophocles directed by Ghotbedin Sadeghi and Atila Pesiani, two renowned directors of Iranian theatre. These two shows were presented in two different halls of the Tehran City Theatre. In an interview, the two directors talk about the political resonance of the play with the country's current social situation and the Iranian theatre (Sadeghi, Pessiani 1987: 56–65). It has to be noted that Pesiani's *Ajax* shows a collective vision contrasting the individualistic aspect of the current Iranian productions (Zivaralam 2023).

Even if they follow two different trajectories, Greek tragedies and myths are present today on the stages of the MENA countries, in Arabic countries as well as in Iran. Since the 1990s, there have been each year in Iran more than a dozen performances of ancient texts: *Oedipus, Medea* and *Antigone* are at the top of the list. The Egyptian critic and academic Nehad Selaiha has reviewed a dozen Greek classics produced on the Egyptian stages in the late 1990s and early 2000s (Selaiha 2019 [2004]). At the end of the twentieth century, the Egyptian professor Munira Karawan translated several Greek classics including Sophocles' *Antigone, Electra, Oedipus the King* and *Women of Trachis*, Euripides' *Medea* and *The Trojan Women, Iphigenia* and Aeschylus' *The Libation Bearers* and *The Suppliants*. Among the most famous plays inspired by Greek tragedy in Egypt, we can mention Abo El Seoud's *Antīgūn fī Ramallāh, Antīgūn fī Bayrūt* (*Antigone in Ramallah, Antigone in Beirut*), a tragic poem in nine parts focusing on the consequences of colonialism. In Tunisia, with *Tsunami* (2013), the couple al-Jaʿāybī-Bakkār discussed the post-revolutionary period evoking Antigone's myth. In 2018, the Palestinian Fidaa Zidan directed *The Last Day of Spring* (*Akhir yawm fī 'l-rabī*), a monologue inspired by Sophocles' Antigone, in the National Palestinian Theatre in Jerusalem. The same year, the Lebanese playwright Roger Assaf was inspired by *Iphigenia in Aulis, The Trojan Women*, as well as *Agamemnon* for his *Trojan War* (*Ḥarb ṭarwāda*), depicting the sordid reality of war (Beirut, Sunflower Theatre). In November 2022, at Falaki Theatre (Cairo), Dina Amin's *Antigone's Law* depicted the sadness of a whole city in the aftermath of a destructive civil war where a brother killed his own brother. The curse on the house of Oedipus passes on to his children.

The renewal of academic approaches on the topic

It is therefore necessary to reconsider the place of Greek materials in non-European countries, linked to Europe by their colonial past. This is the purpose of this 'Classical Diaspora' series. In light of this, we have taken into account the extensive recent studies about Greek classics in the MENA region, such as Hardwick and Gillespie's collective volume on the reception of classics in African countries and the MENA regions (2007), but also Decreus and Kolk's *Rereading Classics in 'East' and 'West': Post-colonial Perspectives on the Tragic* (2004), as well as Cormack's PhD dissertation *Oedipus on the Nile: Translations and Adaptations of Sophocles' Oedipus Tyrannos in Egypt, 1900–1970*, focusing more specifically on the Oedipus myth (2017) and Denooz's studies about al-Hakim's approach to Hellenistic and Pharaonic heritages (2003, 2004 and 2015).

Recent academic research on this subject is accompanied by a revitalization of studies on Greek tragedy and a renewed approach to it. The French academic Florence Dupont has maintained for several years that tragedy must be 'decolonized' (Dupont 2004). Dupont endeavours to distinguish the Greek theatrical model, which is textual and normative (as established by the French Renaissance), from the historical and anthropological reality: that of the ceremony and celebration in which tragedy was presented, and thus its performative dimension (Dupont 2007). According to Pierre Brunel (1988: 11), myth is malleable and can be considered 'enrobé de littérature' ('wrapped in literature'), meaning that it can travel as an entity to which other elements are regularly added. It is therefore necessary to consider tragedy not as a monolithic and unalterable object, but to distinguish the different elements that constitute it: the chorus, the alternation between song and speech, the conflict/*agon*, the scenography, the hero, the mythological content, the metaphysical question, the catastrophe, the terror or the dread, but also the images that are associated with it. In the meantime, we also consider critical perspectives regarding the Western reception of Greek myth. The Italian intellectual and artist Pierpaolo Pasolini, who is commonly appreciated by MENA intellectuals, clearly criticizes what he perceives as the domination of one class, the Western bourgeoisie who locked myth away in academies, operas, theatres and novels (Mouzaïne 2022). Pasolini goes even further as he maintains that Greek culture had become classist, in contrast to the Arab myths, which were handed down to the people in their oral form and remained 'a mythology, which means that it remained popular without becoming the cultural expression of the ruling [*dominante*] class' (2015 [1974]).

The present book, which is a natural extension of the dynamic created by postcolonial studies and cultural studies, seeks to continue these analyses in order to demonstrate the 'paradoxical condition of classical literature' (Hardwick, Keynes 2007: 2). By 'Chasing the Myth', we intend to highlight how this material is hard to analyse in the MENA region as we aim at discussing the historical and contemporary place of Greek materials in the Maghreb, the Near East and the Middle East, but also to question the European look on Greek heritage today. We aim to study the extra-European staging and adaptations of these Greek materials in order to value what Biet defines as:

> A questioning of the fables, a historicization of the plots, their updating to make them present, even contemporary, but also a working on the materiality of the text and the play and on the theatrical performance itself.
>
> 2018: 7

With this in mind, we want to detect how modern and contemporary directors have taken on the task of rereading the repertoire and the 'classics' to dissect them from a normative, eternal conception, consider any contradictions they may contain, highlight the heterogeneity of the classical text itself and, finally, give the texts of the repertoire an impact on modern society without sacrificing any of the multiple meanings they were intended to convey at the time they were written (ibid.: 11).

Organization of the book

This book intends to shed light on this cultural trajectory, on the adaptation and reception of Greek tragedy in the MENA region. It focuses on three important moments that also raise different theoretical issues: first the end of the nineteenth century and the beginning of the twentieth century, namely those periods marked by the Nahda, then the Independences, and finally the present-day situation.

The first part offers a historical perspective presenting the reception of the classics in Egypt and Turkey from the beginning of the twentieth century to the twenty-first century, with focus on the reception of the Oedipus myth and its success in the MENA reception. As we have discussed above, even if contacts of MENA countries with Greek culture have been intense since antiquity, colonization and the settlement of Europeans in the region is a crucial historical moment that needs to be studied in detail. The contributions of this first part consider these developments to discuss this crucial moment, providing a historical perspective on how the classics were received in Egypt and Turkey from the turn of the twentieth century to the twenty-first century, with a special emphasis on how the Oedipus myth was received and how well it did in the MENA region. As we have already established, colonialism and the arrival of Europeans in the region are significant historical events that require close examination, even if MENA countries have had extensive cultural exchanges with Greece since antiquity. To discuss this vital time, the contributions of this first part take these developments into account. The first chapter offers an updated discussion about the translation of Greek tragedy into Arabic in the wake of the Nahda, starting with the controversial Ibn Rushd translation and its difficult reception over the centuries, with a related digression on the translation of the term 'tragedy' itself. With a focus on reception, translational practices, and their subsequent impacts as acts of resistance or acquiescence to domination, in this chapter Roberto Salazar analyses these complicated phenomena by posing the historical context and investigating individual cases. The second chapter explores the extraordinary success of Sophocles' *Oedipus* in Arab countries starting from Najīb al-Ḥaddād's 1905 *Oedipus* (which was based not on Sophocles but on the eighteenth-century version of the story created by Voltaire), until today, with Wajdi Mouawad's (Wajdī Muʿawwaḍ) most recent work, *Tous les Oiseaux* (*All Birds*, 2017). With this contribution, Marvin Carlson demonstrates how the persistence of Arab interest in this story is essential to understanding the growth of contemporary Arabic theatre, as well as the political ramifications of portraying this myth through the various stories of Oedipus' creations. In the third chapter, Erica Letailleur discusses the cultural appropriation of the ancient Greek repertoire in modern and contemporary Turkish theatre. While questioning the notion of artistic and cultural heritage, she demonstrates the influence of ancient Greece both through architectural elements and theatrical texts. She also studies the place of traditional collective forms and their hybridization in this process. In this chapter, the author proposes a set of performances, each of which illustrates an aspect of this appropriation.

The second part focuses on the political dimension of Greek tragedy's reception by MENA artists in the region during the twentieth to the twenty-first century. We investigate how contemporary artists from the region appropriated the tragic model and its set of characters. Furthermore, we highlight how socio-political issues and current events in the countries taken into consideration have expressed themselves in the guise of classical myths. Under specific political circumstances, proclaiming the 'universality' of Greek tragedy can protect against political scrutiny, especially in societies placed under authoritarian/conservative regimes since 'a text can be banned or censored in one context and regarded as canonical in another' (Hardwick, Keynes 2007: 2). Indeed, Greek tragedy gives a voice to the weak and the victimized: 'Greek tragedy grants a hearing to voices otherwise excluded as female, under age, polluted, or insane, and thus involves a temporary and fictional extension of the right to free speech that is normally restricted to male citizens' (Leezenberg 2007: 285). In the fourth chapter, Daniela Potenza engages with Agamben's theory of the permanent state of exception in some contemporary Arab plays which have issued from Greek tragedies. Omar Abusaada and Mohammad Al Attar's *Iphigenia* (2017), Hanane Hajj Ali's rebellious play *Jogging: Theatre in Progress* (2012, latest version 2022) – where she enacts the desperation of different Lebanese Medeas disempowered by their society – and Sulayman Al Bassam's *IMedea* (2017, latest version 2022), about contemporary European hysterias regarding Islam and the power of digital platforms to alter the political space – are compared to the Greek tragedies and their further interpretations. This chapter shows how Greek tragedy today can be the basis for the women's unspoken stories dealing with issues of power, justice, law, war and gender in places where 'the state of exception' has become the norm. This chapter will be in dialogue with the fifth chapter and Yassaman Khajehi's study on the place of Medea in contemporary Iranian and Lebanese theatre, where the social situation is highly politicized. In these countries, demands for women's rights are positioned between a traditional taboo and an 'imported' Western fashion. This is seen as a problem, but the theatrical narrative becomes a loophole through which to present women's place and action. The character of Medea and her relation to the question of motherhood becomes a safe 'place' to address these issues. In addition, beyond the socio-political issues of Euripides' text and its questioning of the margins, the news in Iran pushes artists and spectators to retell Medea's fable in order to reflect on current political issues: give birth to a new generation or stop the economic and social suffering? Through several examples, like Neda Shahrokhi's *Medea* (2015) in Iran and Hanane Hajj Ali's *Jogging* (2016) and Valérie Cachard's *Bloody Mary* (2019–23) in Lebanon, this chapter demonstrates this transformation and updating of Medea between 2015 and 2023. The sixth chapter studies contemporary Iranian theatre through another female figure, Antigone. With several case studies, *Antigone* (2010) by Popak Hidji, *Antigone* (2018) by Ali Razi and *Antigone* (2011) by Homayoun Ghani Zadeh, this chapter make a comparative study of these adaptations to examine how the tragic material is developed and highlight how the universal dimension of Antigone is particularized in the Iranian context. It also shows how the adaptation of tragic material is used as an aesthetic strategy of resistance by Iranian artists to reveal what is not allowed to be expressed, in other words, to circumvent censorship. Through his sociological study of Haythem Abderrazak's *Looking for Oresteia* (2018), Antonio Pacifico identifies in the seventh chapter the multiple obstacles Iraqi stage directors face today in their country. At the same time, he investigates the uneven and often complicated relations between a 'peripheral' field, such as the Iraqi's, and the main 'centres' of international theatre, especially after the American invasion and the fall of the Baathist regime (2003).

The third part questions the idea of Greek materials as 'common/shared' heritage, and deals with issues of interculturality, reception and postcolonial perspectives. It questions the transformation of the Greek materials when they pass through different cultural areas. In the eighth chapter, Emmanuelle Thiébot considers the political dimension of three adaptations of Greek tragedies in Hanoch Levin's theatre. She shows the ambivalence of interpretations of these plays between Israel and France: in Israel, they are considered highly political, while in France they are subjects of a neutral reading as the tragic approach has been replaced by the absurd. If this shows the malleability of the classics, it also questions its approach in different cultural contexts. The two following chapters deal with cases of international artistic collaborations between the MENA region and Europe. Astrid Chabrat-Kajdan studies Adel Hakim's *mise en scène* of *Antigone* as a coproduction between the Théâtre des Quartier d'Ivry in France and the National Palestinian Theatre. This ninth chapter underlines that this show was a success in Europe, when Palestinian productions struggle to find their ways on to European theatrical institutions and postulates that Hakim's choices of adaptation and staging of the Greek tragedy (both as a familiar and foreign object to European audiences) created the conditions of this success. In the tenth chapter, Pauline Donizeau compares two *Oresteia* staged by European directors (Milo Rau in 2019 and Célie Pauthe in collaboration with Haythem Abderrazak in 2018) who adapted Aeschylus' text to deal with the current situation of Iraq at war. She uses the theoretical tools of intercultural theatre studies to analyse the two productions and their very different approaches to both the topic and the tragic materials. Finally, in the eleventh chapter, Omar Fertat focuses on the Moroccan artist Zoubeir Ben Bouchta claiming Greek tragedy as an Arab-Tamazight heritage to relocate the fable to his own city, Tangier in his *Tingitanos*, an adaptation of Hercules' myth. Such a proposal permits a reconsideration of Greek tragedy as an object suitable for creolization and allows us revisit the very concept of 'universalism' if we consider, as Seloua Luste Boulbina does it, creolization as a 'universalism from below' (Luste Boulbina 2018: 49).

Notes

1   This project has given rise to three international study days: 'Performances and performing arts in societies between revolt, unrest and mutations'; 'Submitting, circumventing, revolting against censorship: theatre under control'; 'The springtime

of theatre? The art to the test of the revolutions'. Research programme organized by Sobhi Boustani, Pauline Donizeau, Yassaman Khajehi and funded and supported by the University of Paris Nanterre, the University of Clermont Auvergne, National Institute for Oriental Languages and Civilizations (Inalco), The National Institute of Art History (INHA), Théâtre Européen d'Odéon in France.

2   According to Ibn El Nadim, Aristotle's *Poetics* was translated three times into Arabic, first by Abu Bishr Matta Bin Yunis (died 328 hijra, about A D 940), Ishaq Ibn Hunayn (died 298 hijra, about A D 910), and Yahya Ibn Adi (282–363 hijra, about A D 893–974). Only one translation, that of Abu Bishr Matta, survived, the other two having been lost (Etman 2004: 284).

3   Sulayman al-Bustani (Sulaymān al-Bustānī, 1856–1925) was a statesman, teacher, poet and historian. He hailed from the prominent Maronite Catholic Boustani family well known for their pioneering contributions to the Nahda.

4   Abyad's production was based on the translation by the Syrian born author Farah Antun (Faraḥ Anṭūn, 1874–1922), who most probably used Jules Lacroix's of Sophocles' *Oedipus Tyrannos*.

5   And he managed to do that. In his famous memories, *al-Ayyām* (*The Days*, 1926–67), the narrator describes how one day Hussein – the character protagonist of the novel – told the story of Oedipus to his daughter; at that point the narrative becomes theatrical, with the little girl crying for Oedipus' destiny. In this passage, the reader can enjoy a representation of the myth with the audience's reaction (Cormack 2017: 118).

References

Afnan, S. (1948), *The Poetics of Aristotle*. Translated from Greek to Persian. London: Luzac & Co.

Afnan, S. (1952), *The Persai*. Translated from Greek into Persian. Paris: Adrien Maisonneuve.

Almohanna, M. (2016), 'Greek Drama in the Arab World', in B. Van Zyl Smit (ed.), *A Handbook to the Reception of Greek Drama*, 364–81, New York: John Wiley & Sons.

Anvar, I. and Sh. Kheradman (1972), 'haft hekayat bar sisaye âbed', *Tamasha*, 51, Tehran.

Biet, C. (2018), 'Introduction: La question du répertoire au théâtre', *Littératures classiques*, 95(1): 7–14.

Brunel, P., ed. (1988), *Dictionnaire des mythes littéraires*, Monaco: Éditions du Rocher.

Carlson, M. (2006), *The Arab Oedipus, the English Translation of Four Plays Based on the Oedipus Legend by Four Leading Dramatists of the Arab World*, New York: Martin E. Segal Theatre Center.

Combe, D. (1996), 'La renaissance de la tragédie: Aimé Césaire, Kateb Yacine, et Nietzsche', in A. Bouvier Cavoret (ed.), *Le Théâtre et le Sacré*, 185–207, Paris: Klincksieck.

Cormack, R. C. (2017), 'Oedipus on the Nile: Translations and Adaptations of Sophocles' *Oedipus Tyrannos* in Egypt, 1900–1970', PhD in Islamic and Middle Eastern Studies, University of Edinburgh.

Decreus, F. and M. Kolk (2004), *Rereading Classics in 'East' and 'West': Post-colonial Perspectives on the Tragic*, Gent: Documentatiecentrum voor Dramatische Kunst.

Denooz, L. (2003), 'Œdipe-Roi en trompe-l'œil: Étude d'Al-Malik Œdipe de Tawfīq al- Ḥakīm', *Kernos*, 16: 211–24.

Denooz, L. (2004), 'Tawfīq al-Ḥakīm et les mythologies méditerranéennes', in F. Bauden (ed.), *Ultra Mare: Mélanges de langue arabe et d'islamologie offerts à Aubert Martin*, Louvain-Paris: Peeters.

Denooz, L. (2015), 'Transmission du théâtre européen vers un "modèle théâtral arabe": Étapes de l'arabisation du théâtre dans l'œuvre de Tawfīq al-Ḥakīm', in L. Chaarani Lesourd et al. (eds), *Passeurs de culture et transferts culturels*, Nancy: Presses Universitaires de Nancy.

Denooz, L. (2002), *Entre Orient et Occident: rôles de l'hellénisme et du pharaonisme dans l'œuvre de Tawfiq al-Hakīm*, Liège: Bibliothèque de la Faculté de philosophie et lettres de l'Université de Liège.

Dupont, F. (2004), 'La tragédie grecque: une invention moderne', in P. Vasseur-Legangneux (ed.), *Les Tragédies grecques sur la scène moderne: une utopie théâtrale*, Villeneuve-d'Ascq: Presses Universitaires du Septentrion.

Dupont, F. (2007), *Aristote ou le vampire du théâtre occidental*, Paris: Flammarion.

Etman, A. (2004), 'The Greek Concept of Tragedy in Arab Culture: How to deal with an Islamic Oedipus?', in F. Decreus and M. Kolk (eds), *Rereading Classics in 'East' and 'West': Post-colonial Perspectives on the Tragic*, 281–99, Gent: Documentatiecentrum voor Dramatische Kunst.

Fanon, F. (1963), *The Wretched of the Earth*, trans. C. Farrington, New York: Grove.

Floor, W. (2005), *The History of Theater in Iran*, Washington DC: Mage Publishers.

Hardwick, L. and C. Gillespie (2007), *Classics in Post-colonial Worlds*, Oxford: Oxford University Press.

Hardwick, L. and M. Keynes (2007), 'Introduction' in L. Hardwick and C. Gillespie (eds), *Classics in Post-colonial Worlds*, 1–11, Oxford: Oxford University Press.

Hart, M-L, O. Taplin, P. Hall, P. Sellars, P. Stein and L. Koniourdou (2003), 'Ancient Greek Tragedy on the Stage', *Journal of Humanities and the Classics*, Third Series, 11(1) (Spring–Summer), Boston University.

Idris, Y. (2019 [1978]), *Al-farāfīr*, Cairo; London: Hindawi.

Krebs, K. (2021), 'Definitions: Adaptation and Related Modalities', in V. Liapis and A. Sidiropoulou (eds), *Adapting Greek Tragedy: Contemporary Contexts for Ancient Texts*, 59–76, Cambridge: Cambridge University Press.

Leezenberg, M. (2007), 'From the Peloponnesian War to the Iraq War: A Post-Liberal Reading of the Greek Tragedy' in L. Hardwick and C. Gillespie (eds), *Classics in Post-colonial Worlds*, 265–85, Oxford: Oxford University Press.

Luste Boulbina S. (2018), *Les miroirs vagabonds ou la décolonisation des savoirs*, Paris: Les Presses du réel.

Malekzadeh, S. (2021), 'Minstrels: The Wise Teachers of Ancient Iran' in B. Rahimi (ed.), *Performing Iran: Culture,* 39–45, London: I.B. Tauris Bloomsbury.

Monaco, A. (2022), 'Introduction', in S. al-Bustānī, *Intrcduzione all'Iliade di Omero*, v–li, Rome: Istituto per L'Oriente Carlo Alfonso Nallino.

Mouzaïne, A. (2022), 'Pasolini e il mondo arabo: Un vasto orizzonte da Sana'a al Marocco', *Orient XXI*, 3/12/2022.

Noorani, Y. (2019), 'Translating World Literature into Arabic and Arabic into World Literature: Sulayman al-Bustani's al-Ilyadha and Ruhi al-Khalidi's Arabic Rendition of Victor Hugo', in M. Booth (ed.), *Migrating Texts: Circulating Translations around the Ottoman Mediterranean*, 236–65, Edinburgh: Edinburgh University Press.

Pasolini, P. (2015 [1974]), '3/5 Pier Paolo Pasolini: Dans l'atelier de pensée de P. P. P. (2015 Hors-champs/France Culture)', www.youtube.com/watch?v=r7Nir-W5d1o.

Pavis, P. (1996), *The Intercultural Performance Reader*, London; New York: Routledge.

Pormann, P. E. (2006), 'The Arab "Cultural Awakening (Nahḍa)", 1870–1950, and the Classical Tradition'. *International Journal of the Classical Tradition*, 13(1): 3–20.

Rezvani, M. (1964), *Le théâtre et la danse en Iran*, Paris: Maisonneuve & Larose.

Sadeghi, Gh. and A. Pessian (1987), 'Ajax barandeh ast ya bazandeh?', *Namayesh*, 2, December, Teheran, 56–65.

Said, E. (2019 [1978]), *Orientalism*, Penguin Modern Classics, London: Penguin.

Selaiha, N. (2019 [2004]), *The Egyptian Theatre, Cultural Encounters 1*, New York: Martin E. Segal Theatre Center.

Sibley, E. (2019), 'Redefining Theatre: Yusuf Idris' *Al-Farāfīr* and the Work of Cultural Decolonization', *Alif: Journal of Comparative Poetics*, 39: 31–62.

Sidiropoulou, A. (2021), 'Adaptation as a Love Affair: The Ethics of Directing the Greeks', in V. Lipais, A. Sidiropoulou (eds), *Adapting Greek Tragedy: Contemporary Contexts for Ancient Texts*, 131–54, Cambridge: Cambridge University Press.

Soubrier, V. (2012), 'Une nouvelle renaissance? Les auteurs dramatiques postcoloniaux et l'héritage grec au tournant du XXIe siècle', *Revue de Littérature Comparée*, 344: 475–86.

Zivaralam, E. (2023), 'Fard gerai yek khasteh ya yek ejbar?', *Imaj*, 2, Tehran: Soureh University.

Part One

Adaptations and Translations of Greek Tragedy in a Colonial Context: An Historical Perspective

1

Tragic Ways, Tragic Voices

Translating Greek Tragedy into Arabic in the Wake of the Nahḍa

Roberto Salazar

The purpose of this chapter is to explore how nineteenth and twentieth-century Egyptian writers dealt with the problem of translating ancient Greek tragedy into Arabic and adapting it for the Egyptian public in a context marked by colonial tensions. Works from Western classical antiquity, which allow for ambiguous readings, serve as placeholders for the European tradition, but also as a foundational point of reference for the nascent theatrical tradition of the Nahḍa, the Arab artistic renaissance. Modern theatre in the Arab world developed mainly between the Bilād al-Shām (Greater Syria or the Levant) and Egypt. State-sponsored policies and investment drew many of the most important theatre pioneers from Syria to Cairo and Alexandria. In this context, it was only a matter of time before playwrights and directors would turn their attention towards Greek drama. My aim is to shed new light on the role the translation of Greek tragedy plays in this process.

Studying this reception process, allows one to gain better insight into the inception of theatre in the region,[1] in terms of translational practices which work as acts of resistance or acquiescence to foreign domination. This entails a variety of problems. Adapting an unknown source material from a polytheistic context into an Islamic cultural landscape with an established literary system is not a simple task. Who are the main agents in this process? A further issue is presented by the language of translation: should Greek tragedies be translated into Standard Arabic or into the Egyptian vernacular? We will see that the translation of Greek tragedy set the stage for political tensions, colonial and postcolonial are felt throughout, in which theatrical practices interact with scholarly traditions.

Reception of Greek tragedy in the Arab world is a relatively new field of study. Peter Pormann (2009; 2014; 2015) and Ahmed Etman (1978; 2004; 2007) have contributed general overviews of modern translations and adaptations of Greek works into Arabic. Marvin Carlson (2005; 2013; 2019) has written extensively on the reception of Greek drama in the Arab world, including an edition of four Arabic adaptations of the myth of Oedipus. Raphael Cormack's dissertation on the Egyptian versions of Sophocles' *Oedipus Tyrannos* (Cormack 2017) was one of the first exhaustive case studies in the reception of this Greek tragedy in Egypt. However, insufficient attention has been given to the translation of ancient Greek tragedy, a minor but fascinating episode in the history of modern Egyptian literature. As we shall see, Greek plays have gone from being unknown text to serving as common, recognizable references in Egyptian literature and the Arab theatrical repertoire.

Ibn Rushd's predicament

In his short story 'La busca de Averroes', Jorge Luis Borges ([1949] 1997) famously portrays the Andalusian philosopher Ibn Rushd as he fails to accurately convey the meaning of the Greek words 'tragedy' and 'comedy' into Arabic, which he rendered as 'praise' (*madīḥ*) and 'blame' (*hijā'*) in his synoptic epitomes of Aristotle's *Poetics*. Borrowing from the French Orientalist and Semitic scholar Ernest Renan (1823–1922), Borges claims that Ibn Rushd could not grasp the meaning of these Greek words because he remained a prisoner of his cultural environment ('encerrado en el ámbito del islam, nunca pudo saber el significado de las voces *tragedia* y *comedia*', ibid.: 558), a world in which theatre as such did not exist. Without first-hand experience of dramatic literature, so the narrator somewhat regretfully claims, such culturally specific terms as *komoidia* and *tragoidia* could never have made it into the Arabic text unscathed. The interpretation the philosopher offers of both terms is, therefore, tragically doomed.

The Renanian argument, which Borges uses ironically to frame his own feeling of frustration with the pitfalls of literary representation, has often been taken at face value to explain why Greek drama was not translated into Arabic before the twentieth century. Until the start of the Nahḍa, Greek literature (understood as works of imaginative fiction written in Ancient Greek) remains largely unknown in the Arab world (Pormann 2015; 2009). This is all the more baffling, given that a vast corpus of philosophical, scientific, and medical texts from ancient Greece was translated during the Abbasid era.[2] The names of the greatest ancient Greek poets were known to the translators of *Bayt al-Ḥikma* and their successors (Jihād 2007). And yet, aside from sparse quotes and maxims (Pormann 2014: 6–7), ancient Greek literature was never translated. Even in 1949, in the preface for his *Malik Ūdīb*, the first original adaptation of the myth of Oedipus into Arabic, the Egyptian playwright Tawfīq al-Ḥakīm (1898–1987), is appalled at what he calls Ibn Rushd's lack of curiosity regarding the original texts of which the *Poetics* is a commentary (Etman 2004).

Nuancing Borges' interpretation, Kilito (2002: 48) observes that Ibn Rushd was working on an already faulty translation, that of Abū Bishr Mattā Ibn Yūnus. Therefore, he inherited this creative misunderstanding from the tradition,[3] which construed tragedy and comedy as poetic (not dramatic) genres.[4] Leezenberg (2004: 300) points out that a variety of 'largely contingent factors' determine the 'interpretive differences' between 'the classical Arabo-Islamic understanding of Aristotle's remarks on tragedy' and Western views on the text of the *Poetics*. Whereas in Europe, the *Poetics* shaped the reception of Greek tragedies as forms of drama, for medieval authors writing in Arabic it became an important epistemological tool through which Ibn Rushd and other philosophers conceptualized the Arabic poetic tradition, in terms of native rhetorical categories.[5] This contingency lies at the heart of Borges' understanding of Ibn Rushd's conundrum. Borges interrogates, rather than accepts, the extent to which tradition shapes interpretation. Moreover, Ibn Rushd's mistake arguably arises from Aristotle's own misreading of Greek tragedy. Indeed, Aristotle's reduction of tragedy to poetic mimesis leads him to disregard the importance of performance, allowing foreign traditions to easily ignore it. Ibn Rushd is in fact 'the most Aristotelian' of the medieval commentators, as he makes poetry's 'pedagogical usefulness' his focal point (Gould 2014: 11). His ethical orientation explains his choice of vocabulary. His pedagogical approach and his foreignizing translation foreshadow the approach to tragedy that will characterize the works of various pioneers of Egyptian translation and theatre in the nineteenth century.

Ṭarāghūdhīyā, trajīdiā, ma'sā, riwāya: translating the term 'tragedy'

If Ibn Rushd's translation of the word *tragedy* as *madīḥ* (praise) is a contingent, and perhaps conscious misreading of Aristotle, other translations of the term make their way into the Arabic lexicon.

Broadly speaking, authors use two Arabic terms for the Greek *tragoidia: maʾsā* (distressing event) and *tirajidiya* or *ṭarāghūdhīyā* (two different phonetic renditions of the original Greek word). Strikingly enough, although borrowed from Greek, the first term is far older, used in early adaptations and translations of Greek drama into Arabic. It was first used by Farabi (al-Farābi, 870–950) and Ibn Sina (Avicenna, 980–1037) in their commentaries on the *Poetics*, to correct Ibn Matta's original mistranslation (Gould 2014). Both commentators prefer to transliterate, against a tradition established by al-Kindi (Isḥāq al-Kindī, d. c. 870), whereby Greek literary genres would be identified with Arabic ones (Gutas 1990). In the end, neither term had a very long posterity, so that in the nineteenth century the term is borrowed again into Arabic, this time from French or Italian.[6]

On the other hand, as Jaroslav Stektevych (1970) notes, the word *maʾsā* is a modern derivation from the Arabic root '[ʾ s, a]' (a root associated with the idea of suffering), supposedly coined by Ibrāhīm al-Yazījī, a Greek Catholic from Syria active in Lebanon at the end of the nineteenth century.[7] Today, its use has been generalized across the board in all registers of the Arabic language to refer not only to the literary genre but also to a personal *tragedy* or calamity, just as the adjective *maʾsāwī* is a common word for 'tragic'.[8] It is, therefore, a technical term created to highlight a salient ethic and aesthetic feature of the literary genre: the sense of despair and pain. The need for a new word translates the difficulty of conveying the totality of meanings involved in the storied development of the genre and its many contradictions. To this list belongs also the word *riwāya* ('story', 'narration', 'fabula'), a common translation of 'theatre play' which also sometimes refers to published tragedies.

Greek tragedy through European models: prestige and reform

Variously mistranslated into Arabic, the meaning of the word *tragedy* remains obscure for a further eight centuries. The *iqtibās* of Greek tragedy into Arabic can be seen as a long process of transculturation, a radical form of cultural transfer.[9] Transculturation is defined by Fernando Ortiz as 'the different phases of the process of transition from one culture to another' which involves not only acquiring another culture (acculturation) but also 'the loss [or] uprooting of a previous culture' (deculturation). It also 'carries the idea of the consequent creation of new cultural phenomena, which could be called neoculturation' (Ortiz 1940, quoted by Côté 2017). In the case of Egyptian theatre, interaction with the

European tradition is both willing and constrained. It produces 'theatrical practices' in a 'liminal space that is thoroughly hybrid' (Amine 2006: 145).

The process of creating an original Arab theatre is, as Monica Ruocco (2007) points out, synonymous with adapting European dramatic literature to the taste of Arab audiences. The plays in the ancient Attic tragic corpus are, for the most part,[10] dramatic retellings of pagan myths in verse, traditionally interpreted as conveying a sense of high-stakes (even transcendent) conflict to produce a particular aesthetic effect, mostly through a specific kind of dramatic syntax and the depiction of human suffering.[11] Ancient Attic tragedy, like few other dramatic genres, is deeply rooted in the historical and geographical context of its inception.[12] Paradoxically, it is also one of the genres whose interpretation by literary theory has detached it so much from its original soil in order to fabricate a purportedly universal model,[13] as it was the case of Romantic dialectical interpretation of Oedipus and Antigone.[14] Due to this ambiguity, Greek tragical texts can support different claims from Egyptian translators and writers who see them as either embodiments of European theatre or as a way to bypass direct European influence by, so to speak, cutting out the middleman.

At the end of the nineteenth century, however, Egyptian reception of Greek tragedy is still dependant on the growing influence and prestige of European culture, especially during the reign of Khedive Ismail (1863–79). European theatre had first appeared in Egypt as entertainment for Bonaparte's troops (1798–1800), who had a hall built in the Azbakiyya district of Cairo to stage theatre plays. But it was Ismail's Europhile project of urban development which transformed this neighbourhood into a theatre hub, filled with cafés, cabarets, and music halls.[15] This development is, of course, linked to the influx of European visitors due to the inauguration of the Suez Canal the same year.[16] European companies, led by the likes of Sarah Bernhardt and Jean Mounet-Sully, start visiting Egyptian theatres at the turn of the century.[17] This influence will be perceived even more strongly after 1882 and the beginning of British colonial occupation of Egypt.

All these factors create a real (albeit somewhat marginal) interest in Greek tragedy among Nahḍawī intellectuals, an interest always mediated by modern European literary and theatrical traditions. Writers and translators lack any knowledge of Ancient Greek, which is not taught in any university department across the Arab world at the time. Access to Greek literature is therefore mediated through European languages and literatures, partly through state-funded Bureau of Translation, directed by Rifaa al-Tahtawi (Rifāʿa Rāfiʿ al-Ṭahṭāwī, 1801–73). Tahtawi is also the first to translate Greek myth (in French garb!) for the stage:

the Théâtre de la Comédie (1869) was inaugurated to the tunes of Offenbach's *La Belle Hélène*, which Tahtawi translated as *Hīlāna al-Jamīla* (Isma ʿil 2015).[18]

Modern tragedies, ancient themes

This choice of language is a particularly difficult one to make in diglossic communities.[19] Not only must *Nahḍawī* writers create new words and structures to adapt to modern realities, but also the distinction between vernacular Arabic languages (the Arabic 'dialects') and the standard, a marker of prestige – also tied to religion, as Arabic is the language of the Qur'an – further complicates the issue. This is a common characteristic in early Egyptian translations of the tragic genre.

Najib al-Haddad and Muḥammad ʿUthmān Jalāl (1829–98) chose opposing strategies of hybridization and adaptation to translate French versions of ancient Greek tragedies. Najib al-Haddad, a nephew of Ibrahīm al-Yazījī. As for ʿUthmān Jalāl, mainly known for his successful Arabic adaptations of Molière, translated three of Racine's tragedies in 1893 as *Useful Stories in the Art of Tragedy* (*al-Riwayāt al-mufīda fī ʿilm al-trajīda*, 1893), a rhyming title characteristic of classical Arabic literature.[20] In the preface, al-Jalāl explains that these works belong to a European genre called '*la tragédie*', similar to the classical Arabic genre of *faraj baʿd al-shidda* 'relief after distress', 'treating of the fulfilment of hopes after long denials'.[21] The text is in Egyptian, instead of Standard Arabic, and written in *zajal*, a common form of popular verse.[22] According to Jalal, tragedy is to be understood in relation to European theatre. As Carole Bardenstein (2005) has pointed out, Jalāl, who seeks to bring tragedy to a larger audience, reclaims the text by hybridizing it through Egyptianization (*tamṣīr*). Jalāl uses 'the cultural prestige and authority of the French culture' in order to assert 'indigenous cultural capital and prestige' (Bardenstein 2005: 1). This process engages both Greek culture as a distant and prestigious reference and European literature as an ambiguous political space. The process of translation is more than the decoding and recoding from a language into another: it is a culturally complicated negotiation.[23]

One of the most crucial impulses behind the translation movement of the Nahḍa was the desire for revitalization of culture and literature, political reform, and modernization. A graduate of the School of Languages, Jalāl believed in education as a tool for reform and had high hopes for his Racinian translations.

Perhaps inspired by the Aristotelian tradition of *katharsis*, he attempted to draw the outline for an Egyptian understanding of tragic aesthetics. His project was unsuccessful. Sameh F. Hannah claims that this failure 'established a conventional practice for drama translators in Egypt for more than a century, i.e., the use of '*ammiyya* [Colloquial Arabic] in translating comedy and *fusha* [Modern Standard Arabic] in translating tragedy' (Hanna 2009: 165).

Jalāl's preface also invokes the prestige of the Khedivial dynasty, stressing the importance of patronage. Khedive Ismail seems to have relished being compared to Louis XIV, a patron of the arts, as Moosa suggests (1997: 44).[24] State sponsorship, in no small part, guaranteed the success of a European model of theatre in Egypt.[25] Abbas Hilmi, Ismail's son, even granted funding to actor and director George Abyad (Jūrj Abyaḍ, 1880–1959) from Bilād al-Shām, to study theatre in Paris (Hanna 2007: 34). He would later, upon his return, be the first to stage an original Greek tragedy in Arabic.

George Abyad's and Farah Antun's version of *Oedipus Tyrannos*

In 1912, a decade after the publication of al-Ḥaddād's *Ūdīb*, Abyad's staged an Arabic version of *Oedipus Tyrannos*, translated by Farah Antun (Faraḥ Anṭūn, 1874–1922). Abyad focused on the ambiguous power relations between the suffering people and their leader, a choice that would influence later Egyptian adaptations of the play. The ambiguity of the Greek term *tyrannos* warrants a strong political reading of Sophocles' play as a meditation on the nature of both tyrannical and democratic power (Knox 1954), which makes the *tyrannos* an illegitimate dictator. This theme will become central to later Egyptian adaptations of the myth.

Oedipus had entered the Egyptian stage a few years earlier, in a now lost, yet highly successful, translation of *Demofoonte* entitled *al-Sirr al-maknūn* (*The hidden secret*). The main role was played by one of the most famous Egyptian singers of the time, Salama Hegazi (Salāma Ḥijāzī, 1852–1917), who had also starred in Najib al-Haddad's *Romeo and Juliet* and had his own theatre troupe. Singers were an omnipresent component of early productions in Egypt, influenced by European vaudeville but with a stronger focus on traditional Arabic music. *Al-Sirr al-maknūn* also included a musical number.[26] Hegazi would go on to collaborate with Abyad in his version of Sophocles' *Oedipus*

Tyrannos.[27] The text of the translation, also lost, has been partially preserved as a recording from 1948, available online.[28]

It is the earliest translation of a Greek tragedy into Arabic, although the text might have evolved through the years. The date of the recording is a testament to the play's success. It was performed for over thirty years, and the role of Oedipus became one of Abyad's most iconic (Cormack 2017: 52). The hybrid nature of the play, which catered to both critics (who demanded a serious form of drama) and the Egyptian crowds (who had a taste for musical theatre) is one of the reasons of its undying popularity.

The hybrid nature of both the text and the performance was recently explored by Raphael Cormack (2017). We can gather from the recording of the play that the text owed much to the French dramatic tradition. In fact, in his domesticating verse translation, Lacroix restructured Sophocles' text as a French classical drama in Alexandrine lines, with a five-act layout. In the recording, most Greek names are pronounced as their French counterparts: Oedipus is *Ūdīb* (Fr. Œdipe); *Apollon* and *Kreon*, however, they are pronounced with a stress on the last syllable, which is also nasalized; finally, *Fibūs* and *Laiyūs* are realized as the French Phébus and Laïus. The recording is, thus, heavily mediated by French. The original choral odes, on the other hand, are replaced with original songs by Salama Hegazi.[29] The singer was immensely popular, so the show was sure to draw a crowd.[30] As Ziad Fahmy puts it, audiences were 'voting with their wallets' (2011: 131).[31] The songs combine elements of European Arab music, including rhythms (*iqāʿāt*) and scales (*maqāmāt*).[32] Most use *nahāwand*, a mode very similar to the Western major scale, and *hijāzkār*, a variation on a *maqām* that, despite being often presented in the West as the 'Arabic scale', can also fit a well-tempered chromatic system and would sound relatively familiar to Western listeners.[33] Both are suited to the gravity and distressful atmosphere of Sophocles' tragedy. In terms of rhythms, traditional Arabic patterns (such as *nawakht*) blend in with European waltzes.

By combining elements of the more 'artistic kind of theatre' (Cormack 2017: 53) with popular music, Abyad created a hybrid form of politicized tragedy which harkened back, perhaps unknowingly, to the musical origins of Attic drama. Hegazi's songs were a crucial part of the production. They focused the attention of the spectator on the relationship between the charismatic, yet tainted, *tyrannos* (Nagy 2020), and the people, the saviour of the city being is none other than its polluter, perhaps a form of veiled criticism of the Khedive's increasingly unpopular measures.[34]

A philological paradigm for Greek drama:
Taha Hussein and Louis Awad

Today, the whole of the Attic tragic corpus has been translated into Arabic by Egyptian philologists trained either at the University of Alexandria or at the University of Cairo and participate in state-sponsored translation programmes.[35] This is, to some extent, the realization of one of Taha Hussein's dreams, a dream that the following generation of intellectuals such as Louis Awad (Luwīs ʿAwaḍ) would keep alive. Taha Hussein (Ṭāhā Ḥusayn, 1889–1973), one of the foremost Arab intellectuals of the twentieth century, also translated Sophocles into Arabic. He had become acquainted with Greek and Latin at the Sorbonne, where he also came in contact with the methods of European philology, textual criticism and literary analysis, which exerted a lasting influence on him.

Upon his return to Egypt, Hussein taught Ancient History at the University, including the history of Greece and Rome, from 1919 to 1925. He became a staunch advocate for both classical languages in Egyptian universities and schools. During this period, he penned various works dealing with Greek history and literature, among which the book of *Selected Pages from the Dramatic Poetry of the Greeks* (*Ṣuḥuf Mukhtāra min al-shiʿr al-tamthīlī ʿinda al-Yunān*), published in 1920 (Ḥusayn 2014). The book contains selections from Aeschylus and Sophocles (but, for reasons still unclear, not Euripides), translated into Arabic by Hussein, preceded by a lengthy forty-page introduction in which he calls for engagement with Greek sources, as a steppingstone into a proper understanding of Egyptian history. In 1939, he published a translation of four of Sophocles' tragedies.

For Hussein, philology and translations were also modes of cultural commentary: he saw classics as a gateway to Western culture.[36] As Hussein explicitly states in a review (Ḥusayn 2014b) of Aḥmad Luṭfī al-Sayyid's 1924 translation of Aristotle's *Nicomachean Ethics*: 'Aristotle's philosophy was the foundation of the first Arab [Abbasid] renaissance, and that of the modern European Renaissance. It must, therefore, set the foundations of the intellectual renaissance in contemporary Egypt (*asās al-nahḍa al-ʿilmiyya fī Miṣr al-ḥadītha*).' The translation of the Greek drama should have a similarly galvanizing effect (Hussein 2014a: 9–11). Nevertheless, Greek texts were a shared heritage (Ḥusayn 2014a: 9–12), to which both the European Renaissance and the Abbasid translation movement had equally legitimate claims. In *The Future of Culture in Egypt* (*Mustaqbal al-thaqāfa fī Miṣr*, 1938), Hussein would flesh out the idea that the precedence of the West was neither genealogical nor ontological, but merely temporal.[37] This was a feeling shared by other contemporary Egyptian thinkers.[38]

Hussein's introduction to the translated excerpts also contains a detailed and erudite presentation of the origins of Greek theatre, as well as biographies of Aeschylus and Sophocles, relying on a solid knowledge of contemporary Western classical scholarship, but without being excessively erudite, since he aims to introduce the public to unknown territory.[39] He describes the relationship between Athenian drama, religious and civic life and Athenian politics, as relevant to Egypt's modern political project: 'We want a political renaissance (*nahḍa siyāsiyya*), we want to give a proper home in our country, but we are entirely ignorant of the origins and the rules of politics' (Hussein 2014a: 12).

As May Hawas points out, Hussein's own attempts to find 'balance' or a 'third way' between East and West,[40] modernity and tradition, colonizer and colonized, recognize a right to agency for *Nahḍawī* writers despite the unbalance of cultural and economic capital. This allows Hussein to situate Egyptian literature beyond binary oppositions regarding religious, political and cultural identity.[41] Hussein upends the traditional goals of philology, a notoriously conservative discipline, to locate Greek literature in a space where it can be, at least partly, dissociated from the European classical tradition. Thus philology becomes an instrument of intellectual liberation.

Why does Hussein choose to translate tragedy? First, because theatre had become increasingly popular. Hussein himself had marvelled at Abyad's success in the role of Oedipus (Cormack 2017: 52). Moreover, because of tragedy's foundational position in the European canon. How can Egyptians hope, Hussein asks, to understand Racine's *Iphigénie* without proper knowledge of the original plays by Euripides?[42] Creative engagement with Greek literature requires a sound knowledge of the tradition and of the tools of philology.[43] Finally, Hussein's considerations are pragmatic, pedagogical, and aesthetical. Tragedies are shorter and more manageable than Homer's *Iliad* (which had recently been translated by al-Bustānī, 1904). They are also, according to the translator (Ḥusayn 2014a: 12), of all the ancient genres, the most easily understandable and most pleasing to the soul (*ashal ... fahm, wa-alīn min-hu mulmis wa-aladhdh fī 'l-nufūs mawqiʿ*).

Louis Awad's translations of Aeschylus' trilogy can be seen as a radical continuation of Hussein's work. A Cambridge and Princeton graduate with a PhD thesis on the reception of the myth of Prometheus in European literature, Awad translated Aeschylus around the time of Nasser's defeat in the Six-Day War (1967).[44] He was critical of Nasser's view of economic development driven exclusively by scientific and technical progress, which had 'certainly supplied the country with a large class of technicians, [at the expense of humanistic studies]' but at the same 'depleted our intellectual class' (Awad 1968: 157). In this sense, his translations of Sophocles and Aristophanes can be partly construed as efforts to resist such a technocratic pull.

Translational choices

The edition of Awad's *Agamemnon* includes a thorough introduction like that of Hussein's 1920 book, with fewer lines devoted to history and politics. Instead, he presents Aeschylus' life and works in detail, and discusses the role of masks (based on Julius Pollux), showing interest in the staging process. He also offers a summary of Aristotle's *Poetics* and their modern reception. Unlike Hussein, Awad never uses the word *ma'sā* to refer to tragedy, but either transcribes it (*turajīdiā*), or glosses it as 'dramatic poetry' (*al-shi'r al-tamthīlī*), or as 'sorrowful drama' (*tamthīl muḥzin*). The text of his introduction is peppered with Greek names transcribed into Arabic followed by their English counterpart. A diagram of the structure of a round Greek amphitheatre follows the introduction.

Although an improvement on Hussein's methods, this edition is representative of what Jiménez Ángel calls a 'science without discipline' (Cuervo and Jiménez Angel 2013), that is, the pursuit of scientific endeavours outside of an institutionalized academic framework. Both authors depend on European scholarship: French for Hussein, English for Awad. The latter, who did not know Greek, relied on English-language translations by Morshead, Buckley and Weir Smyth.[45] Hussein's claim that he translated from the Greek has been contested by various scholars.[46] The fact that he only translated the four plays that make up the first tome of Paul Masqueray's edition is a further indication of this.[47] In spite of their reliance on European models, both translations betray a wish to take on Greek literature without mediation. This is clear, for instance, in Hussein's rough phonetic transliteration of Greek names, in contrast with the previous trend of using the French equivalents.[48]

Perhaps more interestingly, both translations operate in radically opposed ways in terms of language, form, and faithfulness to the original. Whereas Hussein's translations use prose without embellishments to convey a faithful idea of the original, Awad chooses to translate Aeschylus' theological dramas (for the most part) into Arabic verse by way of a Islamically inflected poetic language, through the use of sophisticated vocabulary and Quranic phrases. Hussein's stance is less daring than Awad's, which are reminiscent of Jalāl's and Tahtawi's earlier translations. For Richard Jacquemond (2019: 142), translation such as Hussein's are symptomatic of the acculturation of the Egyptian elites, the quest for a translational accuracy being a mere acceptance of European literary canons.[49] Nevertheless, by looking closer at the theory of translation Hussein puts forward in his 1920 preface, one can understand his choice in a different, more pragmatic, light. Hussein deems it objectively impossible for any translator to aptly convey Aeschylus' images and style in all their 'innate beauty' (*jamāluhu al-fiṭrī*, Hussein 2014a: 44–5). Prose is the lesser of two evils: the transposition from verse to prose entails a dislocation of the drama's original harmony, conveying only the 'least delightful and admirable aspects' of the work (*aqallu ajizā'ihā bahjat^{an} wa-raw'at^{an}* Hussein 2014a: 45). Aeschylus cannot be properly read in Arabic any more than the great pre-Islamic poet Imru' al-Qays can be adequately read in French. In that case, why translate? According to Hussein, the goal of translation must be upended. Instead of offering a true picture (*sūra ḥaqīqiyya*, ibid.) of the original, it should only pique the reader's curiosity.

Awad's translation of Aeschylus, on the other hand, is a transcultural hybrid, that was meant for the stage. It was used most notably by Greek director Takis Mouzenidis in a 1968 production at the Cairo Opera House (Cormack 2017: 196). The dialogue is written in blank verse (*al-shiʿr al-mursal*, Aeschylus and Awad 196?: 45), using the *rajaz* meter, one of the oldest and simplest traditional meters, and that is close to prose (Stoetzer 1998). Following Aristotle's remarks, Awad wishes the meter of dialogue to be closer to the natural prosody of conversation. Chorus parts (which Awad translated as *kūrās*, a rough transliteration of the Greek, instead of Hussein's more traditional *jawqa*) are to be sung: the chorus, in every stage direction, 'sings' (*yunshid*). For this purpose, Awad used *ramal*, a 'more musical meter' (*baḥr^{an} ashadd musīqiyyat^{an}*) (Aeschylus and Awad 196?: 17–29).

In the original, the *parodos* (the entrance of the chorus) of *Agamemnon* consists of an anapaestic prologue, six strophic pairs (strophe and antistrophe) and a conclusive epode. The choral odes of Greek tragedy stand out from the rest of the text in terms of meter and language, a challenge often ignored by translators. To translate this *parodos*, Hussein and Awad use diametrically opposed strategies.

The scene is the ancient Greek city of Argos. As the play opens, a watchman has just received news of the Achaean victory at the Trojan war.[50] The chorus of Argive elders enters the scene, singing of Calchas's unhappy prophecy at Aulis.

Each strophic segment ends with the hope that this prophecy will not come true: 'αἴλινον αἴλινον εἰπέ, τὸ δ᾽ εὖ νικάτω᾽.[51] This a ritual formula combines a *linos* (a dirge[52]) and pean (a victory chant), creating an unsettling feeling of impending doom. A literal Arabic translation would be somewhat bewildering, so Hussein translates it as follows: 'let us sing, let us sing a poem full of omens, but may the bad auguries they contain prove false' (*li-nataghanna, li-nataghanna ashʿārᵃⁿ milʾū-ha al-shūʾm, wa-lākin li-yukdhaba mā shtamalat ʿalay-hi min ṭīratⁱⁿ*, Hussein 2014a: 91).[53] The tone is flat and explicative. It elucidates the obscurity of the original but erases its ritual context and any direct references to victory (the verb νικάτω) and good (εὖ). It was almost certainly inspired by the French translation by La Porte du Theil (1795).

Awad offers a remarkable solution to this problem, so much so that the original becomes unrecognizable: 'Sing, o night, o sorrowful eye! May this night bring God-given tranquility!' (*ghanni yā layl, wa-yā ʿayn al-ḥazīna/layta hādhā al-layl yaʾtī bi l-sakīna*).[54] The unequivocally Greek *linos* is translated by a *layālī*, a traditional Arabic musical genre, characterized by the repetition of the phrase '*yā layl, yā ʿayn*' ('o night, o eye'), allowing the singer to freely improvise on a given *maqām*. It often introduces a *mawwāl*, often in dialectal Arabic.[55] The meditative, wailing tone of this phrase has ritual properties, which tie into Greek tragedy's own religious and civic context. The role of the singer in the *layālī*, as an ensemble director, might be analogue to that of the chorus-leader (*coryphaeus*). Awad further meshes the chorus into the fabric of Arabic culture by using Islamic vocabulary, as the chorus hopes not for victory for *sakīna*, the tranquillity of the presence of Allah (Blecher et al. 2012).

The same strategy permeates the whole *parodos* (and all chorus passages), especially the hymn to Zeus (160–83 in the Greek text). Whereas Hussein prefers to add explanatory footnotes on mythology and Greek religion, Awad modifies the text to tell the myth of Uranus and Cronus in detail: the hymn takes up twice as many lines as in the original Greek (48 instead of 22). By the same token, the Greek pagan worldview is adapted to an Islamic setting. To illustrate, Awad gives Zeus names that are commonly associated with Allah: *dhūʾl-jalāl, al-qahhār, āyyuha al-wāḥid*,[56] as well as words that are common in Sufi musical traditions to refer to either God or the Prophet. Even more glaringly, while the Greek chorus declares that 'whoever willingly sings a victory song for Zeus ... shall gain wisdom altogether', in Awad's version, the pious man who sings the praises of Zeus becomes *mahdī* (God-guided) and follows the *ṣirāṭ al-mustaqīm* (righteous path),[57] an obvious reference to the opening surah of the Quran. He also refuses to associate the cult of Zeus with that of other gods (*atā bāb Zyūs ghayr mushrik*).[58] Louis Awad, who hailed from a Christian background, was nonetheless aware of the unique relationship that exists between the Arabic language and Islam.[59]

The Islamic tone of these lines is unmistakable to an Arab listener. It helps carry over an understanding of the tragic sense of human feebleness in the face of adversity in a relatable way for a monotheistic audience. Greek tragedy finally speaks the language of praise that was at the heart Ibn Rushd's misunderstanding. And yet, a perceivable tension between both traditions remains. The effect is one of simultaneous harmony and dissonance, a thorough, yet ambiguous, transculturation of the original. Awad's translational experiments do not *domesticate* the text. They use egregiously Islamic passages in a text that is an obviously pagan context, somehow underlines the grafting process of translation: Awad adapts Greek tragedy to Egyptian culture, while systematically exposing the gaps between antiquity and present, East and West, Europe and Egypt, creating unavoidable tensions. Awad's work thus echoes Tawfīq al-Ḥakīm's momentous *al-Malik Ūdīb* (1949), the first Egyptian retelling of the story of Oedipus in dialogue with Islamic metaphysics.[60]

Conclusions: into the twenty-first century

In less than a century, a network of Arab translators, writers and directors active in Egypt in the nineteenth and twentieth centuries attempt a transculturation of Greek tragedy, from the page to the stage. Misunderstood by the medieval philosophical tradition, in the modern era, Greek tragedy steadily becomes a genre that the Egyptian public and literary milieu can recognize. Spurred by political and economic domination, which highlights the imbalance between Europe and the Arab world, the agents of this transculturation resort to ancient Greek tragedy as a paradoxical, albeit marginal, instrument to rethink and redefine the stakes of modernity in literature and culture. The varying masks tragedy successively takes on underscore the anxiety produced by the process of translating ancient dramatic artifacts (read through the lens of the European literary tradition) into an Arabic and Islamic context. This, in turn, illuminates the original hybridity of the genre. With the further development of classics departments in major Egyptian universities from the 1960s onwards, translations from Greek also became the standard. Hussein may have been unable to entirely cut out European mediation, but he was able to create a new philological paradigm for the reception of Greek tragedy, which affects it both as literature and as drama. This process also sheds light on the role of state-sponsored cultural activities (translation, education, theatrical productions, and infrastructure), which still shape the relationship between Egyptian writers, philologists, directors, and conflicting literary and theatrical models. Egyptian treatments of Greek tragedy point to an eristic dialogue with world literature and the world stage, which has yet to be explored by scholars in the larger context of the development of theatre as a global phenomenon.

Notes

1 That is to say, the inception of forms of institutionalized theatre, partly inspired by Western models and literary sources and staged in spaces dedicated exclusively to this endeavour. Prior to the nineteenth century, there existed a variety of non-Western theatrical practices throughout the Arab-Islamic world. See Ruocco (2007).

2 'Comment les arabes auraient-ils pu contribuer à la formation de l'héritage grec alors que la culture grecque existait bien avant la culture arabe? . . . C'est que j'ai trouvé – parmi les trésors de manuscrits arabes qui n'étaient pas encore étudiés – des textes très importants et assez abondants attribués aux grands penseurs de la Grèce' (Badawi 1987: 7).

3 See Gutas (1990: 95): 'Normally, the meaning of the text in the various stages would be by and large identical; but with a text as alien to Syriac or Arabic culture as that of the *Poetics*, the meaning gets deformed at each successive stage of the transmission.'

4 As Gould has shown, Ibn Rushd did not need to understand the nature of theatre to be able to apply Aristotle's conceptual framework to his own poetic tradition. This is not surprising, as Aristotle devotes little attention to the theatricality of tragedy: according to him, tragedy and comedy are poetic forms operating their mimetic function through language. Furthermore, poetic genres have ethical implications, since they imitate the actions of human beings entangled in moral dilemmas. This understanding minimizes the gap between text and performance and assimilates theatre to its literary features, as suggested by Dupont (2011).

5 '[If] a misreading is entailed in the rhetoricization of Aristotle's genre typologies, this misreading must be ascribed to an entire exegetical tradition originating in late antiquity. Like the later Arabic philosophers, this early Arabic exegetical tradition had little use for a theory of poetics based on drama' (Gould 2014: 9).

6 Farabi's transliteration is consistent with the pronunciation of medieval Greek, but not so the word *turajīdiā* (or even *trajīdia*), which is closer to its French and Italian equivalents. The same can be said of the feminized Arabic ending used by medieval translators.

7 The word seems to be attested in medieval times, but never as a translation for the word tragedy.

8 For instance, a *mawwāl* from rural Egypt cites a personal *maʾsā* as a source of poetic inspiration See Serafin Fanjul (1977). The *mawwāl* is a traditional Arabic song of lament.

9 *Iqtibās* a term often used by *Nahḍawī* writers to refer to borrowing through translation and adaptation. On the notion of iqtibās and appropriation during the Nahḍa, see Ruocco (2007) and (Khayat 2019).

10 Aeschylus' *Persians* is the only extant example of a historical tragedy.

11 This partial definition attempts to reconcile various accounts of the nature and function of tragedy from Aristotle onwards. Wilamowitz-Moellendorff (1907), Schadewaldt (1991) Dupont (2011) and Marx (2012) relocate tragedy in its cultural, political, religious and even topographical context. Hall (2010) emphasizes the relationship between the depiction of suffering and ethical behaviour.

12 On the nature of Greek tragedy and its relationship to Athenian civic life, see Wilamowitz-Moellendorf (1907), Pierre Judet de la Combe (2010), Vernant and Vidal-Naquet (Vernant 1981).

13 Peter Szondi (2011: 151) provides a historical and philosophical interpretation of this phenomenon in his *Versuch zum Tragischen*: 'Seit Aristoteles gibt es eine Poetik der Tragödie, seit Schelling erst eine Philosophie des Tragischen.'

14 See Billings (2014 and 2017).

15 See Ruocco (2007: 169–71). Cf. P. C. Sadgrove (1996).

16 See Trabelsi (2018).

17 Cormack (2017: 62).

18 See Cormack (2019).

19 On diglossia see Bassiouney (2020) and (on Greek diglossia) Mackridge (2009).

20 He also translated Corneille, La Fontaine and Boileau.

21 I quote Shamma's English edition of the text (Shamma and Salama-Carr 2021: 254). Note that al-Haddad's translation of Racine bears a similar title.

22 On the use of *zajal* in Egyptian popular theatre see Ziad Fahmy (Fahmy 2011), Chapter III. Dialect featured prominently in popular dramas at the time. See Fahmy, ibid.: 64.

23 Bardenstein's views have been nuanced by Tageldin (2011: 290).

24 This was met with resistance. See Trabelsi (2018).

25 'Ces dépenses attiraient également des critiques féroces de la part des paysans égyptiens qui vivaient encore dans une pauvreté extrême', ibid.

26 Hegazi's songs have been preserved and published by Fatḥallah (2002).

27 Cormack (2017: 32) mentions a staging of an Italian translation of Sophocles' *Oedipus* by Ernete Novelli in 1899.

28 See www.youtube.com/watch?v=V_DlfLed7GI, accessed: 22 November 2022.

29 For a detailed study of Salama's songs in the play see Cormack (2021).

30 On Hegazi, see Ruocco (2007: 173–4, 187).

31 Fahmy refers to the rise of theatre in colloquial Egyptian Arabic, at the expense of the standard language, but the same case can be made for musical theatre.

32 See Fathallah (2002).

33 On the nature of the Arabic and their performance in twentieth-century music, see Farraj and Shumays (2019).

34 See Cormack (2017: 70–5).

35 See Etman (2007). Most philological translations from the original Greek are published and sponsored by the Egyptian National Centre for Translation.

36 Besides the 1920 selections from Greek drama, Hussein publishes translations of Aristotle's *Constitution of the Athenians* (1925), Racine's *Phèdre* (1933) and Gide's *Thésée,* as well as a selection of translations from Western drama under the title *Western Dramatic Literature.*

37 For a summary of the main ideas in this book, see Pormann (2009), and Barbulesco (2002).

38 Ahmad Lutfi al-Sayyid and Mahmud Fahmi, the author of a *History of Greece*, were amongst these figures. See Reid (2002: 165, 170–1).

39 Further research needs to be conducted on the scholarship used by Hussein.

40 Hawas (2018: 83) 'For Hussein (and many in the Nahḍa), metaphors of balance were often used to locate Egyptian politics, literature, and religions between "East" and "West," or "ancient" and "modern." This middling location was not seen as weakness, but strength. Standing at a crossroads theoretically afforded Egypt a better position to navigate its cultural conflicts.'

41 Barbulesco (2002) interprets the resistance to Hussein's theory as an opposition to his Egyptian nationalist intellectual project, which was in contradiction with pan-Islamic identity.

42 Paradoxically, Euripides is the only tragic author Hussein did not translate into Arabic.

43 A persistent view among Egyptian intellectuals. Ahmad Etman (2007: 150), writes claims such an engagement must rely on 'a systematic study of the origins of drama'.

44 The exact date of publication of this translation is unclear.

45 See Pormann 2009: 219.

46 He admitted to Paul Cachia 'that he made use of French translations to check doubtful passages' (Cachia 1956: 185). Cormack shows to what extent this was an understatement (Cormack 2017: 112).

47 Sophocles and Paul Masqueray, *Sophocle: Ajax. Antigone. Œdipe-Roi. Électre.*, Vol. 1 (Paris: Les Belles Lettres, 1922).

48 One noteworthy example is the transition from the earlier Ūdīb (the French pronunciation used in earlier versions, including Farah Antun's translation) to Oidībūs.

49 According to Jacquemond (2019: 142), Egyptian translators 'turned to what has been defined by Western culture as its classics, thus imposing them upon their national culture without questioning the validity of such a transposition of a Western value system'.

50 For a study of the *parodos* see Coward (Andújar, Coward and Hadjimichael 2018: 39–64).

51 'Sing the song of woe, the song of woe, but may the good prevail!', translation by Weir Smyth (Aeschylus 1963: 16). In the Greek text, the line is repeated on lines 121, 139, 159.

52 See Coward (2018).

53 This is clearly an interpretation of La Porte du Theil's rendition of the line: 'Chantons, chantons des vers lugubres; mais que le présage en soit démenti!' in *Théâtre des Grecs, par le P. Brumoy.* Edited by Pierre Brumoy. Translated by Joseph de La Porte du Theil. Vol. 2. Paris: Cussac, 43.

54 See Aeschylus and ʿAwad (196?: 42). The line is then repeated on 43 and 45.

55 See Farraj and Shumays (2019: 350).

56 'Lord of Majesty', 'Absolute Conqueror', 'the One'. These are among the ninety-nine traditional names of Allah. Zeus thus shares the unicity, majesty and omnipotence of the God of Islam.

57 'He is rightly guided, and a leader, and a wiseman/, and he walks the righteous path' (*wa-huwwa mahdī, wa-hādⁱⁿ wa-ḥakīm/ wa-yamshī fī ṣirāṭ al-mustaqīm,* Aeschylus and Awad 196?: 47).

58 'He visits Zeus's door without associating him [with other deities]', ibid.

59 The interactions between the Qur'an and the Arabic poetic tradition are well-known (Sperl 2020; Neuwirth 2019).

60 On al-Hakim's *al-Malik Ūdīb* see Denooz (2002).

References

Aeschylus (AD 196), *Maʾsāt Agāmimnūn*, trans. L. ʿAwad. Cairo: Dār al-Qawmiyya li-l-Ṭibāʿat wa-l-Nashr.

Aeschylus (1963), *Aeschylus: In Two Volumes.* Edited by Hugh Lloyd-Jones. Translated by Herbert Weir Smyth. Vol. 2. 2 vols. Cambridge, MA: Harvard University Press.

Amine, K. (2006), 'Theatre in the Arab World: A Difficult Birth', *Theatre Research International*, 31(2): 145–62. https://doi.org/10.1017/S0307883306002094.

Andújar, R., R. P. Coward and T. A. Hadjimichael (2018), *Paths of Song: The Lyric Dimension of Greek Tragedy*, Berlin: De Gruyter.

Awad, L. (1968), 'Cultural and Intellectual Developments in Egypt since 1952', in P. J. Vatikiotis (ed.), *Egypt Since the Revolution (RLE Egypt)*, New York: Routledge.

Badawī, A. (1987), 'La Transmission de la Philosophie Grecque au Monde Arabe', *Études de Philosophie Médiévale*, 56. Paris: J. Vrin.

Barbulesco, L. (2002), 'L'itinéraire hellénique de Tâhâ Husayn', *Revue des mondes musulmans et de la Méditerranée*, 95–8 (April): 297–305. https://doi.org/10.4000/remmm.237.

Bardenstein, C. (2005), 'Translation and Transformaticn in Modern Arabic Literature: The Indigenous Assertions of Muḥammad 'Uthmān Jalāl', *Studies in Arabic Language and Literature*, 5, Wiesbaden: Harrassowitz.

Bassiouney, R. (2020), *Arabic Sociolinguistics: Topics in Diglossia, Gender, Identity, and Politics*, 2nd edn, Washington, DC: Georgetown Ur.iversity Press.

Billings, J. (2017), *Genealogy of the Tragic: Greek Tragedy and German Philosophy*, Princeton, New Jersey: Princeton University Press.

Blecher, J., M. T. Houtsma, R. Hartmann, R. Basset and T. W. Arnold (2012), 'Al-Sakīna', *Encyclopaedia of Islam*. Koninklijke Brill NV. https://doi.org/10.1163/2214-871X_ei1_SIM_5087.

Borges, J. L. (1997), *Obras completas*. Edited by Carlos V. Frías. Barcelona, Spain: Emecé.

Cachia, P. (1956), *Ṭāhā Husayn: His Place in the Egyptian Literary Renaissance*, London: Luzac & Co.

Carlson, M. (2005), *The Arab Oedipus: Four Plays from Egypt and Syria*, New York: Martin E. Segal Theatre Center Publications.

Carlson, M. (2013), 'The Arab Aristophanes', *Comparative Drama* 47(2): 151–66.

Carlson, M. (2019), *Theatre and Islam,* London: Macmıllan Education.

Cormack, R. (2017), 'Oedipus on the Nile: Translations and Adaptations of Sophocles' Oedipus Tyrannos in Egypt, 1900–1970', PhD diss., Edinburgh: The University of Edinburgh.

Cormack, R. (2019), 'Lords or Idols?', in M. Booth (ed.), *Migrating Texts*, Edinburgh: Edinburgh University Press. www.jstor.org/stable/10.3366/j.ctvnjbgb3.16.

Cormack, R. (2021), 'Who's Afraid of Musical Theatre? George Abyad's 1912 Oedipus Rex', in A. Gorman, S. Irving (ed.), *Cultural Entangl*ement *in the Pre-Independence Arab World: Arts, Thought and Literature*, 33–50, Lcndon: Bloomsbury Publishing Plc. https://doi.org/10.5040/9780755606313.

Côté, J. (2017), 'VI. From Transculturation to Hybridization: Redefining Culture in the Americas', in A. Benessaieh (ed.), *Amériques Transculturelles/Transcultural Americas*, 121–47, Ottawa: University of Ottawa Press. http://books.openedition.org/uop/363.

Cuervo, R. J. and A. Jiménez Angel (2013), *Correspondencia y Formación de Redes Intelectuales: Los Epistolarios de Rufino José Cuervo, 1865 y 1882*. Primera edición, Bogotá: Instituto Caro y Cuervo.

Denooz, L. (2002), *Entre Orient et Occident: rôles de l'hellénisme et du pharaonisme dans l'oeuvre de Tawfiq al-Hakīm*, Genève, Suisse: Droz.

Dupont, F. (2011), *Aristote ou le vampire du théâtre occidental*, Paris: Flammarion/Aubier.

Etman, A. (2004), 'The Greek Concept of Tragedy in the Arab Culture, or How to Deal with an Islamic Oedipus?', *Documenta*, XXII(4): 281–99.

Etman, A. (2007), 'Translation at the Intersection of Traditions: The Arab Reception of the classics', in L. Hardwick, C. Stray (eds), *A Companion to Classical Receptions*, 141–52, Oxford, UK: Blackwell Publishing Ltd. https://doi.org/10.1002/9780470696507.ch11.

Fahmy, Z. (2011), *Ordinary Egyptians: Creating the Modern Nation through Popular Culture*, Stanford, California: Stanford University Press.

Farraj, J. and S. Abu Shumays (2019), *Inside Arabic Music: Arabic Maqam Performance and Theory in the 20th Century Middle East*, New York, NY: Oxford University Press.

Fatḥallah, Ī. (2002), *Salāma Ḥijāzī*, Cairo: Dār al-Shurūq.

Gould, R. (2014), 'The Poetics from Athens to Al-Andalus: Ibn Rushd's Grounds for Comparison', *Modern Philology*, 112(1): 1–24. https://doi.org/10.1086/676464.

Gutas, D. (1990), 'On Translating Averroes' Commentaries', *Journal of the American Oriental Society*, 110(1): 92–101. https://doi.org/10.2307/603913.

Hall, E. (2010), *Greek Tragedy: Suffering under the Sun*, Oxford: Oxford University Press.

Hanna, S. F. (2007), 'Decommercialising Shakespeare: Mutran's Translation of "Othello"', *Critical Survey*, 19(3): 27–54. www.jstor.org/stable/41556231.

Hanna, S. F. (2009), 'Othello in the Egyptian Vernacular', *The Translator*, 15(1): 157–78. https://doi.org/10.1080/13556509.2009.10799275.

Hawas, M. (2018), 'Taha Hussein and the Case for World Literature', *Comparative Literature Studies*, 55(1): 66–92. https://doi.org/10.5325/complitstudies.55.1.0066.

Ḥusayn, Ṭ. (2014a), *Ḥadīth Al-Arbiʿāʾ*, Cairo: Mūʾassasat Hindāwī.

Ḥusayn, Ṭ. (2014b), *Ṣuḥuf Mukhtāra Min Al-Shiʿr al-Tamthīlī ʿinda al-Yunān*, Cairo: Mūʾassasat Hindāwī.

Ismaʿil, S. ʿA. (2012), '"Al-Masrah al-Almāni"', *Kawalis*, 31: 86–93.

Ismaʿil, S. ʿA. (2015), *Hīlāna Al-Jamīla: Awwal Masraḥiyya Manshura Bi-l-ʿarabiyya Fī Miṣr Sanat 1868: Athar Adabī Majhūl li-l-Shaykh Rifaʿa al-Tahtāwī*, Cairo: General Egyptian Book Organization.

Jacquemond, R. (2019), 'Translation and Cultural Hegemony: The Case of French-Arabic Translation', in L. Venuti (ed.), *Rethinking Translation: Discourse, Subjectivity, Ideology*, 139–58, Abingdon: Routledge.

Jihād, K. (2007), *La Part de l'étranger: La Traduction de la Poésie dans la culture arabe: essai critique*, La Bibliothèque Arabe. Série Hommes et Sociétés, Paris; Arles: Sindbad Actes Sud.

Judet de La Combe, P. (2010), *Les tragédies grecques sont-elles tragiques? Théâtre et théorie*, Montrouge: Bayard.

Khayat, N. (2019), 'What's in a Name? Perceptions of Authorship and Copyright during the Arabic Nahda', *Nineteenth-Century Contexts*, 41(4): 423–40. https://doi.org/10.1080/08905495.2019.1622948.

Kilito, A. (2002), *Lan tatakallama lughatī*, Beirut: Dār al-Ṭalīʿah.

Knox, B. M. W. (1954), 'Why Is Oedipus Called Tyrannos?', *The Classical Journal*, 50(3): 97–130. www.jstor.org/stable/3292487.

Leezenberg, M. (2004), 'Katharsis, Greek and Arab Style: On Averroes's Misunderstanding of Aristotle's Misunderstanding of Tragedy', *Documenta*, 22(4). https://doi.org/10.21825/doc.v22i4.10331.

Mackridge, P. (2009), *Language and National Identity in Greece, 1766–1976*, Oxford; New York: Oxford University Press.

Marx, W. (2012), *Le tombeau d'Oedipe: pour une tragédie sans tragique*, Paris: Les Éditions de Minuit.

Moosa, M. (1997), *The Origins of Modern Arabic Fiction*, Boulder, CO: Lynne Rienner Publishers.

Moreh, S. (1966), 'Blank Verse ("al-Shiʻr al-Mursal") in Modern Arabic Literature', *Bulletin of the School of Oriental and African Studies, University of London*, 29(3): 483–505. www.jstor.org/stable/611471.

Nagy, G. (2020), *The Ancient Greek Hero in 24 Hours*, Cambridge, MA: Belknap Press.

Najjar, F.M. (1976), 'State and University in Egypt during the Period of Socialist Transformation, 1961–1967', *The Review of Politics*, 38(1): 57–87. www.jstor.org/stable/1406436.

Neuwirth, A. (2019), 'The Qur'an and Poetry', in Neuwirth, A. and Wilder, S. (eds), *The Qur'an and Late Antiquity: A Shared Heritage*, Oxford: Oxford University Press. https://doi.org/10.1093/oso/9780199928958.003.0013.

Ortiz, F. (1940), *Contrapunteo cubano del tabaco y el azúcar: (advertencia de sus contrastes agrarios, económicos, históricos y sociales, su etnografía y su transculturación)*, La Habana, Cuba: Jesús Montero Editor.

Pormann, P. E. (2009), 'Classics and Islam: From Homer to al-Qāʿida', *International Journal of the Classical Tradition*, 16(2): 197–233. https://doi.org/10.1007/s12138-009-0120-8.

Pormann, P. E. (2014), 'Arabs and Aristophanes, Menander among the Muslims: Greek Humour in the Medieval and Modern Middle East', *International Journal of the Classical Tradition*, 21(1): 1–29. www.jstor.org/stable/24716606.

Pormann, P. E. (2015), 'Greek Thought, Modern Arabic Culture: Classical Receptions since the Nahḍa', *Intellectual History of the Islamicate World*, 3 (1–2): 291–315. https://doi.org/10.1163/2212943X-00301011.

Reid, D. M. (1990), *Cairo University and the Making of Modern Egypt*, Cambridge Middle East Library 23, Cambridge; New York: Cambridge University Press.

Reid, D. M. (2002), *Whose Pharaohs? Archaeology, Museums, and Egyptian National Identity from Napoleon to World War I*, Berkeley: University of California Press.

Ruocco, M. (2007), 'La Nahḍa par l'Iqtibās: Naissance du théâtre arabe', in B. Hallaq, H. Toelle (eds), *Histoire de la littérature arabe moderne. Tome 1, 1800–1945*, Arles: Actes Sud.

Sadgrove, Ph. (1996), *The Egyptian Theatre in the Nineteenth Century: 1799–1882*, Berkshire: Ithaca Press.

Schadewaldt, W., M. Schadewaldt, I. Schudoma and W. Schadewaldt (1991), *Die Griechische Tragödie*. 1. Aufl. Tübinger Vorlesungen, Bd. 4. Frankfurt am Main: Suhrkamp.

Serafin F. (1977), 'The Erotic Popular "Mawwa:L" in Egypt: Note on Transcription', *Journal of Arabic Literature*, 8: 104–22. www.jstor.org/stable/4182981.

Shamma, T. and M. Salama-Carr (2021), *Anthology of Arabic Discourse on Translation*, Translation Studies in Translation, London; New York: Routledge.

Sperl, S. (2020), 'The Qur'an and Arabic Poetry', in M. Shah, M. Abdel Haleem (eds), *The Oxford Handbook of Qur'anic Studies*, Oxford: Oxford University Press. https://doi.org/10.1093/oxfordhb/9780199698646.013.16.

Stetkevych, J. (1970), *The Modern Arabic Literary Language: Lexical and Stylistic Developments*, Publications of the Center for Middle Eastern Studies, 6, Chicago: University of Chicago Press.

Stoetzer, W. (1998), 'rajaz', in J. Scott Meisami, P. Starkey (eds), *Encyclopedia of Arabic Literature*, London: Routledge.

Szondi, P. and C. König (2011), *Schriften*. Edited by Wolfgang Fietkau, Jean Bollack, and Henriette Beese. 2 vols. Berlin: Suhrkamp, 2011.

Tageldin, S. M. (2011), *Disarming Words: Empire and the Seductions of Translation in Egypt*, Berkeley: University of California Press.

Tageldin, S. M. (2016), 'Fénelon's Gods, al-Ṭahṭāwī's Jinn: Trans-Mediterranean Fictionalities', *Philological Encounters*, 2 (June). https://doi.org/10.1163/24519197-00000023.

Trabelsi, O. (2018), 'L'essor du théâtre occidental dans l'Égypte khédiviale et les premières aspirations des Égyptiens à un théâtre moderne arabe', *Horizons/Théâtre: Revue d'études théâtrales*, 12: 26–46. https://doi.org/10.4000/ht.292.

Venuti, L. (2008), *The Translator's Invisibility: A History of Translation*, 2nd edn, London; New York: Routledge.

Vernant, J.-P. (1981), *Mythe et société en Grèce ancienne*, Fondations, Paris: F. Maspero.

Wilamowitz-Moellendorff, U. von (1907), *Einleitung in die griechische Tragödie*, Berlin: Weidmann.

2

Oedipus of Thebes on Arab Stages

Marvin Carlson

Even though Aristotle, the dominant theatre critic in the Western tradition, considered Sophocles' *Oedipus* the most perfect tragedy, few of the most highly regarded Western dramatists have attempted to create their own versions of this classic. Rival stories, such as that of Electra and Orestes, Medea, even Oedipus' daughter Antigone, have proven much more attractive.

The situation has been quite different in the Arab world. The Oedipus story has inspired leading Arabic dramatists and no other Greek myth has so significant a tradition of adaptations and translations in this dramatic tradition. The reasons for this difference are difficult to determine. Perhaps Aristotle's high praise for Sophocles' version discouraged Western authors from attempting rival versions. Perhaps the political dimensions of the play, especially its exploration of the dynamics of the pride and fall of the powerful ruler, always a major concern in the Arabic theatre, attracted authors from that tradition. Perhaps the national and geographical conditions of the arrival of Western drama in the Arab world, about which I will have more to say presently, worked to the advantage of this story. Nor can one discount the coincidence that Oedipus' home city of Thebes had the same name as a famous city in Egypt, causing not a few readers over the centuries to mistakenly consider Oedipus Egyptian. Whatever the reasons, the continuing Arab interest in this story is central to an understanding of the development of the modern Arabic theatre, and the aim of this chapter is to explore the dramatic results of that interest.

The first known appearance of the Oedipus story in the Arab World was in 1905, and was among the first examples of Western-style drama in the Arab world. Drama in this style was introduced in the very European-oriented city of Beirut, now in Lebanon, which was then a part of Syria. In 1848, a Beirut businessman, Marūn al-Naqqāsh, presented in his home an Arabic play, *al-Bakhīl* (The Miser), inspired by Molière's *The Miser*. The new form gained popularity in Beirut, and during the 1878s was introduced to Egypt by actors from Syria. Syrian actors and authors dominated this early theatre, and among the most popular of them was the prolific Najib al-Haddad (Najīb al-Ḥaddād), especially remembered for his adaptations of major European classics, beginning with *Romeo and Juliet* in 1890.

al-Haddad's 1905 *Oedipus* was based not up Sophocles but on the eighteenth-century version of the story created by Voltaire. The choice of this version was not surprising, since France dominated the cultural life of European-oriented Syria at that time and Voltaire was far better known and more highly regarded than any of the classic dramatists. Indeed, the first tragedy in Arabic, created in 1872, was an adaptation of Voltaire's tragedy *Mérope*.

This first Arabic *Oedipus* has not survived, but contemporary reports survive that allow us to gain a general understanding of al-Haddad's approach. Of particular interest is the report that al-Haddad's text was in prose, but that the company presenting the play added poetry in the form of songs and chants. Were a modern reader to encounter the actual performed text, they might reasonably assume that these musical passages were an attempt to replicate the choric odes of the original, but such a project would surely have been the concern of al-Haddad himself, a leading literary scholar. Clearly this material was added by the actors to make the literary drama more accessible to a public familiar with song and dance entertainment but not yet with purely spoken drama. The same mixture is found throughout the early Arabic adaptations of European drama as well as in the first original Arabic dramas.

The second Arabic *Oedipus* appeared in 1913 and was the work of another prominent Syrian dramatist, Farah Antun (Faraḥ Anṭūn), whose works dominated the repertoire of the early Arabic theatre. His *Oedipus* has a special place in the modern Arabic theatre. It was created especially as the opening production of the recently formed company of Georges Abyad (Jūrj Abyaḍ) in Cairo, the first company in Egypt supported by the state. Unhappily for the company, the Khedive who supported them was deposed in 1914 and, deprived of his support, the company left Egypt to try their fortunes at touring. They thus brought the first modern theatre into what is now Palestine and travelled as far to the West as Tunisia and Algeria. Although Antun's *Oedipus* was a popular offering and remained in the company's repertoire until the 1940s, drama was still not considered a significant literary form in the Arab world, and like the al-Ḥaddād's version, all copies of Antun's *Oedipus* have disappeared. Its general form was probably similar to that of al-Haddad, but it was probably still not close to the Greek original because it was apparently translated, not from Sophocles but from an unknown French intermediary, not Voltaire.

The first surviving Arabic *Oedipus* thus comes, not coincidentally, from the literary rather than the theatrical world, and is the work of one of Egypt's leading men of letters in the early twentieth century, Taha Hussein (Ṭāha Ḥusayn). Hussein, a champion of the Western literary tradition, published an Arabic version of the contemporary French *Oedipus* of André Gide in 1931 as well as the first Arabic version of *Oedipus* based directly on the Greek original in 1939, in a volume which also included *Ajax*, *Electra*, and *Antigone*. Whatever their literary merits, however, Hussein's translations aroused no interest in the theatre world, which continued to offer the proven stage-worthy version of Antun.

It was not until 1949 that the Arab world produced a version of the Greek classic that was praised both by the literary and theatrical communities, and it was, appropriately, the creation of the first Arab dramatist to achieve a significant international reputation, Tawfiq al-Hakim (Tawfīq al-Ḥakīm). The appearance of al-Hakim's play, *The People of the Cave*, which was chosen to open Egypt's first national theatre in 1933, immediately established its authors as one of Egypt's leading literary figures. Among the most enthusiastic supporters of the new author was Taha Hussein, who called the new work 'epoch-making', a milestone 'not in modern Arabic literature alone, but in the whole of Arabic literature'. Hussein went on to hail the play as 'the first work in Arabic literature which may properly be called drama' (quoted in Badawi 1987: 27).

Given Hussein's continuing and critical support of the young al-Hakim, it is tempting to think that the example of the older author may have influenced al-Hakim's choice to create his own version of the Oedipus legend, but al-Hakim himself cites a variety of other inspirations. Like Hussein, and many other Arab intellectuals of the period, he spent some of his formative years (1925–8) in Paris, where he was much influenced by the French literary and theatrical tradition. In his autobiographical writings he even relates how impressed he was by a performance of Voltaire's *Oedipe* at the Comédie-Française, with Albert Lambert, the leading tragedian of the period, in the title role. This was by no means his introduction to the work, however. Al-Hakim reports that while still a schoolboy, he often went to see his favourite actor, Georges Abyad, performing *Oedipus* and *Othello* at the Cairo Opera and that he was able to recite 'whole pages' of these works to his schoolmates (al-Hakim 1992: 140).

In a lengthy preface to his version of the story, al-Hakim discusses how as a dramatist with an Islamic background, he has reconsidered the European Oedipus story. The Western story, he argues, emphasizes a conflict between the human will and fate, a conflict which has diminished in power as religious belief has declined in the West. al-Hakim suggests another potentially equal source of conflict, which he feels is still accessible in Islamic religion although which some might consider more philosophical than religious – a conflict between what al-Hakim calls fact and truth. The fact in Sophocles is the physical events of the play, the truth, the hidden world of unknown events and unacknowledged assumption that undermine the apparently stable world of fact. Although al-Ḥakīm argues that this restores something of the original religious power of tragedy, the effect is on the whole more secular. Along with fate, the Gods (or God) have disappeared, a shift particularly noticeable in the character of Tiresias, not a divine seer, but a very contemporary political manipulator, primarily concerned with power and control over the ruling house. Indeed the central story of the defeat of the Sphinx is revealed to be a political fabrication to elevate Oedipus, a fabrication created by the wily Tiresias. This much more secular and political orientation of al-Hakim's *Oedipus* has led some critics, most notably Sami Munir, to read the play basically as a political allegory, inspired by the British manipulation of the Egyptian government in the 1940s, while the play was being written (Munir 1979).

The degree of specific political inspiration in al-Ḥakīm's version remains a matter of debate, but no such disagreement exists in the case of another major Egyptian reworking of the Greek legend, which, strikingly, was published the same year as al-Hakim's *Oedipus*, 1949. This was the *Tragedy of Oedipus* created by Ali Ahmad Bakathir ('Alī Aḥmad Bākathīr), one of the important new dramatists to appear during the 1940s in the wake of al-Hakim's success. Unlike al-Hakim, Bakathir specifically cited current politics, specifically the crushing defeat of the Arab armies in Palestine in 1948 as causing him the 'deep, heavy pain' which the creation of the play sought to relieve (quotes in Selaiha 2001: 3).

Bakathir's path to the Greek legend was very different from that of al-Hakim. The latter was born in Egypt, exposed to the European classics from his earliest day, and further internationalized, like many well-to-do young Egyptians of his generation, by several years in Paris. Bakathir was born to Arab parents in far-off Indonesia and before coming to Cairo in 1934 (at roughly the same age when the young al-Hakim departed for Paris) had a traditional Islamic education, which included no exposure at all to European culture or classics. While studying at Cairo University, however, Bakathir became fascinated by English literature, and especially by Shakespeare, whose *Romeo and Juliet* he translated into Arabic.

Bakathir remained, however, a strong supporter of Islam and of Arabic nationalism, both major themes in his first plays, in the early 1940s, dealing with classic and Islamic Egyptian history. These two concerns were growing in importance in Egyptian society even before the 1948 war and were probably most clearly expressed in one of the most popular books of the day, Sayyid Quṭb's *Social Justice in Islam (al-ʿAdāla al-ijtimāʿiyya fī-l-Islām)* which appeared in 1949, the same year as Bākathīr's *Oedipus*. Clearly these two works reflect the same intellectual world. Quṭb calls for an integrated, coherent Islamic theory of social justice in response to the growing power of secular Marxism. Bakathir's *Oedipus* can be taken almost as an illustration of this project. He begins as a kind of proto-Marxist who preaches social justice and confiscates the goods of the Temple to distribute to the people, but who is ultimately led by the inspired guidance of Tiresias to an understanding that his social aims can in fact only be achieved by faith in God and total submission to his will.

Thus, although the two *Oedipus* plays of Bakathir and al-Ḥakīm both have a strong political dimension largely lacking in the original, their messages and implications are strikingly different. This can probably be seen most clearly in the almost diametrically opposed depictions of the key figure of Tiresias, who is in al-Hakim's version a totally amoral political intriguer, while in that of Bakathir he is a devout Muslim who speaks in a language redolent of the Qur'an and whose advice at last leads to Oedipus' religious enlightenment. The role played by Tiresias in al-Ḥakīm is essentially filled in Bakathir by Lucasius, the high priest, a wily, calculating politician intent on preserving the riches of his Temple. The plot grows almost entirely from his intrigues. From the first prophecy to Laius through the killing of the Sphinx and Oedipus' ascension to the throne, all results not from the working of fare or the gods, but from the manipulations and deceptions of the evil Lucasius.

Up until this time, it was Egyptian dramatists alone in the Arab world who created modern reworkings of the Oedipus story, perhaps not surprising since Egypt has almost from the beginning dominated the modern Arab theatre in production, playwrighting and publication. During the 1940s and 1950s however, the establishment of a National Theatre and the inspiration of Egyptian work encouraged an important new generation of playwrights in Syria. One of the leaders of this generation was Walid Ikhlasi (Walīd Ikhlāṣī), who, like al-Hakim, experimented with a wide range of dramatic subjects and modes, from reworking of European classics to works in the manner of the theatre of the absurd. Both influences are present to some extent in his Oedipus, which appeared in 1978, just a year before those of Bakathir and Fahmi (Fahmī) in Egypt.

Ikhlasi's version is strikingly different, however, not only from those of his contemporaries, but from any Arabic version to date. Although all of the Egyptian versions have distinct contemporary echoes, Ikhlasi frankly transfers his *Oedipus* into the most contemporary of settings – a modern computer laboratory. Even the names are gone, although the protagonist Sufiān is clearly modeled on Oedipus and his colleague, the computer scientist Dr al-Bāhī bears some resemblance to Tiresias, especially in his expository functions. The prophecy comes not from an oracle, but, in appropriate late-twentieth century fashion, from a super-computer.

This prophecy however shifts from the generation of Sufiān's parents (the murder of his father and incest with his mother) to that of his children (the murder of his son and incest with his daughter). Sufiān's daughter, Sulāf, is the closest parallel to Jocasta, but after the fateful revelation, late in the play, she disappears from the action and attention focuses entirely on the suffering of Sufiān. Rather surprisingly in this contemporary retelling, Ikhlasi restores the classic chorus, universally omitted in the Egyptian adaptations, and uses it to provide short poetic meditations on the story, especially at the opening and closing of scenes.

Here and in other aspects Ikhlasi's version, while obviously the further removed from the Greek original, most importantly it is almost entirely devoid of the distinct political orientation of most Egyptian versions, returning to the highly personal study of an individual who imagines that he is in control of his universe and finds that he is in fact the plaything of forces beyond his control or comprehension. Ikhlasi does not position the computer as the dark force that shapes his protagonist's fate. Its role is closer to that of the traditional oracle, which can look deeper into the cosmic mystery than the most intelligent human but ultimately has no power over it. Although Sufiān himself has much less trust in the computer than his colleague (an echo of Oedipus' distrust of the oracle), clearly the computer serves to emphasize that even in a world dominated by science and rational thought, the primal forces that destroyed Oedipus, that early champion of rationalism, have lost nothing of their power.

After the almost simultaneous appearance of three versions of the Greek myth by three of the leading dramatists of the Arab world, a full generation passed before another Arab dramatist undertook a retelling of the story. This was *The Return of the Absent One* (*'Awdat al-Ghā'ib*), one of the first plays by Fawzi Fahmi, who became a leading figure in the Cairo literary scene and president of the Cairo Academy of Arts. Like his Arab predecessors and indeed like Arab tragic dramatists in general, Fahmī was much more concerned with the political implications of his source stories than with their explorations of fate or destiny. This tendency was reinforced in Egypt by events between the versions of al-Hakim and Bakathir and that of Fahmi, especially the disastrous 1967 war, followed by the resignation of Nasser and his return to power by popular support. The obligations and actions of a good ruler, a clear concern for both al-Hakim and Bakathir, became even more central an issue for Fahmi.

His Oedipus, like Bakathir's, is a noble political visionary surrounded by corruption and intrigue. At first, again recalling Bakathir, he at first tries to reform the state without laying bare its corruption, but he then experiences a conversion, not a religious one as in Bakathir, but a personal and political one, exposing the corruption and conspiracy in the state and taking measures to similarly, but privately cleanse himself as well. In order to achieve this, without undermining the nobility Fahmi wishes to give his hero, the dramatist has to make radical changes to the traditional story. To begin with, when Oedipus learns from a messenger of his incestuous marriage, he understands and accepts the truth at once. He and Jocasta swear to each other never to reveal their true relationship (a moderately easy matter since in this version they have produced no children)[1] and far from blinding himself, leaves Jocasta to marry a pure young woman, Euryganeia, who will be his companion in ruling the new reformed and cleansed Thebes. This reformed version was praised by some critics for its attempted recuperation of the incest motif,[2] but others felt that whatever moral elevation this reworking achieved did not fully redeem the protagonist[3] and Fahmi's version has proven less attractive to both scholars and producers than its two immediate predecessors or its two successors.

The next Arabic Oedipus to appear departed even more radically from the dramatic tradition, but also has enjoyed the greatest success. This was the creation of Ali Salim ('Alī Sālim), who first appeared on the literary scene in the 1960s and immediately established himself as an inspired satirist, taking as his targets Egyptian bureaucracy, the jargon of scientists, politicians and literary critics, the new middle class of post-Revolutionary Egypt, and despotic activities of all sorts. Not surprisingly, every one of his first five plays had difficulties with the state censor, and his *The Comedy of Oedipus*, in 1979, was the first to reach the stage uncut. It was a great success at the now defunct Al-Hakim Theatre, but its very popularity apparently aroused the concern of the censors, who demanded a more subdued version shortly after it opened.

It is a bit surprising that Salim's play was approved without reservations in the first place. Perhaps it was the use of a foreign classic already treated by some of the country's most respected dramatists that mollified the censors, or perhaps it was the claimed remoteness of the action, which was described by the author as occurring 'a long time, a very long time ago' (Salim 2005: 287). Despite this claim, however, the play's characters, unlike those of earlier versions of the legend, are clearly contemporary or very recent and again, unlike his Egyptian predecessors, Sālim transports his action from the Greek to the Egyptian Thebes. It has been suggested that this change was inspired at least in part by the 1960 book *Oedipus and Akhenaton* by Immanuel Velikovsky, which advanced the theory that the Greek myth was originally inspired by the life of the visionary pharaoh.[4] Salim in his introduction to the play cites this interpretation, not only claiming that Akhenaton and his family were the original inspiration for the Oedipus story, but that Sophocles' version itself was based on an earlier Egyptian version of the story (quoted in Etman 2004, 297). No historical evidence has been discovered in support of this theory, but the coincidence of the name Thebes in ancient Egypt and classic Greece encouraged this convergence, as did the central figure of the Sphinx, which holds an important position in the mythology and iconography of both cultures.[5]

The subtitle of Sālim's drama, *You Who Killed the Beast* (*Enta illi 'atalt al-waḥsh*) provides an excellent insight into the focus and dramatic strategies of this adaptation. In fact the encounter with the Sphinx is the only significant element Salim retains from the original myth. The city suffers from no plague (other than the continuing fear of the half-mythologized beast that threatens its inhabitants), Oedipus is not an outsider but a popular commoner, the city's chess champion. There is no murder of a father not marriage of a mother. Even the famous victory over the menacing Sphinx turns out ultimately to be an illusion. After the Sphinx has devoured several university professors who tried to defeat it through their superior intelligence, the commoner Oedipus offers to destroy the monster if he is made king and married to Queen Jocasta as a reward.

With this promise, he leaves the city and returns to claim, falsely, that he has killed the monster. His claim is supported by the city's corrupt functionaries, the chief of police, the president of the chamber of commerce and the rector of the university. The situation is quite reminiscent of that in Bākathīr or Fahmī's versions, where an idealistic and visionary Oedipus is surrounded by corrupt officials who turn his work to oppressive and self-serving ends. They are happy to encourage the god-like stature of the heroic Oedipus in order to cover their own manipulations, while all hesitations, all questions of the authority of Oedipus and his regime are here answered by the public's mindless chant of 'You're the one who killed the beast'. This image of the God-like defender of the nation permeates the society, with images of the killing of the beast appearing on television, in posters, in dramatic representations, even on children's toys.

Despite its complete shift in tonality, Salim's version shares with Bakathir's a distinct political orientation, very much reflecting the tensions and concerns of its society at the moment of its creation. Behind the Oedipus of each is clearly the figure of Gamal Abdel Nasser, the dominant political figure in the Arab world. Bakathir's play, although created in the wake of the 1967 defeat, still saw, as did most Egyptians, their leader as the heroic figure who had freed Egypt from British influence, nationalized the Suez Canal, and instituted major political and social reforms. Although he resigned after the disgrace of 1967 he was almost immediately recalled to power by crowds shouting 'Gamal, we are all your soldiers', a chant which is very likely echoed in Sālim's 'You're the one who killed the beast'.

Anwar Sadat, Nasser's ally and confidant, became president upon Nasser's death in 1970, and although he regained the occupied Sinai Peninsula lost in the 1967 war, he never achieved anything like the heroic position in the popular imagination enjoyed by his predecessor. Nasser remained for many in the Arab world a model for the sort of figure that could protect the people of that world from the continuing threats from the old colonial powers and Israel. That continuing faith in a strongman who would lead and save the people is the basic target of the satiric spirit that drives Sālim's work. Once again Tiresias provides use with the key to understanding the action, though his role is very different in this version than it has been before. Here he is essentially the chorus and *raisonneur* of the play, renouncing the illusionary cult of the hero which has

Figure 1 *The Comedy of Oedipus*, Ali Salim, directed by Jennifer A. Kokai, 1970. Credit: Weber State University.

allowed corrupt authorities to remain in power. When Oedipus first goes out to confront the beast, Tiresias tries to warn the people that even if Oedipus succeeds, their emancipation will not be the result. 'What of the beast within you? Who is going to kill that – that stupid beast that makes you forever wait for the one who will solve your problems for you' (Salim 2005: 303).

When a beast (perhaps the same one) again menaces the city and Oedipus confesses that his first claim of victory was a falsehood, he urges the people to follow the advice of Tiresias and to confront the beast themselves. In fact they are defeated as well, and Tiresias explains to the devastated Oedipus that generations of repression by the authorities and the police have created a culture of fear that leaves the people vulnerable and unable to exercise their real power. Oedipus banishes ʿAwālih, the chief of police, who has been primarily responsible for this culture, but although Tiresias applauds this action, he warns Oedipus that the solution is not so simple. 'It's easy to banish ʿAwālih from Thebes', he cautions, 'but it's impossible to expel him immediately from the hearts of the people' (Salim 2005: 347). Developing a people that can act without fear is a goal not quickly or easily achieved. At the end of the play, Oedipus departs in search of enlightenment, leaving Tiresias alone to remind us that in this version of the story 'it is not important that we know what happened to Oedipus', since the story, and the future, belong to the awakening people of Thebes, 'a people which has truly begun to know the solution' (Salim 2005: 350).

Since the comic classic of Ali Salim, Oedipus has largely disappeared from Arabic stages, but his spirit has recently re-emerged in the work of one of the most prominent playwrights of the Arabic diaspora, the Lebanese-Canadian Wajdi Mouawad (Wajdī Muʿawwaḍ). His 2003 play *Incendies* (*Scorched*), which brought him to international attention, is shot through with Oedipal echoes. In its contemporary setting and its use of the themes of murder and incest but presented with different generational perspectives, it somewhat resembles the adaptation of Ikhlasi, but while Ikhlasi had emphasized the personal tragedy, Mouawad, like most Arab adaptors, foregrounds the political dimensions of his story. He embeds his characters in the ongoing brutal conflicts of the Middle East, inspired in particular by his experience of the Lebanese Civil War.

Incendies opens with the funeral of a Canadian woman emigrated from Lebanon who leaves two envelopes to her twin children, one asking them to find their father, whom they thought dead, and the other to find a brother that they never knew existed. The play depicts their quest to Lebanon and the secrets of the Lebanese War's effects on their family. They slowly reconstruct a tale of betrayals, shifting loyalties, atrocities and daring acts of kindness at the heart of which is the imprisonment of her mother for political reasons and her torture and rape there. Though neither of them knows this at the time, she later discovers he was her son, long separated from her by the war and brought up on the opposing side. In this reworking the actual Oedipus figure only appears briefly at the end of the play, and the Jocasta is already dead at the beginning (although she has a major role in the many flashbacks). The bearers of the action are the twin brother and sister, whose Greek parallel would be the four children of Oedipus, although this parallel is not developed. Although the brother and sister are profoundly affected and changed by their discoveries, the real focus of the play is on the war itself and upon the suffering, inhumane actions, and degradation it brings to all parties on both sides. Thanks to its rich symbolic structures, its powerful depiction of the physical and mental effects of war, and its psychological power, this seems of all of the Arabic adaptations of the Oedipus story the one that comes closest to recapturing the power of the original.

The ghost of Oedipus also hovers over Mouawad's most recent work, *Tous les Oiseaux* (*All Birds*), created in Paris in 2017 and since a major international success. The focus this time is directly on the Israel-Palestine conflict and its tragic impact on the lives of three generations of a Jewish family. Again the play is driven by a quest, an American/Israeli student and his girlfriend, of Palestinian descent, to discover a hidden family secret that for decades has divided his grandparents. The central tragic figure is the student's father, David, an Israeli living in Berlin whose passionate Zionism parallels the overweening intellectual confidence of Oedipus and who suffers a similar fate, when the tragic secret at the heart of the play is revealed. This is, that like Oedipus, David was unknowingly a foundling, raised by a couple not his parents in another home and environment. What gives this secret a tragic dimension is that it is discovered that David is actually the son of Palestinians, the hatred of whom lies at the base of his psychic world. By shifting the Oedipal echo from the unconscious incest to the (symbolic) destruction of an unknown father, Mouawad has found in the classic legend another way of developing the tragic dilemma of Oedipus, who did not know who he was, and blindly followed that lack of knowledge to destructive self-awareness.

Like *Incendies*, *Tous les Oiseaux*, with its multiplicity of cultural references, density of poetic expression, relevance to contemporary concerns, and richly developed characters, draws its emotional power from many sources beyond the Oedipus myth which both clearly reference, but the imaginative, original and effective way that Mouwad utilizes this myth demonstrates once again its continuing hold on the imagination of playwrights and audiences across the centuries and around the world.

Notes

1 In order to avoid as much as possible the matter of incest, Fahmī utilized a little-known variant of the Oedipus legend, according to which Oedipus divorced Jocasta upon learning of their true relationship and married Euryganeia, who was in fact the mother of Oedipus children.

2 Safi Mahfouz calls it 'the only Arab Oedipus acceptable to an Islamic audience' (2012: 180).

3 Nehad Selaiha has argued that even though Fahmi's Oedipus has purified the kingdom, he has not in fact purified himself, and is still afflicted by the tragic flaw of hiding the truth about himself from his people (2001: 564).

4 Akhenaton has also inspired several modern Egyptian dramatists, Mahdī Bunduq with *The Last Days of Akhenaton* in 2002 and Wagdi Zeid (Wajdī Zayd) with *The Last Pharaoh* in 2012.

5 The figure of the Sphinx, with a human head, the body of a lion, and the wings of a bird, is widely found in the mythology of both Egypt and Greece, although the head is normally seen as male in Egypt, female in Greece. The word Sphinx itself is Greek from the verb *sphingo*, 'to squeeze', but some historians have argued that it may be a corruption of the Egyptian *shesepankh*, meaning living image. The Greeks themselves thought that their Sphinx originally came from Aethiopia, or Upper Egypt, so the roots seem inextricably intertwined.

References

Badawi, M. M. (1987), *Modern Arabic Drama in Egypt*, Cambridge: Cambridge University Press.

Etman, A. (2004), 'The Greek Concept of Tragedy in the Arab Culture: How to Deal with an Islamic Oedipus', *Documenta Jaargang*, 12(4): 281–99.

Al-Hakim, T. (1992), *The Prison of Life*, trans. P. Cachia. Cairo: American University Press.

Mahfouz, S. (2012), 'The Arab Oedipus: Oriental Perspectives on the Myth', *Modern Drama*, 55(2): 171–96.

Munir, S. (1979), *The Egyptian Theatre after World War II*, Cairo: Anglo-Egyptian Bookshop.

Salim, A. (2005), 'The Comedy of Oedipus', in M. Carlson (ed.), *The Arab Oedipus: Four Plays*, 285–350, New York: Segal Publications.

Selaiha, N. (2001), 'Manifold Oedipus', *Al-Ahram*, 563 (6–12 December).

3

From Ancient Greek Theatre to Turkish Theatre and Back

State of the Art

Erica Letailleur

In this chapter, we will try to define the contours of the influence of ancient Greek theatre on contemporary Turkish theatre – from the first published adaptation of an ancient tragedy by Selahettin Batu in 1942 (Batu 1942), to the present day. In this way, we will question the notion of heritage, through a theatre that bears the archaeological traces of ancient Dionysia, but also through the practical reminiscences in traditional performances. We will also question the notion of cultural appropriation by looking at the presence of the authors of ancient tragedies in the repertoires of the country's theatrical institutions, using their themes and plays rediscovered indirectly through European languages and not directly from the Greek source, as we shall see. In this way, the question of heritage as well as that of cultural appropriation, which will be discussed here, will allow us to take a critical look at the construction of a Europeanized art that seeks universality, through identification with ancient Greek works. This is a highly political process, the power of which has been demonstrated by researchers such as Samir Amin (Amin 1988).

As we will see from this study, Turkish theatre is multifaceted. On the one hand, it feeds on ancient sources in a quasi-physical way, due to the significant presence of archaeological remains in the country. On the other hand, Turkish theatre is also shaped by popular traditions that have endured for centuries: for historians such as Metin And, the origins of certain forms must be traced back to ancient sources (And 2012). Finally, as far as contemporary theatre is concerned, since the Republican era starting in 1923, dramaturgy, themes and repertoire have been borrowed from European models: this leads to some borrowing of forms, themes and works from ancient Greek sources.

Thus, we will see that questioning the way in which the Greek theatre of antiquity manifests itself in Turkish theatre – which can be said to have existed since the end of the nineteenth century – is tantamount to questioning the very identity of this theatre. How does Turkish theatre bear the traces of antiquity? Given the enormous time span between the end of Greek antiquity and the beginning of Turkish theatre, especially the moment when the first works of antiquity were adapted for Turkish theatre in the 1940s, is it appropriate to think in terms of heritage? Would it be more appropriate to speak of cultural appropriation or reappropriation given the way in which the intelligentsia has embraced Western models that claim to be based on the heritage of antiquity? This is what we are going to discuss here.

In the first part of the chapter, we will discuss the tangible traces and supposedly intangible remnants of ancient Greek theatre practices in contemporary Turkey. Secondly, we will discuss the ways in which Turkish playwrights have reappropriated the themes of Greek antiquity, starting with the Republican period, which corresponds to what historians consider to be the moment when Turkish playwriting emerged. Finally, it seems important to question the way in which the stage has also appropriated the theatrical works of ancient Greek tragedy: for this purpose, in a third part, we will see a commented inventory of the translations registered in the repertoire of the main institutions of Turkish theatrical life.[1]

Before embarking on this analysis, it seems necessary to recall that the Turkish theatre as we know it today is the rational fruit of the process of modernization and westernization that has taken place since the end of the Ottoman Empire, under the reign of Sultan Mahmut II. In his work *From the Beginnings to 1983, History of Turkish Theatre*,[2] the historian Metin And has developed a taxonomy that has been adopted by scholars to describe this phenomenon (And 2004). There are two main categories: traditional Turkish theatre on the one hand, and the Western-influenced Turkish theatre on the other. According to him, each of these two categories is divided into subcategories. On the one hand, he distinguishes between subcategories of genre for traditional theatre: there is, in particular, a difference between village traditions and urban folk traditions. Metin And also distinguishes subcategories of period for the Western-influenced theatre, with three main currents: the theatre of the Reforms era (1839–1908), the theatre of the Constitutional era (1908–23), the theatre of the Republic from 1923 to the present (And 2004).

Focusing particularly on the Republican period from the 1940s onwards, which is when the first Greek tragedies were adapted and translated for the

Turkish stage, we will see how each of these perspectives reveals a different aspect of the history of Turkish theatre as a specifically contemporary performing art: a new art form invented from ancient roots, itself reformulated through the filter of the modernity of each era. Before doing so, we will look at an aspect that could almost be considered timeless with regard to this question: the material and immaterial presence of heritage elements that seem to exist across time and space through archaeological remains and living traditions.

Ancient Greek theatre in Turkey: a heritage?

As mentioned above, it seems appropriate to distinguish two modalities of the presence of ancient Greek theatre in Turkey. The first of these could be considered as the tangible and intangible traces of the heritage of ancient practices. This is the one we are going to discuss in this first part. We will thus distinguish two basic traces: on the one hand, the archaeological remains, which are a tangible manifestation of the presence of ancient Greek theatrical practices on the land of today's Turkey. On the other hand, we will discuss the supposed traces of ancient practices in the popular rituals and performative traditions that persist in Turkey today. As we shall see, this second hypothesis of an intangible heritage of Greek antiquity in contemporary Turkey, was put forward by Metin And (And 2004). Through these two aspects of the traces of ancient Greek theatre in Turkish landscapes and traditional performance practices, we will question the notion of cultural heritage as a newly manufactured idea (Chakrabarty 2020).

The archaeological sources: tangible remains of antiquity

Let us begin this reflection with an example. In 2021, excavations in İzmir by a team of archaeologists uncovered the remains of an ancient theatre with an estimated seating capacity of around 21,000. According to Erdoğan Aslan, this stone theatre was built, as was often the case, on the site of a smaller wooden theatre that originally stood next to a temple dedicated to Aphrodite Stratonikis and a place of Dionysian worship, from the third century BC (Aslan 2020). In the second century BC, and then under the reign of the Emperor Augustus, the theatre was rebuilt in stone and enlarged for the needs of Roman performances. Much later, parts of the building would have been used as a glass and ceramics workshop. Finally, during the Ottoman period, part of the theatre would have been dismantled, and some blocks used to construct monumental buildings in the city. The theatre building gradually disappeared. At present, archaeologists are reconstructing the puzzle in order to restore the stone theatre to its original form (Ritzman 2022).

The example of the successive transformations of this building, built on the remains of an ancient Greek theatre, shows the changes in social, cultural and religious life in the lands of modern Turkey. Here, the old can be synonymous with the new. People build on the remains of the past, which simply change identity and purpose. What is no longer in use serves as the basis for new needs: tradition evolves hand in hand with the invention of the present. The same is true of this theatre in İzmir: for centuries, oblivion has slowly taken the place of the people on the stage, until the building is rediscovered and new possibilities for its use are opened up for the future – as in the theatres in Efes (İzmir district) or Aspendos (Antalya district), where performing arts festivals are now organized every year by the Ministry of Culture and Tourism of the Republic of Turkey.[3]

In fact, the landscape of present-day Turkey is physically marked by the presence of ancient Greek theatre remains. Among the Roman theatres that have survived, archaeologists have found traces of older theatres of Greek architecture, such as those at Xanthos (Antalya district), Termessos (Antalya district), Efes (İzmir district), Bodrum (Muğla district) or Hierapolis (Denizli district) (Aslan, 2020). In addition, several of these sites and others not mentioned above have been declared World Heritage Sites by UNESCO: Hieropolis-Pamukkale (since 1988), Xhanthos-Letoon (since 1988), the archaeological site of Troy in Çanakkale district (since 1998) and Efes (since 2015), notably.[4]

The archaeological remains of antiquity clearly show how the Greek theatre was gradually incorporated into the daily life of populations whose culture and habits changed over time. It was only at the end of the twentieth century that these monuments were recognized and treated as part of the world's cultural heritage. As such, they are now being reinvested and used as the setting for major cultural events, as we have seen. This seems to link Turkey's contemporary creation to its ancient heritage: it links Turkish cultural policy to the universal heritage of humanity and affirms the Republic of Turkey as a power capable of competing with others in terms of artistic creation, but also and above all in terms of cultural heritage. Finally, to hold international festivals today in ancient theatres, such as Efes or Aspendos, is to affirm in a certain way a kind of transmission that would have taken place between the territories of Greek antiquity where Western civilization is said to have been born, and republican Turkey, which claims its share of the inheritance. One could think that there was a rupture and that theatre, as it was practised in the ancient form of Greek culture disappeared in these territories before being reappropriated for political reasons in the twentieth century, with the birth of the Western model of theatre. This would be an interesting echo of the universal history of theatre as told in the West (Nutku 2000). However, this is not so simple, because for Metin And, certain ancient forms have persisted in Turkish popular practices. This is what we are going to talk about now.

Traditional Turkish theatre and ancient Greek theatre: a complex relationship

According to Metin And, Anatolian folk theatre forms – be they village plays or traditional urban forms – have their roots in Eastern Mediterranean culture, in ancient and remote times. For him, they are the very essence of contemporary European theatre (And 2004). He considers that these numerous traditions share several common features with the theatre of antiquity. First of all, these traditions share the notion of *mimus*, the imitation of an action – which, according to And, is reminiscent of Aristotle's observations. This includes imitation of people, animals and even inanimate objects. Second, it involves interaction with one or more characters. Thirdly, dance, music, song, acrobatics and clowning are a necessary part of the performance. According to him, these observations are complemented by other specific features, for example the inclusion of other traditional forms of playing in the performance, implying a kind of theatre within the theatre, or the spectacular features of the performance (e.g. make-up, masks and costumes), from which the theatrical aesthetic emerges.

Another point that we feel is important to highlight here is the practice of ritual sacrifice, which recalls the original goat song of the ancient Dionysia and can be observed in certain village traditions such as the *Koç Katımı* ('ram slaughter'). This tradition includes various performative elements such as songs, dances and theatrical imitations. Although the tradition is now associated with Islamic religious festivals, historians say this type of village celebration is much older (And 2004: 23–4). For them, these practices are reminiscent of the beginnings of ancient Greek festivals.

In contemporary Turkish repertoire inspired by ancient themes, there are explicit references to these sacrificial traditions. For example, this is the case in Güngör Dilmen's *Kurban* – a play written in 1967, which will be discussed in more detail below. In a speech by one of the characters in the play, the author refers to the sacrificial lamb of the Bible (Abraham's sacrifice), which he explicitly links to the sacrifice of Medea's children, as well as to the ritual sacrifice of the goat in ancient tragedy competitions.[5] This speech shows very clearly the various ingredients that link the European model of theatre in Turkey to ancient sources, through traditional practices such as those just mentioned.

To think about the influence of ancient Greek theatre on the contemporary Turkish stage is to think about the history of Turkish theatre in terms of a syncretism that identifies itself with both ancient roots and traditional sources: one being the continuation of the other. Metin And, however, underlines how fragile this remains, from a theoretical point of view, since what underlies the theatrical culture of Turkish society is not to be found in the imposed Western dramaturgical models, but in what has crossed the millennia and completely transformed itself. This phenomenon which goes beyond the simple question of repertoire, makes the very idea of a Turkish theatre in the Western sense obsolete, according to him (And 2004: 201).

In fact, the presence of ancient Greek theatre on contemporary Turkish stages, like the fate of the archaeological remains, does not follow the train of history from antiquity to the present day in a way that might seem fluid and natural. Although the population has continued to occupy the ancestral lands, the country has been deeply marked by major historical events that have had an impact on cultural activity – notably the Roman invasion beginning in the second century BC, the conquest of Constantinople by the Muslims in 1453, or the dissolution of the Ottoman Empire in 1922 and the emergence of the Republic of Turkey in 1923 (Şener 2004).

In this way, the subject of Greek tragedy in Turkey can be approached from numerous perspectives, which, when they intersect, tell the story of how Turkish theatre narrates itself to the world today: how it may have continued from the earliest times, how it has been constructed according to Western models since the Tanzimat era, and how it exists today in different forms.

Turkish repertoire inspired by ancient Greek theatre

We will now discuss in more detail how themes and characters from Greek antiquity are staged in different plays of the Turkish theatrical repertoire after the emergence of the Republic of Turkey – for it is from this moment that Turkish-speaking authors really begin to write works based on the Western model, as part of Atatürk's policy of making Turkey a state comparable to

European nations, in all fields, including, of course, art and culture (Çongur 2017). Thus, while there are no explicit sources that we are aware of that attest to a political need to appropriate Greek themes in the Turkish repertoire, the examples that we will examine here show that the presence of themes inspired by antiquity has a dimension that goes beyond the simple question of aesthetics.

In this sense, the plays that are based on or inspired by ancient Greek themes are referred to as 'plays whose sources are fairy tales, epics, legends, folk tales and mythology' in Enver Töre's typology, which includes nine categories of dramaturgical sources that make up the contemporary Turkish repertoire (Töre 2009: 2018–2348): in other words, it is a tiny fragment among the number of plays in the Turkish repertoire since 1876.

To understand this subtlety, it is important to remember that the creation of a specific Turkish-language theatre repertoire by Turkish-speaking authors only began at the end of the Tanzimat period (around 1876), and that this repertoire was initially mainly influenced by the French theatre of the seventeenth and eighteenth centuries. Therefore, historians do not mention any direct influence of authors such as Aeschylus, Sophocles or Euripides on the early Turkish repertoire. Metin And even goes so far as to say that the non-appropriation of ancient Greek sources calls into question the very legitimacy of the Turkish dramatic repertoire (And 1994: 5).

In any case, it would be interesting to study the extent to which the Turkish repertoire is shaped by the indirect influence of classical European works, which in turn are shaped according to the dramaturgical rules reappropriated from the Aristotelian model (e.g. the rule of the unities, the notion of character, the *mimesis* paradigm, etc.). It would also be highly relevant to examine the place of the chorus in contemporary Turkish drama and to establish links with ancient models. However, there is neither the time nor the space in this chapter. Therefore, we will limit ourselves to mentioning the interest that such an undertaking could represent. Thus, we propose here simply to examine the access to Aristotle's foundational text for artists and theatre scholars in Turkey, before giving an overview of how the contemporary Turkish repertoire has been inspired by the themes of ancient Greek mythology and theatre.

Translations of Aristotle's' *Poetics* into modern Turkish

The first translation of Aristotle's *Poetics* into modern Turkish was published by Atatürk University Press (Erzurum) in 1961, in a translation by İsmail Tunalı (Amanet 2022: 3–4). After Remzi Kitapevi republished the book in 1963, seven other translations followed in the 2000s. In 2003, the work was published by K Kitaplığı in a translation by Samih Rifat, and then republished in the same translation by Can Yayınları in 2007. In 2005, the book was published by Bilim ve Sanat Yayınları (Istanbul), in a translation by Nazile Kalaycı. In 2008, Yılmaz Onay published his translation of the *Poetics* at Mitos Boyut Yayınları. In 2011, a translation by Murat Temelli was published by Ark Kitapları. In 2016, an annotated translation by Ömer Aygün and Ari Çokona was published by İş Bankası Kültür Yayınları. Finally, in 2021, a new translation by İpek Çorumlu was published by Platanus Publishing (Amanet 2022).

Even if it is difficult to draw conclusions that would be purely speculative, it is interesting to note after 2000, the significant number of translations into modern Turkish of this major work which shapes the identity of global theatre. Is there an implicit and distant link between Republic of Turkey's obtaining the status of candidate to the European Union in 1999 following the Helsinki Council and this flowering of translations? Did Turkish intellectuals, from that moment on, seek a tangible link with the sources of European theatre? It is impossible to say, although the hypothesis is tempting. In any case, there is no official directive to confirm this hypothesis.

Themes of ancient Greek tragedy in modern Turkish theatre

Although it is difficult to determine the extent to which Aristotelian dramaturgy has contributed to shaping the dramaturgical identity of contemporary Turkish theatre, it is possible to discern an influence of the ancient Greek texts through the use of themes and patterns inherited from antiquity. For example, some Turkish playwrights have used themes from Greek mythology, especially characters from ancient tragedy, to create their own work: Antigone, Helen and Iphigenia, for example, have been adapted by Turkish writers. Thus, in 1942, the first work in the contemporary Turkish repertoire inspired by ancient tragedies was *İphigenia Tauris'te* (Iphigenia in Tauris) by Selahettin Batu (Batu 1942), who also translated Goethe's *Iphigenia in Tauris* (Arslan 2015: 492–503). In 1954, the same author published *Güzel Helena* (*The Beautiful Helena*; Batu 1959), inspired by the Trojan War motif. These works, written in verse, have a very poetic language and were chosen to represent Turkey in international exchanges with Germany and Austria. In 1966, Kemal Demirel published *Antigone*. This play is a 'Turkish' adaptation of Sophocles' work: it borrows linguistic motifs and expressions from popular culture, while remaining within the ancient structure (plot, division into scenes, presence of the chorus and the protagonists, etc.). In short, these first works seem to testify to a desire to translate ancient texts by adapting them to Turkish language and culture.

There are also plays inspired by ancient Greek themes that do not originate in the theatre. In 1959, Güngör Dilmen wrote his famous trilogy about King Midas: *Midas'ın Kulakları* (*Midas' Ears*), *Midas'ın Altınları* (*Midas' Gold*) and *Midas'ın Kördüğümü* (*Midas' Knot*; Dilmen 2015). Here, Güngör Dilmen uses myths to critique his time, liberating historical and mythical identities from the petrified image of the past, elevating their contradictions, inclinations, and passions, and positioning them in the here and now of the theatre (Dağ Gümüş 2019: 28–41).

However, the ancient Greek figure that has probably inspired contemporary Turkish playwrights the most is Medea, who is considered by Turkish writers to be one of the most powerful archetypes of Greek mythology when it comes to stage representation (Küçük 2017: 416). Six plays based on the myth can be counted to date: Munis Faik Ozansoy's *Medea* (1963), Güngör Dilmen's *Kurban* (*Sacrifice*, 1967), Yüksel Pazarkaya's *Mediha* (1993), Kemal Kocatürk's *Medeia* (2005), Tarık Günersel's *Altın Post* (*The Golden Fleece*, 2007), and Ali Ihsan Kaleci's *Ay Kadın Ay* (*Moon Woman Moon*, 2018).[6]

In her article 'Medea Myth in Modern Turkish Theatre', Sena Küçük presents and compares five of these works with particular emphasis on the universality that the Turkish repertoire gains by appropriating an ancient myth such as that of Medea (Küçük 2017: 415–40).

According to Küçük, these works can be divided into two main categories. In the first category, are plays directly adapted from Greek mythology. These are *Medea* by Munis Faik Ozansoy and *Medeia* by Kemal Kocatürk. The first, the only play written by the poet Munis Faik Ozansoy, is a tragedy in two acts dating from 1963 and premiered in 1966 at the Ankara National Theatre. The second, written in 2004, is an adaptation of Euripides' tragedy written by the actor, playwright and director Kemal Kocatürk. For the second 'Turkey-Germany Bridge Theatre festival' (Hamburg 2019), the play has been re-adapted in three languages (Turkish, Zaza, German) in the form of a monologue and produced by Kocatürk himself. Both plays are written according to a dramaturgical model that respects the unity of time, place and action. The plot and characters are those of the ancient tragedy. There is a chorus on stage. In Kocatürk's play, there is even a parodos and an exodos.

Tarık Günersel's *Altın Post* could also be included in this category, although it does not deal with the tragedy of Medea, but with the myth that preceded it. It is a sixteen-scene play that presents the epic of the Argonauts, the meeting between Medea and Jason, Medea's betrayal of her father and the murder of her brother.

Remarkable enough to be highlighted here, unlike the other plays in this repertoire, *Altın Post* is a comedy.

The second category evoked by Sena Küçük concerns works inspired by Greek mythology and transposed into the socio-cultural reality of Anatolia. They are *Kurban* by Güngör Dilmen and *Mediha* by Yüksel Pazarkaya: both plays are inspired by the myth of Medea and set in contemporary Turkey.

The first, considered by Sevda Şener to be one of the most important Turkish plays (Şener 1970), was written in 1967 and premiered the same year by the company of Gülriz Sururi and Engin Cezzar, with the actress Ayşe Emel Mesci in the first role (Letailleur 2019). The second, written in 1992, is the work of Yüksel Pazarkaya, a German-speaking intellectual whose work represents an important link between Germany and Turkey, with a recurring theme of Turkish immigration to Europe from the 1960s onwards.

In *Kurban*, the action takes place in an Anatolian village. A villager, Mahmut, takes a second wife: his actual wife, Zehra, rejects this situation and decides to sacrifice their two children before killing herself during the wedding (Dilmen 1987). As for *Mediha*, the work presents the character of Hasan, who, in order to obtain a residence permit in Germany, contracts a sham marriage with a German woman and divorces his wife Mediha. After signing the divorce papers, Mediha murders her children before killing herself.

Ali Ihsan Kaleci's play *Ay Kadın Ay* stands out from the crowd in that it is free of any explicit reference to ancient mythology – indeed, the central character is simply called Woman. The general theme of the play is the woman, the witch, the foreigner who kills her children in reaction to her husband's remarriage. The work, written in 2018, includes an older poem that the author wrote years ago as a tribute to the actress Ayşe Emel Mesci, who played the role of Zehra in first production of Güngör Dilmen's *Kurban*.[7] Kaleci's work thus contains a reference within a reference, a nod to the contemporary Turkish scene within what could be called a 'double acculturation phenomenon' of the modern West and the ancient West.

Ultimately, the adaptation of these works from the ancient repertoire to the repertoire of modern Turkey seems to serve political interests that converge on the objective of spreading the influence of Turkish theatre on the world stage, either because these works are suitable for export, or because they allow the expression of socio-cultural realities within frameworks that are intended to be universal. For example, *Altın Post* was chosen to represent Turkish–Georgian friendship in 2001. Another example: Kemal Kocatürk sees *Medeia* as an allegory representing the unsolvable conflict between East and West. The final example,

Kurban, is considered the most performed Turkish play abroad since its premiere (Küçük 2017: 435).

Brief inventory of ancient Greek tragedies in contemporary productions in Turkey

Turning now to the staging of works from the ancient Greek repertoire on the Turkish theatre scene, it is important to point out first of all that a list of all the creations on the public and private stages of the country would constitute a work of considerable scope, which we do not have the opportunity to undertake in this chapter. We will limit ourselves here to general observations and the mention of some interesting examples. We have worked mainly with the repertoire archive of the National Theatres of Turkey's Head Dramaturgy Office,[8] as well as from the repertoire archive of Istanbul Municipal Theatre.[9] The repertoire of the National Theatres includes works that have been validated by a reading committee for future productions: whether the play has been performed or not, the work is listed in this archive called the 'repertoire'. The repertoire of the Istanbul Municipal Theatre does not make a similar distinction and only includes works that have been staged. It is important to note that the online archive of the Head Dramaturgy Office of the National Theatres of Turkey is not up to date and many productions were not listed as of 2016. The archive of the National Theatre of Istanbul is not up to date either, as it stops in 2014. For practical reasons, we propose to look at these repertoires as they currently exist in their official, publicly accessible versions.

According to our observations, the repertoire of the National Theatres of Turkey has thirty-six entries related to the Greek repertoire of antiquity. As for the repertoire of the Istanbul Municipal Theatre, it has eight entries related to the Greek repertoire of antiquity. These include works by Aeschylus, Sophocles, Euripides and by Aristophanes. Here we will focus only on works related to the tragedies of Aeschylus, Sophocles and Euripides. It is worth noting that not all of the plays of these three authors are included in the repertoire of these major theatre institutions in Turkey.

The works of Aeschylus included in these repertoires are: *The Oresteia* (*Agamemnon, The Libation Bearers* and *The Eumenides*), translated from English and directed by Ebru Sonuç at İstanbul State Theatre in 1991–2 (the show was also repeated the following season); *The Persians*, translated from Greek by Güngör Dilmen and added to the repertoire of the National Theatre of Turkey in

1999; and *Prometheus Bound*, translated from English by Furkan Akderin and added to the repertoire of the National Theatre of Turkey in 1999. Thus, according to this overview, only *The Oresteia* trilogy has been performed on major Turkish stages between 1962 and 2016.

Eight tragedies by Sophocles are included in the two repertoires examined. Although *Oedipus Rex* was performed at the Ankara National Theatre as early as 1942, the first registered translation of this work was submitted by Bedrettin Tuncel in 1955 in a translation from Greek. The play was performed at the Ankara headquarters from 1959 to 1961, and again from 1965 to 1967 in the same translation. In 1996–7, Bedrettin Tuncel's translation was also used at the Istanbul Municipal Theatre, in a creation directed by Cüneyt Tuncel, in the form of a diptych entitled *King Oedipus at Colonus*. *Oedipus at Colonus* was also added to the repertoire of the National Theatres of Turkey in 1999 by Nurullah Ataç, but has not been performed.

Electra was submitted to the Head Dramaturgy Office of Turkish National Theatres by various translators between 1952 and 2007. A first translation from English was submitted in 1952 and was staged by Afif Orbay at the Ankari Headquarters. Another project was submitted in 1962 by Oktay Rifat with a translation from Greek, but was not performed. In 1999, Azra Ehrat submitted a new translation from English. This too was not performed. Finally, in 2007, Zeynep Avcı directed Sophocles' *Electra* at the National Theatre of İzmir. The same translation from English was used by Işıl Kasapoğlu for his production of *Electra* at the National Theatre of İstanbul in 2017–18 (to be repeated in 2018–19).

Ajax was translated from Italian by Suat Sinanoğlu and added to the repertoire of the National Theatre of Turkey in 1988, but it was never staged. *The Women of Trachis* has been translated from Greek by Şaziye Berin Kurt and was added to the repertoire of the National Theater of Turkey in 1999, but has not been staged. There are also two versions of *Philoctetes* in the repertoire of the National Theatres of Turkey. The first was submitted by Nurullah Ataç in 1999. The second was submitted by Sükran Yücel and Bengi Heval Öz in 2008. None of these translations has been performed on the stages of the National Theatres. In 2004–5, a translation of *Antigone* by Güngör Dilmen was staged at the Istanbul Municipal Theatre by the actor and director Macit Koper.

As for Euripides' work, six of his tragedies are included in the repertoires studied here. There are four different translations of *Medea*. The first dates from 1966 and was written by Munis Faik Ozansoy for the repertoire of the National Theatres of Turkey. It was performed in Ankara in the same year. A second translation, by Talat Sait Halman, was staged by the American director Arthur Housman at the Istanbul Municipal Theatre in 1985 (for the 1985–6 season, revived in 1986–7). A third translation by Ahmed Hamdi Tanpınar and Kemal Kocatürk was added to the repertoire of the National Theatres of Turkey in 2006 – it was not produced by the national institution. However, the same translation of Euripides' play was used for the production of *Medea* by Ljupço Gorgievski in the 2003–4 season of the Istanbul Municipal Theatre. The fourth and most recent translation of *Medea* dates from 2015 and was submitted to the repertoire of the National Theatres of Turkey by Metin Balay. It was directed by Gökhan Kocaoğlu at the National Theatre of Trabzon in the same year. Subsequently, Adonis Filipi, an Albanian director, adopted this translation for his production at the National Theatre of Izmir in 2021–2.

Three translations of *The Trojan Women* are listed by the Head Dramaturgy Office of the National Theatres of Turkey. The first is from 1979 and was translated from French by Güzin Dino. It was performed by Mehmet Atay at the National Theatre of Trabzon during the 2008–9 season. The second play, translated from Greek by Ülkü Taner, was staged in 1987–8, before being revived by Yücel Erten in 2000. Another translation by Sema Sandalcı was submitted in 2004.

The Bacchae first appeared in the repertoire of the National Theatres of Turkey in 1990, in a translation from French by Sabahattin Eyüboğlu, which was produced in the same year. Engin Orbey directed the play at the National Theatre of Ankara for the 2000–1 season (it was revived in 2001–2). Another translation from Greek, submitted by Güngör Dilmen in 2002, has never been performed on national stages. However, a third translation by Tarık Günersel was performed in a show directed by Mihai Maniutiu in the 2009–10 season of the Istanbul Municipal Theatre.

Two versions of *Helen* have been added to the repertoire of Turkey's National Theatres. The first by Vahdi Hatay in 1999; the second by Yılmaz Onay in 2013. Neither of them has been performed. At least translation of *Rhesos* was submitted to the national repertoire by Sema Sandalcı in 2007 but it was never performed.

As can be seen from this inventory, several issues arise when looking at the staging of ancient Greek tragedies in the major public theatres of Turkey. First, it is interesting to note that not all translations into Turkish are based on the original Greek texts, but on translations from other languages (mainly French, English, Italian and German). This translation bias once again draws attention to the fact that the repertoire of modern Turkish theatre, especially from the

Republican period onwards, has been constructed with a kind of urgency to imitate the repertoire of Western stages. The founding texts are thus exploited by those who have access to them, according to the means they have at their disposal. The link between the linguists who have access to the original texts and the theatre people is not always established.

It should also be noted that several foreign directors have been invited by these institutions (especially the Istanbul Municipal Theatre) to produce Greek tragedies from the ancient repertoire. This is the case of Arthur Housman, who directed the first production of Euripides' *Medea* in Istanbul in 1985, or Ljupço Gorgievski, who directed the same play in 2003–04. This is also the case of Mihai Maniutiu, who directed *The Bacchae* in 2009–10.

When we look at the photographic archives of these productions of ancient Greek tragedies on contemporary Turkish stages, we also notice that the aesthetics, often stylized, seem to convey a certain antique 'taste', through the hairstyles of the actors and actresses, the costumes that evoke a certain idea of antiquity, and the contrasting colours, for example.

All these elements make it possible to affirm once again that the Turkish theatre taking up Greek tragedy shows how much Turkey has integrated the world repertoire on its own stages. In this sense, the historian Elif Çongur points out that the Turkish theatre of the Republican period has three major qualifiers: it is nationalist, secular and contemporary (Çongur 2017: 42). Insofar as it allows Turkish theatre to reach the level of international programming in terms of repertoire, guest directors, aesthetics, etc., the Greek repertoire's appropriation seems to reinforce the idea of a connection to the universal heritage of theatre – if one can express it in these terms. Through its religious neutrality, inasmuch as it presents myths that touch on universal beliefs, the tragic repertoire of ancient Greece also allows the Turkish stage to prove and test its secularity. For all these reasons, the Greek tragedy of antiquity on the Turkish stage of the twentieth century seems, to be like a guarantee of modernity.

In many ways the idea of theatre in Turkey is imbued with Greek antiquity. On the one hand, the ruins of its theatres are still present on the country's own soil. On the other hand, the traditions passed down from century to century in the remotest parts of Anatolia, would carry the almost genetic trace of ancient theatre forms and raise the question of their origins. Finally, because the contemporary repertoire draws on the sources of antiquity to forge a strong identity: no matter how many works have been adapted or translated, ancient Greek tragedy forges the identity of post-Republican Turkish theatre by allowing it to reach the idea of universality and, in this sense, to join the global movement of world theatre.

Widely discussed in postcolonial studies, this notion could, of course, be questioned. The idea that Turkish theatre is universal because it joins the history of Western theatre, which supposedly originated in ancient Greece, as Chakrabarty points out about the European intellectual tradition is now recognized as obsolete (Chakrabarty 2020: 43). While some Turkish scholars continue to see their theatre as Western (and therefore universal) in nature because of its reminiscences of Greek tragedy, we should not forget that historians such as Metin And, in search of Turkey's own cultural specificity, point to the absence of the notion of drama in the country's performative traditions. In this sense, the very existence of a specifically Turkish theatre is consequently denied. For Metin And, the term 'theatre' then refers to the notion of a dialogical performative practice, involving the idea of imitation and characters, on the model of Aristotelian thought: it does not exist in this form in traditional practices.

Perhaps, in the light of the elements we have examined in this chapter, we could make two observations. The first is that Turkish artists have indeed drawn on the repertoire of ancient Greek tragedy: whether in the context of writing new works or translating works from the past. The second observation is that beyond the notion of repertoire, there are palpable traces of ancient practices in the life of Turkish performance (through archaeological remains, but also through the supposed real survival of practical elements in certain traditions). Finally, we are faced here with the whole contradiction of the idea of linking cultural practices in Turkey to the Western models: they are both integrated into it and resemble it, because they are the result of a clearly defined political will since 1876 and the Tanzimat laws, but they integrate it in a way that is not necessarily Western. So in the end, it is necessary to decentralize in order to understand it.

Notes

1 The repertoires of the National Theatres of Turkey and some municipal theatres (such as the Istanbul City Theatre) represent banks of dramatic texts listed according to a validation system carried out by a reading committee and authorizing the possible production of works. Field notes, 2019.

2 Original title: *Başlangıcından 1983'e Türk Tiyatro Tarihi*, İstanbul: İletişim Yay, 2004 (first issue 1992). Title translated from Turkish by the author.

3 See www.operabale.gov.tr/en-us/Pages/festival.aspx last consulted on 26 September 2022.

4 'UNESCO Dünya Mirası Listesi', website of the Turkish Delegation at the UNESCO, www.unesco.org.tr/Pages/125/122/UNESCO-D%C3%BCnya-Miras%C4%B1-Listesi, last consulted on 28/09/2022.

5 Güngör Dilmen, *Kurban*, in *Toplu Oyunları 2*, İstanbul: Mitos Boyut Yayınları, 1987, p. 59. Also see Sevda Şener, *'Kurban' üzerine bir inceleme*, Ankara Üniversitesi Dil, Tarih ve Çoğrafya Fakültesi, Tiyatro Bölümü, 1970.

6 Unpublished. The manuscript is in the author's personal archives.

7 Interview with Ali Ihsan Kaleci, Paris, 25 January 2016.

8 See www.devtiyatro.gov.tr/DevletTiyatro/tr/Basdramaturgluk/9018, last consulted on 26 September 2022.

9 Abdullah Topal, '1985-2014 Oyunlar', https://stcdn.ibb.istanbul/Uploads/2017/9/1985-2014-Oyunlar-1.pdf, last consulted on 30 September 2022.

References

Amanet, H. (2022), 'Aristoteles'in Türkçe'ye Çevrilen Eserlerinin Listesi'. Available online: www.academia.edu/28714099/Aristotelesin_T%C3%BCrk%C3%A7eye_%C3%87evrilen_Eserlerinin_Listesi_Ocak_2022_

Amin, S. (1988), *L'Eurocentrisme: Critique d'une idéologie*, Paris: Anthropos.

And, M. (2004), *Başlangıçtan 1983'e Türk Tiyatro Tarihi*, Istanbul: İletişim Yayınları.

And, M. (2012), *Ritüelden Drama: Kerbelâ-Muharrem-Ta'ziye*, Istanbul: Yapı Kredi Yayınları.

Aslan, E. (2020), Antalya İl Kültür ve Turizm Müdürlüğü, Müğla İl Kültür ve Turizm Müdürlüğü, İzmir Efes Müze Müdürlüğü, Selçuk Üniversitesi Edebiyat Fakültesi Sualtı Arkeolojisi Anabilim Dalı. Available online: www.kulturportali.gov.tr/portal/tarihin-taniklari-antik-tiyatrolar

Arslan, M. (2015), 'Euripides, Goethe ve Selahattin Batu'da Ortak Mitolojik Kahraman olarak İphigenie', in C. Sakallı (ed.), *Yerel Bağlamlar Küresel Yakınlıklar. Edebiyatta, Kültürde ve Sanatta Geçişler, Kopuşlar, Yenileşmeler. Bildiriler*, 492–503, Mersin: Mersin University Press.

Batu, S. (1942), *İphigenia Tauris'te: Manzum Dramı*, Ankara: Yenişehir Kitapevi.

Batu, S. (1959), *Güzel Helena*, Ankara: Maarif Basımevi, Ankara.

Chakrabarty, D. (2020), *Provincialiser l'Europe: La pensée postcoloniale et la différence historique*, Paris: Amsterdam.

Çongur, E. (2017), *Ulusal Kimliği Tiyatro ile Yaratmak: Türk Tiyatrosunun Kimlik İnşasındaki İşlevi*, Ankara: İmge Kitabevi.

Dağ, Ü. (2019), 'Euripides'in "Helene" ve Selahattin Batu'nun "Güzel Helena" Eserlerinde Kadın İmgesinin Karşılaştırılması', *Turkish Studies*, 14(3): 1355–70.

Dağ Gümüş, P (2019), 'Güngör Dilmen'in Midas Üçlemesinde Mitik Yapı', *Avrasya Uluslararası Araştırmalar Dergisi*, 7: 28–41.

Dilmen, G. (2015), *Toplu Oyunları 1: Midas'ın Kulakları – Midas'ın Altınları – Midas'ın Kördüğümü*, Istanbul: Mitos Boyut Yayınları.

Dilmen, G. (1987), *Toplu Oyunları II*, Istanbul: Mitos Boyut Yayınları.

Demirel, K. (1966), *Antigone*, Istanbul: Yankı Yayınları.

Faik Ozansoy, M. (1963), *Medea*, Ankara: Ankara Üniversitesi Basımevi.

Günersel, T. (2007), *Altın Post*, in *Toplu Oyunları I*, Istanbul: Mitos Boyut Yayınları.

Kocatürk, K. (2011), *Medeia*, in *Toplu Oyunları I*, Istanbul: Mitos Boyut Yayınları.

Küçük, S. (2017), 'Modern Türk Tiyatrosunda Medea Miti', *The Journal of Academic Social Sciences Studies: International Journal of Social Science*, 55(II): 415–40.

Letailleur, E. (2019), '*Kurban* de Güngör Dilmen: une tragédie médéenne en Anatolie', in F. Quillet (ed.), *Médée sur la scene Mondiale aujourd'hui*, 155–70, Paris: L'Harmattan.

Nutku, Ö. (2000), *Dünya Tiyatro Tarihi*, Istanbul: Mitos Boyut Yayınları.

Nutku, Ö. (2018), *Atatürk ve Cumhuriyet Tiyatrosu*, Istanbul: Kaynak Yayınları.

Pazarkaya, Y. (1993), *Mediha*, Ankara: Kültür Bakanlığı.

Ritzman, N. (2021), 'Le théâtre antique d'Izmir d'environ 21 000 places sort de terre peu à peu', *Le Petit Journal*. https://lepetitjournal.com/istanbul/comprendre-turquie/le-theatre-antique-dizmir-denviron-21-000-places-sort-de-terre-peu-peu-307189, 25/09/2022.

Şener, S. (1970), '*Kurban* üzerine bir inceleme', Ankara: Ankara Üniversitesi Dil, Tarih ve Çoğrafya Fakültesi, Tiyatro Bölümü.

Şener, S. (1972), *Çağdaş Türk Tiyatrosunda İnsan (1923–1972)*, Ankara: Ankara Üniversitesi Dil ve Tarih-Çoğrafya Fakültesi Yayınları.

Şener, S. (1998), *Cumhuriyet'in 75: Yılında Türk Tiyatrosu*, İstanbul: Türkiye İş Bankası Kültür Yayınları.

Şener, S. (2004), *Gelişim Sürecinde Türk Tiyatrosu*, İstanbul: Mitos-Boyut Yayınları.

Töre, E. (2009), 'Türk Tiyatrosunun Kaynakları', *Turkish Studies, International Periodical for the Language, Literature and History of Turkish or Turkic*, 4(1–II): 2181–348.

Üulü, A. (2006), *Türk Tiyatrosunun Antropolojisi*, Ankara: Aşina Kitaplar.

Yüksel, A. (2011), *Türk Tiyatrosu Üstüne Notlar: Uzun Yolda Bir Mola*, Istanbul: Cumhuriyet Kitapları.

Zerenler, D. (2005), 'Antigone'nin İki Farklı Yorumu', *Selçuk Üniversitesi Türkiyat Araştırmaları Dergisi*, 18: 263–72.

Part Two

The Model as Diversion: A Tool to Tackle Political Issues on the Contemporary Stage

4

Brave Women in a Mad World

Euripides and the State of Exception in Arab Theatre

Daniela Potenza

In his famous study titled 'State of Exception', the philosopher Giorgio Agamben explores what he calls the 'no-man's-land between public law and political fact, and between the juridical order and life' (Agamben 2005: 1), where laws define spaces in which authorities possess extensive extra-legal authority. The state of exception is based on the ancient Latin maxim according to which *necessitas legem non habet* (necessity has no law), implying that the state of necessity, on which the exception is founded, cannot have a juridical form. Necessity's ability to overrule the law leads to Agamben's following reflection on the idea of necessity:

> ... the extreme aporia against which the entire theory of the state of necessity ultimately runs aground concerns the very nature of necessity, which writers continue more or less unconsciously to think of as an objective situation. This naive conception – which presupposes a pure factuality that the conception itself has called into question – is easily critiqued by those jurists who show that, far from occurring as an objective given, necessity clearly entails a subjective judgment, and that obviously the only circumstances that are necessary and objective are those that are declared to be so.
>
> Ibid.: 29–30

Studying some cases of state of necessity in history, Agamben infers that the voluntary creation of a permanent state of emergency has become one of the essential practices of contemporary states, including so-called democratic ones (ibid.: 2). For instance, the state of exception applies today to many categories of migrants such as refugees who are confined to camps, asylum seekers in detention facilities, temporary workers whose legal status depends on the discretion of their employers, irregular migrants who live in constant fear of deportation. Such situations imply that many migrants are in a dangerous permanently temporary status (De Genova 2012).

Trained in the unscrupulousness and spiritual freedom of the Athenian society of the time following the Persian wars, through his tragedies, Euripides expresses the need to re-examine everything, with a moral, political, philosophical, literary and social criticism that often reaches the point of controversy or irony. In Euripides' tragedies we find the seeds of some fundamental concepts – such as state, politics, moral critics and the opposition between human and divine laws – allowing us to think about the state of exception. The link between Euripides' works and the state of exception is drawn by the same Agamben, who quotes the gesture of Antigone, since she opposes the written law to the *agrapta nomina* (unwritten laws; Agamben 2005: 28). Similar considerations can apply to Iphigenia. Agreeing to die when she sees how important the expedition is to everyone, Iphigenia performs an act of great generosity, qualifying herself as the only character with a noble soul in the whole tragedy. On the other side, her father's inhumanity will be punished by the gods through a number of misfortunes befalling himself and his whole family. *Iphigenia in Aulis* is therefore a work that unmasks the mechanisms of power, revealing how man-made laws disrupt all moral norms when it comes to power and its exercise. Likewise, Medea acts as a civil disobedient when Jason dishonours her with infidelity in the name of power. Medea's gesture appears as a desperate self-affirmation against the oppression suffered within the human context in which the woman finds herself living and acting.

This chapter aims to highlight the links between the brave protagonists of three successful contemporary Arab adaptations of the Greek myths of Iphigenia and Medea and the Greek heroines as they have been delivered by Greek tragedies and further interpretations. More precisely, it aims to show how Greek tragedy today can be the basis for women's unspoken stories dealing with issues of power, justice, law, war and gender where the state of exception has become the norm, such as in refugee camps and towns ravaged by conflict. I first study them individually in a direct comparison with their Greek source and with more recent adaptations of Greek myth to retrace an evolution of the state of exception critique. Some final remarks concerning the three plays outline their common points in tackling the question of the permanent state of exception.

In the shoes of Iphigenia

Iphigenia (2017) is the latest successful play by Omar Abusaada ('Umar Abū Sa'ada) and Mohammad Al Attar's (Muḥammad al-'Aṭṭār) Greek trilogy also including the *Trojan Women Project* (2013) and *Antigone of Shatila* (2015), whose genesis is rich in experimentation.[1] Responding to a request from an English production company which wanted to make a documentary film linking Syria and Troy, in November 2013, together with the actress Nanda Mohammad and the set designer Bissane Al Charif, Abusaada creates a play that uses the framework of the tragedy of Euripides' *Trojan Women* to present testimonies of Syrian women refugees in Jordan.[2] Back in Damascus, Abusaada works on therapeutic theatre projects with displaced teenagers. Meanwhile, in August 2013, Al Attar was in northern Syria, where he held drama seminars with mostly Syrian and Palestinian refugee women in Shatila Camp in Beirut. Starting from Al Attar's project, the two collaborate on *Antigone of Syria*, for the Al Hamra Theatre in Beirut. This time, on the stage, twenty-two women recall their lives in Syria during the revolution, then recount their flight from Syria and their arrival in Lebanon. The final show does not satisfy the two artists who rework the play during the year and create a new version with a reduced number of participants. The second version of the Lebanese project becomes *Antigone of Shatila*, which is staged in May 2015 at the Al Madina Theatre and is then scheduled for the Rencontres à l'échelle (Marseille) and at the Thalia Theatre in Hamburg.[3]

Iphigenia is co-produced by Volksbühne, in Berlin, where Al Attar has been living since 2015. Inspired by the Greek tragedy, nine Syrian and Iraqi women refugees in Berlin unfold their personal stories; their testimonies are reworked (thus using the verbatim theatre technique) to create the theatrical text, then recited by the women themselves. As in the previous projects, *Iphigenia* is based on drama therapy workshops, organized to give contributors – Syrian refugee women – the chance to tell their stories and help alleviate their trauma of displacement.

The play is organized in nine scenes, one for each audition for the role of Iphigenia in the homonymous play by Euripides. It opens with the audition of Diana, a young Syrian woman, who is interviewed by another Syrian woman, Riham, who also records the auditions. Riham interrogates Diana about her experiences as an actress and motivation in the show, then she asks her to play a scene from *Iphigenia*. As the audition progresses, questions become more and more private and Riham as well as the audience get to know more about Diana.

From the first audition, the idea of meta-theatre develops as a main element of the play while Iphigenia's story invites the women to tell their own stories. Each of the nine women interviewed by Riham points out one or more topics that are related to Iphigenia's myth. Diana's interview, for instance, centres on the idea of fame and sacrifice (she plays Iphigenia's monologue, 'Mother, Your raging against my father has no purpose. His decision is made, resistance is useless'), while the next scene, corresponding to Layla's audition, is more about sacrifice and love, drawing another direct line to Iphigenia's myth. At the same time, a

Figure 2 *Iphigenia*, directed by Omar Abusaada, Mohammad Al Attar, 2017. Credit: Reem Alghazzi.

reflection about acting and appearance is settled. Rahaf, the next auditioned woman, is nervous. From her conversation with Riham, it emerges that she was born in Syria, then she went to Italy, then to the Emirates and at the end she moved to Germany. Regarding Iphigenia's story, Riham thinks that Iphigenia should have tried to fight against her father's decision, indeed, she has prepared Iphigenia's monologue to Agamemnon. However, when she is about to play, she cannot remember it because of the fear of missing the chance. Her frustration appears clearly in the comparison with her idea of Iphigenia.

Nour's reflections on Iphigenia's myth and her vision of the Iphigenia and Agamemnon relationship – 'an unconditional, but at the same time suffocating love' – bring in the father–daughter relationship with the related issue of power balance. Sajida too finds analogies between her and Iphigenia in their relationships with their respective families as she performs Iphigenia's monologue pleading with her father not to kill her. For her audition, Alaa has written a letter reminiscent of Iphigenia's words to calm her mother Clytemnestra (in the fifth episode) and so, they link the idea of sacrifice to fame, glory and honour. As for Hiba, she feels like Iphigenia in many ways:

> Hiba
> ... She [Iphigenia] lived through a war and did things she didn't want to do. That's exactly what happened to me. We're the same age. In my imagination, we even look the same.
>
> Ibid.: Scene 6

Again, sacrifice and martyrdom are discussed in relation to war, a phenomenon that Hiba has experienced in Syria, despite her young age (seventeen years old). The girl admits she could not learn any part of the play because the language was too difficult, so she does not play any monologue from *Iphigenia*. A sense of displacement – new to the myth of Iphigenia – runs through the play accompanied by the pervading topic of war, existing also in the Greek myth:

HIBA
    . . . When the fighting started in Aleppo, we saw death with our own eyes. And when we decided to leave Lebanon and come here, death was everywhere. Every time I thought: if something happens to us, then please let me die. If only nothing would happen to my family, especially my little sisters and brothers. I couldn't go on if I knew something happened to them.

Ibid.: Scene 6

Zeina's improvised scene of a suicide recalls Iphigenia's sacrifice and allows her to speak about her traumatic experiences in a refugee camp in Lebanon, in a mix of topics from the ancient myth and innovations.

Portions of Euripides' play are brought on stage by the actresses as well as the chorus, who often introduce them.[4] Working as a palimpsest, Iphigenia's myth conveys the old topics and messages from the Greek play, such as the nature of heroism, free will, familial loyalty versus the common good, and the individual sin of pride (hubris). Iphigenia's Greek myth works as a leitmotiv of the play, but it also allows for a theatre of testimony. Moreover, being employed like a play within the play, it allows for metatheatre and, through a reflection about the Greek myth, it aims at a transformative role for society, represented both by the audience and the actresses.

The new context of *Iphigenia* offers space for new topics of reflection such as migration, marginalization and the refugee crisis. For instance, although Diana's interview is not centred on the topic of migration, while recounting her studies, she mentions that on moving to Beirut, she had to live in a difficult situation as she could not extend her visa and General Security was harassing her. In the new place, Berlin, she still feels lost because of bureaucracy and because she wants to work in the arts, but she does not feel safe. Similarly, Sajida is at the audition because she wants to disengage from the job centre. Nour arrives late to the audition because she had to deal with the job centre and the Immigration Office. Asked by Riham about her experience in Germany, she admits feeling 'lost and confused', without sense of security. Rahaf has lived in two other countries before getting to Germany. Hiba feels 'like a foreigner' as she 'can't settle in'.

The topic of displacement is not directly linked to the tragedy of Iphigenia. However, it becomes a marginal but unavoidable subject in the new adaptation of the myth. Moreover, even if the term 'refugee' is never used, to avoid labelling the women as such, most of the issues these women face are linked to their status as Arab refugees in Germany.[5] At the same time, Agamemnon's extra-legal

Figure 3 *Iphigenia*, directed by Omar Abusaada, Mohammad Al Attar, 2017. Credit: Reem Alghazzi.

authority over Iphigenia, which is allowed because of a necessity (namely, to put an end to the war), mirrors the women's condition as refugees in Germany, who are in a 'permanently temporary status' dictated by their dependence on bureaucracy since they are *de facto* legal non-citizens.

Medea, the (Lebanese) mother

Jogging: Theatre in Progress (*Jogging, Masraḥ qayd al-Taṭwīr*, 2012, latest version 2022),[6] text and performance by Hanane Hajj Ali (Ḥanān al-Ḥājj ʿAlī), is a partly autobiographical performance that tackles the taboos of religion, politics and sex in Lebanon presenting a radical challenge to the stereotypes and prejudices that afflict global perceptions of Arab women. With *Jogging*, Hajj Ali toured both in local (Lebanese) towns and in prestigious international theatres and festivals, such as the Avignon Festival in 2022. She won the Vertebra Award for Best Actress at the Fringe/Edinburgh International Festival in August 2017 and the 2020 Gilder/Coigney International Theatre Award.[7]

During her daily morning jog in her city, Beirut, the protagonist of the play, Hanane, runs and thinks about dreams, desires, hopes, disillusions, characters and roles, especially of women from her country who had to make the terrible choice to kill their children to avoid their suffering in a catastrophic world. In her reflections, Hanane evokes the myth of Medea, expressing her fascination for this myth, especially after her seven-year-old son was diagnosed with cancer. In an interview Hajj Ali explains (Ghosn 2021):

> One day while I was running, I had a dream that was like a spark. I imagined that I was smothering my son with a pillow to relieve him of cancer and this country that had made him sick. After that, I was paralyzed for several days and thought of Medea. I had never accepted to play this role because I was not convinced by her act.
>
> Since then, Medea has lived in me. I have become a fragment of her being and I have been searching for years among the women I meet, the other fragments. I am thinking about how I can approach this myth today. Who is Medea in a worn-out and cunning city like Beirut? If tragedy is a past theatrical genre, why does the smell of horror still haunt my nostrils when I run around Beirut?[8]

Hanane tells the story of Medea as a parody, expressing her feelings of repulsion for her act and the attraction it exercises on her. She claims to see the plight of Medea in the lives of women throughout her country while she is on her morning run. While the myth is evoked in its most tragic dimension, the structure and the ethos of the play clearly do not mirror the Greek tragedy.

The first 'Medea' Hanane enacts is Yvonne, a forty-two-year-old Lebanese woman.[9] Yvonne decides to put an end to the days of her three young daughters before joining them in death. She prepares a fruit salad that she garnishes with honey and whipped cream, and sprinkles copiously with rat poison before offering it to her daughters. Once they are asleep, she records a tape of the scene for her husband, eats the rest of the fruit salad, and goes to bed next to her daughters. The film she leaves behind disappears within hours. But one sentence remains: 'I left and I took my daughters with me, so that they will never know the suffering that was mine, and to ensure their future'. Hanane intertwines Yvonne's words with Medea's (from Euripides' and Heiner Müller's versions). As she could not find the tape with the record, she also comments on the reasons why this woman would ever come to kill her daughters. The first cause is seen in Lebanon's catastrophic political state.

With a similar technique, Hajj Ali shows Zahra's story, aiming at adding another piece 'in the giant puzzle of her character' (Ghosn 2021).[10] Zahra is a married woman from the south of Lebanon, fifty years old. Since she met her Jason/Muhammad, her life has drastically changed, and she has enrolled in resistance movements. They have two sons, but Zahra eventually discovers that Muhammad loves another woman:

ZAHRA

What's wrong Muhammad? Why are you looking at me strangely? Why are you sour? Why your body is tense? Your kiss is awkward? Your saliva pinches? Your odour repulsive?

Am I undesired? Three weeks have passed Jason and you did not come near me! Not with your voice or hands or eyes! Look me in the eye . . . Look at me . . .

> wow . . . this is not you, you are not Muhammad . . . you are a cheater and in love
> . . . Love can reveal what's inside you.
>   I disowned my family for your sake.
>
> Hajj Ali 2018: 24

Zahra's words addressed to Muhammad mix with Medea's confrontation with Jason, echoing Muller's text (in bold in the original text). Zahra prays to God, invoking his eternal justice and she becomes a pious woman. Hanane tells the audience that two of Zahra's children died in the 2006 war against Israel, as they fought against the 'enemy' in the south of Lebanon. Zahra, like Medea, sacrifices two of her children. 'But Zahra has no magic chariot and her grandfather is not the god of the sun' – says Hanane (ibid.: 26) – and, in 2013, her third son also died while fighting in the North of Syria.

At this point, it is interesting to note that a first version of the play closes with Hanane reading the letter this third son left before dying, in a clear denunciation of the war's hypocrisy. This letter makes it clear that, even though Zahra didn't kill her son directly, he died for the ideas and ideals she raised him in.[11] The latest version of the play, instead, after the letter's reading, leads to a direct reflection on the myth of Medea, restoring attention to *Jogging*'s leitmotiv and reinforcing the presence of the myth:

HANANE
Who's Medea today?
Me? You?
Beirut? This world never stopping
sinking in the violence?
How many thousands of Medeas are there?
And nobody will ever tell their story.
. . .
Lebanese, Syrian, Palestinian, Iraqi mothers . . . and all
unable to secure the future
of their children.
Other than depositing them in
the boats of death
to try to reach either the northern shores or paradise lost.[12]

The play closes with excerpts from the poem *Home* by Warsan Shire[13] and Hanane commenting that she is incited by Beirut's voice to wake up and run, to keep jogging.

In *Jogging*, the myth of Medea is employed as a leitmotif and in its deeper, substantial meaning: for all *Jogging*'s Medeas, the killing of their children is a momentous but necessary act. Medea's myth is derived from Euripides' version, which is summoned at the beginning of the play. Hanane also quotes Pier Paolo Pasolini's *Medea* (1969), which she criticizes for its screenplay. Quotes from Heiner Müller's *Medeamaterial* (1984)[14] introduces his ethics of cruelty, aimed at reflecting, through Medea's brutal and bloody rebellion, the violence she has received. But on the other hand, because she internalizes the male value system, Müller and so Hajj Ali seems to suggest that it ultimately destroys her feminine identity. Müller explores Medea's potential by using her not as a character but as material, creating various irresolvable juxtapositions and contradictions of character, structure, narrative and performance. Hajj Ali does the same thing partially with her different Medeas on stage.

Despite all these international intertextual allusions – enriched by references to Virginia Woolf, Shakespeare, Reyhaneh Jabbari (Reyḥāne Jabbārī) and even Guy Béart's song 'L'eau vive' – *Jogging*'s Medeas are all women from Lebanon. While Hanane insists on focusing on women from her country – a corrupted country, she says – the end of the last version of the play also includes Syrian, Palestinian and Iraqi women, 'all unable to secure their children's future' says Hanane. The women's tremendous act is directly linked to the instability of the place they live in. However, allusions infer that this act has a universal dimension. Anywhere laws and rights in a context of war and/or destruction do not ensure mothers' ability 'to secure their children's future', acting like Medea is an inescapable fate.

Medea, the Other

IMedea (2021–2) by Sulayman Al Bassam (Sulaymān al-Bassām) is the second part of Al Bassam's ambitious cycle of new texts and dramatic performance projects inspired by ancient texts, disappeared civilizations, forgotten languages and the fragments of lost histories titled *The Icarus Cycle*. The first play of the cycle, *Ur* (2015–18) derives from an ancient Sumerian text – A *Lamentation for the Destruction of the City of Ur* – dating from 2000 BC and held today in the Louvre Museum in Paris. The Sumerian text is considered the first poem written in memory of a destroyed civic entity in the history of mankind. Intertextuality is a common trait of Al Bassam's production, whose *Kalila wa-Dimna*'s adaptation – *The Mirror for Princes: Kalila Wa Dimna* (2007) – takes its inspiration from these ancient fables to write a parable of the American invasion of Iraq.[15]

Like *Ur*, *IMedea* explores thematic concerns around social justice, the nature of power structures and female apotheosis. While *Ur* was created at the Rezidenz

Theatre in Munich in 2018, an initial draft of *IMedea* was developed during Al Bassam's fellowship on the Visiting Global Faculty Programme at The Gallatin School of Individualized Study, New York University, in 2017, then the play was reworked following the rehearsals in collaboration with the actors.[16] Major changes were made due to the pandemic, as for practical reasons Al Bassam had to reduce the number of actors and so, to modify the text of the play. The characters of Creusa, Glauce, the Influencer, Medea's maid and the Engineer were suppressed, while Al Bassam decided to take the role of both Creon, Jason, and the TV host. He also took the role of the dramatist, impersonating himself. As for the protagonist, Medea, she was played by the Syrian actress Hala Omran, who won the prize for best actress at the Carthage Theatre Festival in 2021. Lebanese electro-acoustic duo made by Abed Kobeissi and Ali Hout played 'Two (or the Dragon)' and performed the play's music, while Oussama Jamei, from Tunis, was Aghadiz, a new migrant to Corinth.

Like in the Greek tragedy, Medea is a foreign woman who has killed her own brother to marry Jason. After a few years of marriage, Jason has decided to leave Medea and marry the daughter of Creon, king of Corinth, the city they live in. Jason repudiates Medea, but she does not accept his decision. Creon condemns her and her two sons to exile. Confronted with the oath-breaking hypocrisies of Jason and the punitive social mores of Corinth, Medea is led to take terrible vengeance on Corinthian society by murdering her children. When Jason appears to take revenge on her in turn, as in Euripides' play, dragons appear to take her to the kingdom of Aegean, where she has obtained asylum.

The main variations from the Greek tragedy concern the setting, while many features of the play show a deep study of the myth and an intention to make it relevant to the present, with a discursive topicality running through the play. *IMedea*'s action strays far from Euripides' Corinth. Taking place in a contemporary Corinth, where the media and the digital platforms have the power to alter political space, it stages Medea as a blogger who advocates for migrants' rights. Representing the refugees' voice, her vengeance is linked to her battle against the xenophobia promoted by politicians.

From the prologue onwards, *IMedea* recalls Euripides' *Medea* arrangement. After a background note to the play by the dramatist, three short scenes introduce the topic. Medea is interrogated about two videos of her killing her two children that she posted on the media. While she listens to the interrogator, she remains silent. Then she is at a TV show where she confesses to the interviewer that she does not recognize herself anymore. In the following scene, she describes a dream she had:

MEDEA
The truth is I don't recognize myself anymore.
I dreamt I was barefoot in a field,
my feet sinking into the mud.
I look down and see a house
with no roof and no walls
and a woman standing with a large box next to her feet:
That woman is me.
That box contains my children.

Al Bassam 2021: Act I, Scene 2

Such an introduction mirrors Medea's nurse's prologue in Euripides' play (vv. 44–55):

NURSE
Her suffering has taught her the advantages
of not being cut off from one's homeland.
Now she hates her children. When she sees them,
there is no joy in her. And I'm afraid
she may be up to some new mischief.
Her mind thinks in extremes. I know her well.
She'll not put up with being treated badly.
I worry she may pick up a sharp sword
and stab her stomach, or else she'll go
into the house, in silence, to that bed,
and kill the king and bridegroom Jason.
Then she'll face an even worse disaster.

In Euripides' *Medea* the prologue establishes the tone and the ethos of the play. Likewise, in *IMedea*, the mood of regret, the might-have-been opposed to the reality, is fixed from the first.

From Euripides' tragedy, *IMedea* absorbs the question of being an outsider with all the consequences it implies. In Euripides' play, Medea tells Creon:

MEDEA
You have this city and your father's home, enjoyment of life, and the companionship of friends, but, alone and without a city, I am abused by my husband, carried off as plunder from a foreign land, I have no mother, no brother, no relative to offer me a safe haven from this disaster.

Euripides, *Medea*: vv. 252–57

This idea of Medea being an exile is underlined by the Chorus in the first stasimon, where they explain that Medea lives 'on foreign soil, abandoned' and she is going to be chased from Corinth, despite her being 'well loved in exile by those whose land she'd moved to', as the Nurse asserts (Euripides, *Medea*: vv. 11–12). Similarly, from being a migrant, Medea in *IMedea* could become a Corinthian citizen with a certain weight in Corinthian society, as she is an influencer in a time when digital platforms are the new agora. Indeed, at the beginning of the play, she affirms she is 'Corinthian and proud'. However, Creon informs her that because of her 'political deviancy', she has lost her right to stay in Corinth and has become an illegal immigrant:

> CREON
> You've shown yourself an enemy to the project of this Republic. Your citizenship was granted on condition of respecting the laws and *spirit* of this Republic. Your citizenship has been revoked.
>
> Al Bassam 2021: Act II, Scene 3

In both cases, Medea is well loved by the Corinthian people, but she will face exile because she is an outsider. Moreover, Al Bassam's play shifts Medea's condition of being a foreigner, the stranger *par excellence*, to make her a Corinthian citizen with a different perception of reality compared to her fellow citizens, especially regarding migrants' conditions and ecological issues. In the same logic, the fact that Medea does not eat, as her Nurse announces in Euripides' prologue (Euripides, *Medea*: vv. 32–35) is transformed into detoxing and a hunger strike in *IMedea*. Such a political turn, with Medea's revenge as a political act mirrors the *Medea* of Seneca, dating from the first century BC – as the author explains during the play (Al Bassam 2021: Act III, Scene 3).

Presumably inspired by Ovid's and other Latin versions of *Medea*, Seneca's *Medea* shifts from the idea of Medea's primitive vengeance to a desire for power (Henry, Walker 1967: 171). Moreover, Seneca's Medea could represent the anxieties of imperialism as Jason's desire for power and gaining a kingdom led him to bring devastation to Colchis and Greece (Benton 2003: 271). Indeed, Seneca emphasizes the Corinthians' view of Medea as a barbarian, as well as Medea's culture shock of living in a foreign land. That same barbaric view characterizing the Latin Medea is a main aspect of Pier Paolo Pasolini's Medea played by Maria Callas in his homonymous film (1969). In the first scene of the second act of *IMedea*, the author claims to have found Medea's company in Pasolini's film after he broke up his marriage. With his rebellious Medea, Pasolini stood up for the non-European, postcolonial Other and all the people who are socially endangered in the twentieth century (Stevanović 2013: 219–20).

Figure 4 *IMedea*, directed by Sulayman Al Bassam, 2022. Credit: Ahmed Bousnina.

Like Pasolini, Al Bassam mixes elements from different cultures – Medea is black, like Jason, she is a Greek wife and mother, she brandishes/wields a Japanese blade, wears a veil recalling the hijab and speaks Arabic and English – questioning, like him, the concepts of nation and national cultures that stigmatize the Other. Like the Italian artist, Al Bassam exalts the barbarian origin of Medea and maintains her ancestral charm, making it a positive force.[17]

Once she loses her identity, Medea is under the dominion of an overwhelming force that is within her and faced with which she recognizes that she is powerless. It is Medea's Otherness – in Seneca's, Pasolini's and Al Bassam's *Medeas* – that forces her to fight. Medea, who has lost everything, becomes an emblematic victim of the dissolution of the strongest values that supported order, balance and social harmony: modesty and respect for oaths (Seneca, *Medea*: vv. 439–41).

Women stand out as the exception (in the state of exception)

Iphigenia, Jogging and *IMedea* engage viscerally with Greek myth and its universe to make it relevant to the present and discuss matters of power and law especially in a world where the state of exception has become the norm, such as cities devastated by war, refugee camps, but also Europe with its migrant reception system(s). In doing so, they never contradict the original topics and messages of the Greek tragedies, but they also research within the chains of re-elaborations of the myth – especially in the case of *Jogging* and *IMedea* – to be in line with (or deny) recent interpretations of the same myth.

In the new plays, we notice a process of identification of the protagonists with Greek heroines. This is the case of most of the actresses in *Iphigenia*. In *Jogging*, Hanane's identification with Medea recalls the author in *IMedea*, who claims: 'Medea was a corridor that invited me in. I walked down that corridor and found a mirror in which I could see the contours of myself' (Al Bassam 2021: Act II, Scene 1). The individual self-identification with Iphigenia and Medea implies recognizing oneself to be a subject of a major power that is unfair, as it breaks moral and social norms in the name of a superior good (the state). This process of self-identification with the myth forces a confrontation with the cultural and theatrical legacy of Greek tragedy for our present-day crisis of democracy.

It is not by chance that, in the three plays, specific attention is given to the act of recording. The actresses in *Iphigenia* are recorded by Riham, and the whole play is based on the original dialogues recorded during the auditions. In *Jogging*, Yvonne records her infanticides and Hanane outlines this aspect of the terrible act, describing it as a show where the mother prepares the camera and the tape; she has charged the camera; she picks the right angle; she dresses her daughters in new pyjamas. Similarly, Medea records her sons' murder and posts the video on Twitter. She alleges the importance of their impact and confesses that she knows that they will provoke riots in the migrant camps. More than due to the murder, Medea is chased for the messages and videos she shared on social media. In a Corinth where digital platforms are social spaces, she is 'the voice of the voiceless' (Al Bassam 2021: Prelude, Scene 2), with a reference to the refugees. On his part, Aghadiz, the new migrant, presents himself as 'the one who's spoken about, who doesn't speak' (Al Bassam 2021: Act I, Scene 4).

The question of representation (and misrepresentation) is central to the three plays, where women care that their stories should not be mediated by others' voices. Medea (in *IMedea*) is an influencer; Sajida (in *Iphigenia*) warns Riham that she would not take the part if the play is about 'Syrian refugee women, how they came here, how their lives have changed, stuff like that' because she 'can't keep hearing the same story over and over', she asserts (Al Attar, Abusaada 2017: Scene 5); Hanane assumes that Yvonne's tape is not legally available as the truth it contained 'was buried along with her' (Hajj Ali 2018: 20–1). In this context of self-narration, in *Iphigenia* and in *Jogging*, Greek tragedy acts as a stimulus both to reveal the women's unspoken stories and also to observe them. Moreover, in *Iphigenia*, Greek tragedy is at the basis of drama therapy.

Another point concerning the three plays, like the Greek myths, is that they present female protagonists. From their marginal positions of individuals subjugated to men's decisions, Iphigenia as well as Medea express their perspectives about the situations involving them and act according to their will. In the new *Iphigenia* there are only female characters disclosing their memories, desires and everyday life expressing their opinion about the life they lead. *Jogging* and *IMedea* emphasize this aspect of the myths to explicitly contest the implicit laws of patriarchy in today's societies – especially in the state of emergency – taking for granted the exclusive control of domestic, public and political authority by the older males of the group. It suffices to mention that, in the final commentary, Hanane describes the Lebanese women as women exiled to the very land where they were born and do not even have the right to transmit their nationality to their children, while men rehash the same discourse exemplified in a line evoking the Lebanese Anthem that exalt the men's force. In *IMedea*, Jason comes to provoke Medea by accusing her of having fought patriarchy for her own gain ('You spoke your conscience, denounced your patriarchy', Al Bassam 2021: Prelude, Scene 3).

Directly or indirectly, the three plays address the question of the hijab. Hajj Ali does it implicitly as she wears a headscarf (a '*manādīl*') and so do Hanane and Yvonne, while Zahra has a black hijab that the actress wears to gradually enter in the character. At the beginning of her performance, Hanane ironically defines herself as 'a cool hijab woman' (Hajj Ali 2018: 10). Such an ironic description together with Hajj Ali's performance (wearing her headscarf) defy common sense that a veiled woman cannot play any role, as *Iphigenia* infers.[18] In *Iphigenia*, Riham asks Sajida if she sees any conflict between acting and wearing a hijab. 'Personally, no, I don't see a big conflict. But for lots of people, it's unacceptable' (Al Attar, Abusaada 2017: Scene 5), answers the girl with a disarming simplicity that in a few words denounces prejudices. *IMedea* addresses the issue directly. In Corinth, covering one's face is illegal and when Medea wears a black veil, Jason tries to take it off her head. Jason calls it a 'stupid symbol of male oppression', 'erasure of female identity', 'neutering of female sexuality', while Medea defines it a 'little cloth', a 'rag', a 'black piece of nothing' (Al Bassam 2021: Act I, Scene 3).[19] Jason's ascending climax is contrasted by Medea's descending climax provoking a clear contradiction between the woman's ironic words and Jason's serious chauvinism. Using different tools, each play defies prejudices about the hijab together with its basis of racism, patriarchy and Orientalism.[20]

With the importance of the question of representation (and misrepresentation) in the three plays, and also the fact that they present female Arab and/or Muslim protagonists with a specific address to the question of the hijab, let us assume that the ideal audience for these plays is presumably Western rather than Middle Eastern. This is clear at least for *Iphigenia* and *IMedea*. Co-produced by Volksbühne, *Iphigenia* is clearly created to be represented in Europe and until today it has been staged only in Berlin. As for *IMedea*, after having been represented in the MENA (Tunis, Cairo, Beirut and Kuwait), it was staged in Italy and Mexico (and then back in the MENA, in Casablanca). With its international support and awards, and its participation in the Avignon Festival, *Jogging* has gained international success, despite the play being created to address Lebanese society.[21]

Iphigenia, *Jogging* and *IMedea* are deliberately thought-provoking. Placing women's history in the cleavage between the lack of application of the norm and the cruel enforcement of the law, the three plays show how women are themselves the exception of the permanent state of exception. In other words, in the case of *Iphigenia*, *Jogging* and *IMedea*, recourse to Greek myth produces conscious brave women in a mad world (ruled by men). Dignifying and humanizing Iphigenia and Medea's suffering, the three plays exhibit the universality of Greek myth. The agora for thinking about this permanent state of exception, together with its exceptions, seems also to be universal.

Notes

1 Both Abusaada and Al Attar completed their theatrical studies at the High Institute of Dramatic Arts in Damascus, but following the outbreak of the Syrian protest in March 2011, they reacted differently: Al Attar publicly took a stand against the government by writing an article that appeared in the pan-Arab daily *al-Ḥayāt* in June 2011 and was therefore forced to move to Beirut; Abusaada, on the other hand, refused to leave Syria and continues to reside in Damascus, producing theatre in increasingly difficult circumstances. In 2012 Abusaada directed *Could You Please Look into the Camera?*, written by Al Attar, based on interviews with political prisoners.

2 The play, performed in December 2013 in a theatre of the Jordanian National Center for Culture and Arts, is harshly criticized for the ambiguous political positions that run through it and which are perceived as close to the official Syrian discourse (the revolution being the Trojan horse of discord) and the absence of any real theatricality (Halima 2013).

3 On these two projects, see Ruocco 2016.

4 The chorus appears twice. Once it introduces Diana's monologue, then it ends the play. In this case all the actresses join it, taking the form of the coryphée.

5 In an interview conducted on 16 September 2021, the actress Layla Shandi admitted to me that, despite the fact that the actresses were all refugees, the word 'refugee' was not to be used to describe them.

6 In this chapter I quote the English translation, published in 2018. However, the author kindly provided me with the new conclusion dating from 2022.

7 Hanane Hajj Ali's career as an actress began in 1978 with the Hakawati Theatre, which revived the Lebanese tradition of storytelling and was founded by the man who later became her husband, Roger Assaf. Her several roles in plays and films include, in 2005, the main role of the mother in *Les Paravents/Les Écrans* by Jean Genet at the Palais de Chaillot in Paris. Throughout her forty-year career, she has become an eminent figure on the Lebanese cultural and artistic scene, facilitating and supporting hundreds of colleagues, students and communities in Lebanon and throughout the entire Middle East-North Africa (MENA) region. It has been co-produced by AFAC (Arab Fund for Arts and Culture) and Heinrich Böll Stiftung – MENA Office (Beirut) with the support of: SHAMS Association, Collectif Kahraba, Al Mawred Al Thaqafy (Culture Resource), Moussem (BE), Zoukak/Focus Liban 2016, Artas Foundation, l'Institut Français au Liban, The British Council, Vatech, Khalil Wardé SAL.

8 Like the other stories in *Jogging*, this episode comes from a real fact, as the author has declared in many interviews (see, for instance, Ghosn 2021).

9 The name is invented, but the story is real. This educated mother had learnt that her husband, living and working in the Gulf Emirates in the service of a rich emir, had a dissolute life. On Thursday, 19 October 2019, she killed her daughters and herself, as *Jogging* recounts. Her neighbours discovered the bodies the next morning.

10 The character of Zahra was inspired by a woman from South Lebanon known by Hajj Ali. Married very young by her family to a much older man, at the age of twenty she meets Muhammad and courageously decides to divorce her husband. She then becomes a journalist and earns enough money to build their house. But Muhammad changes with time, and she eventually discovers that he loves another woman. She asks for a divorce and becomes a pious woman. She works with the families of the martyrs and raises her children in this ideology.

11 In a private interview, Hajj Ali explains to me that Zahra's third son's letter started a crisis in Zahra's life and it encouraged her to delve into the character of Medea (interview with Hanane Hajj Ali, Beirut, 24 November 2022).

12 This part was added in 2022. The author kindly sent me this new version of the conclusion. English translation is mine.

13 Warsan Shire (1988) is a British writer, poet, editor and teacher, who was born to Somali parents in Kenya. In 2013 she was awarded the inaugural Brunel University African Poetry Prize.

14 Heiner Müller (1929–95) emerged as Germany's most influential playwright during the second half of the twentieth century, giving with his 'enigmatic and fragmentary pieces' a significant contribution to postmodern theatre. *Medeamaterial* is the central part of his dramatic triptych *Despoiled Shore Medeamaterial Landscape with Argonauts* (1983), part of Müller's exploration of classical Greek drama for its relevance to the present.

15 Al Bassam has adapted Shakespeare as well. His *Arab Shakespeare Trilogy* (2002–11) is inspired by *Hamlet, Richard III* and *Twelfth Night*; see Holderness 2013.

16 *IMedea* was produced by Sabab, an independent touring theatre company led by Sulayman Al Bassam and coproduced by Fondazione Campania dei festival, Campania Teatro Festival, AFAC – the Arab Fund for Arts and Culture. It has premiered at Carthage Theatre Festival, in Tunis (Le 4ème Art, 9 December 2021), Carthage Theatre Festival, in Tunis (Le 4ème Art, 9 December 2021), and has been performed at Cairo International Festival for Experimental Theatre, in Cairo (Hanager Arts Center, Opera House, 15–16 December 2021), in Beirut (Al Madina Theatre, 28–30 January 2022), in Kuwait (Yarmouk Cultural Centre – Dār al-Athār al Islamiyya, 26 March 2022), at Arabisches Theatertreffen Hannover (Pavillon Hannover, 8–9 June 2022), at Campania Teatro Festival, Naples (Teatro Politeama, 2 July 2022), at Requiem for Justice, an International Rally of Artists and Writers for Social Justice (Centro Cultural del Bosque INBAL, Mexico City, 27–8 October 2022), at the 13th edition of the Arab Theatre Festival (Mahrajān al-Masraḥ al-ʿArabī, Theatre Mohammed VI, 23 January 2023), in Casablanca.

17 Pasolini provocatively claimed that Barbarism is the word he loved the most in the world (see Fusillo 1994).

18 In a video interview with Dima Wannus, Hajj Ali explains that she feels free wearing the hijab and that wearing it during her performance is not a political position to demonstrate anything when she performs abroad (Hajj Ali – Wannus 2016: minutes 11'–13').

19 In a few aspects, Al Bassam's Medea recalls Jean Anouilh's sensual character in the homonymous play (1946) pointing out (and criticizing) Medea's sexual sacrifice in her marriage life with Jason. Like Anouilh, Al Bassam analyses male–female relationships more in depth than the Greek/Latin version.

20 Fighting prejudices about hijab was at the basis of the Egyptian feminist movement at the start of the twentieth century. While Qāsim Amīn advocated the abolition of the hijab, which was seen as a symbol of oppression and to grant women's emancipation, Malak Ḥifnī Nāṣif (better known as Bāḥithat al-Bādiya), criticized him believing that men should not tell women how to dress. With the concept of 'gendered orientalism', Lila Abu-Lughod (2013) explains how Muslim women's rights have been exploited to justify US military intervention. So, she traces the history of the Western representation of 'Muslim women' and their rights after 11 September 2001, when even a current of feminism supported the imperialist cause. She worries about the practical and political consequences of such depictions of women's suffering and wonders why many Westerners, including human rights activists, assume that Muslim women lack agency and cannot express themselves because they dress a certain way.

Al Bassam's Medea encapsulates a variety of social battles. One perspective may attribute this to the extraordinary power of the female character. However, a further analysis reveals a prism of postcolonial ideology at stake. Medea, an Arab migrant regardless of social class, embodies various forms of resistance manifested in any deviation from the certainties of European liberalism such as the use of social media, migration, veiling, terrorism, or environmentalism.

21 The play toured in Lebanon and was a remarkable success. It was even staged in the southern city of Nabatieh (Hajj Ali's hometown), whose inhabitants are predominantly Shi'a Muslims, in its school theatre in 2016.

References

Abu-Lughod, L. (2013), *Do Muslim Women Need Saving?*, Cambridge, MA: Harvard University Press.

Agamben, G. (2005), *State of Exception*, Chicago: University of Chicago Press.

Al Attar, M. and O. Abusaada (2017), *Iphigenia*, trans. A. Galt.

Al Bassam, S. (2022), *IMedea*: Unpublished play's scripts.

Anouilh, J. (1967), *Medée*, Paris: la Table Ronde.

Benton, C. (2003), 'Bringing the Other to Center Stage: Seneca's "Medea" and the Anxieties of Imperialism', *Arethusa*, 36(3): 271–84.

De Genova, N. (2012), 'Bare Life, Labor-Power, Mobility, and Global Space: Toward a Marxian Anthropology?', *CR: The New Centennial Review*, 12(3): 129–51.

Euripides (2008), *Iphigenia in Aulis*, trans. I. Johnston. Arlington: Richer Resources Publications.

Euripides (2012), *Medea*, trans. A. Elliot. London: Oberon Books.

Fusillo, M. (1994), '"Credo nelle chiacchiere dei barbari": Il Tema della barbarie in Elsa Morante e in Pier Paolo Pasolini', *Studi Novecenteschi*, 21(47/8): 97–129.

Ghosn, N. (2021), 'Hanane Hajj Ali: Portrait of a Theatrical Trailblazer', *The Markaz Review*, 14 February 2021.

Hajj Ali, H. (2018), *Jogging: Theatre in Progress [Jogging Masraḥ qayd al-Taṭwīr]*, trans. H. Abdulrazzak.

Hajj Ali, H. and D. Wannus (2016), 'Anā min hunā', Orient TV, available at the following link: www.youtube.com/watch?v=7bISmwrL76Y [last access: 25 November 2022].

Halīma, S. (2013), 'Nisā' ṭurwādiyāt, 'arḍ masraḥī yabta id 'an al-wāqi' wa-yumawwih hawiyat al-ǧānī', *Al- 'Arab*, 22 December 2013.

Henry, D. and B. Walker (1967), 'Loss of Identity: Medea Superest?: A Study of Seneca's Medea', *Classical Philology*, 62(3): 169–81.

Holderness, G. (2013), 'Sulayman Al Bassam – Portrait of a Contemporary Arab Theatre', *Recherchen 104: Theater Im Arabischen Sprachraum – Theatre in the Arab World* (12/2013).

Müller, H. (1983), *Despoiled Shore Medea-material Landscape with Argonauts*, trans. M. E. Demeglio, T. P. Liontiris. Sussex: University of Sussex.

Ruocco, M. (2016), 'Migration and Memory: Displacement Narratives of Syrian
    Refugees Women on Stage', in G. Cataldi (ed.), *A Mediterranean Perspective on
    Migrants' Flows in EU: Protection of Rights, Intercultural Encounters and Integration
    Policies*, 207–21, Naples: Editoriale Scientifica.
Seneca, L. A. (1956), *Medea*, trans. M. Hadas. Indianapolis: The Bobbs-Merril Company.
Stevanović, L. (2013), 'Between Mythical and Rational Worlds: Medea by Pier Paolo
    Pasolini', in A. Renger and J. Solomon (eds), *Ancient Worlds in Film and Television:
    Gender and Politics*, 213–27, Leiden: Brill.

5

So Many Medeas!

Medea in Iran and Lebanon since 2015

Yassaman Khajehi

The status of women in a society is in one way or another a social and political cursor that artists in history have often reproduced in their works. Euripides' plays are a case in point as they have an important socio-political dimension and give a central place to women's issues (Saxonhouse 2005; Mendelsohn 2002). In this chapter, I will study the play *Medea* and its contemporary representations to show how this play and its main character become the space of a socio-artistic expression in a contemporary 'complex society' (Goldhill 2004 [1986]). To develop this hypothesis, I will focus on two fields of research that may be at first glance different in terms of the status of women but are very similar at a deeper level. To conduct my research, I interviewed several artists in Iran and Lebanon between 2017 and 2023. This chapter is the result of a reflection based on these exchanges as well as my studies of Iranian and Lebanese societies.

While in Lebanese society the influence of French culture is omnipresent, the Iranian state has tried to erase all traces of westernization and the cultural and social life of the Islamic Revolution of 1979. In Iran, the social situation is often politicized and the demand for women's rights is seen as a taboo or an imported Western fashion. They are even seen as an invasive problem of Western culture that is opposed to Islamic culture and Sharia law. These issues exist differently in Lebanon, because the fact that in this society several religions and ideologies coexist makes the social positioning of women more diverse. However, in these circumstances, we must not forget the major place of morals that ultimately brings together Lebanese and Iranian society. While direct demands for women's rights do not seem obvious, theatrical narration can become an escape route to present, without too much 'commentary', the place of women and their action in society. Moreover, the theatrical space is more secure if it is a foreign text, showing a society outside our time and space. Through case studies and exchanges and interviews with Iranian and Lebanese artists, this chapter studies the functioning of Euripides' play *Medea* in the construction of a social and political discourse about the status of women knowing that this play seems a perfect place to question gender and patriarchy (Bungard & Deno 2021).

Social and political upheaval

To understand the adaptations of *Medea* in contemporary Iran and Lebanon, it is necessary to schematize the socio-political and economic turmoil of these societies. This helps to understand that the contemporary situation in these countries can indeed be described as 'tragic'. The traces of war, extreme conflicts over power distribution, a strong belief in fatalism, a deep lack of social justice, and wide social divides are very conspicuous in these societies. A simple review of events over a defined time demonstrates this. For example, since 2019 a series of misadventures and significant events have occurred in both countries. In Iran, in the autumn of 2019, there were very large protests, with more than a thousand victims, in reaction to the economic situation and increases in the price of petrol. Several thousand people received threatening official text messages, aimed at dissuading them from participating in the protests. The state cut off access to the Internet, and people lost contact with the outside world for the first time, which was already very limited due to US embargoes and the geopolitical situation. For a majority of Iranians, the Internet was the only means of economic survival. Later, on 8 January 2020, a Ukrainian aircraft – Flight 752, flying from Tehran to Kiev – was shot down by a missile shortly after take-off from Tehran airport. There were 176 deaths, and this, according to the official Iranian discourse, was due to 'human error'. This event, like a great tragedy of contemporary times, has significantly marked the Iranian people, and notions of power, but also fate, murder and responsibility, have been raised amongst other issues. Three years later, this event contributed to the formation of another movement. Indeed, after the death of Mahsa Amini, the young Iranian woman arrested by the morality police in Tehran in September 2022, Iran entered a turbulent period with a series of political and social but also artistic protests.

On the Lebanese side, the protests known as *thawra* – meaning 'revolution' – accompanied by various political, economic, and social demands, took place from October 2019. The starting point seems to have been related to a tax on WhatsApp services, the increase in the price of petrol, etc. Indeed, this was the trigger for an economic collapse, the bursting of a financial bubble, which now seems irreversible. As in Iran, the Covid-19 pandemic has exacerbated the situation, and has affected an already weakened and wounded people. Finally, in Lebanon, the so-called 'gaping hole' occurred with the explosion on 4 August in the port of Beirut, killing 218 people. There was a gap, both in a literal and figurative sense produced by the event itself, but also by a demonstration of the depth of corruption and/or ignorance: people in power were aware of this danger. The explosion practically destroyed and, in any case, emptied the area called downtown Beirut of its population. The Lebanese people also lost Alexandra Najjar, the three-year-old girl who had become one of the symbols of the *thawra*, as she participated with her parents, Lebanese flag in hand, in the demonstrations.[1] Her photograph was circulated in the media and symbolized the hope of the revolutionaries. This reality of endless collective suffering was described as a tragedy.

These elements represent only a part of the news of these two countries. We can then see the presence and abundance of events that directly influence artistic creation shared notably on social networks.[2] Indeed, when society enters a period of turmoil, artistic production is more closely related to social and political expression. One example is the set of iconographic installation and performative productions inspired by the idea of 'Woman, Life, Freedom' since September 2022.[3] For example, an unknown artist coloured the water in Teheran's fountains and urban water basins red. The image symbolized the blood of the protesters and victims. Nevertheless, as regards the character of Medea, she is presented first in Iran and Lebanon as a woman-mother who kills her children to take revenge on Jason. The socio-political and economic reasoning behind Medea's situation as a foreign woman on the margins who wants to protect her children comes later. This is also evident in the way the artists discuss their discoveries of the text. I also think that this second understanding of the character is more accepted and widespread in Iran than in Lebanon. This is interpreted as a sign of the longstanding societal, political, and economic crisis in Iran, and also shows the history of female oppression that is more prominent in Iran.

Medea, woman-mother confronting her society

In recent years, the play and its adaptations have been performed many times in Iran. The character and her story, while moving away from its 'strangeness', are becoming familiar on the Iranian stage. Far from the socio-political issues of

Euripides' text and its marginal questions, the set of everyday events in Iran pushes the artist and the spectator to retell the *Medea* fable. This helps to reflect on current events and social demands that are looking for a place to emerge. In other words, here, theatre and narrative shape a place in which the 'staging' of socio-political reality is allowed.

The stage representation of *Medea* and its narrative are indeed opposed to the representation of the ideal mother-woman of the Iranian official discourse. Although this is part of the characteristics of the Medea myth as narrated and emphasized by Seneca, for example, I am more interested here in its social and expressive dimension. The reality of Iranian women in the face of *Medea*'s theatricality directs us towards a reflection on the very meaning of the events: representation is at the heart of Iranian society, and more precisely of Tehrani society, where the 'ideal image' of women is disseminated within urban spaces and the media. This representation, as Annie Le Brun says in *Du trop de réalité*, invites or forces the public to 'get out of the real' to 'enter the real' (Le Brun 2012: 25) and tell a set of stories, sometimes real, sometimes fictional, belonging to ancient Greece and highlighting the issue of women in today society.

To examine the dominant vision of the woman-mother in Iranian society, three evocations are proposed here, each of which illustrates an aspect of this vision. The first: in April 2015, a video of a young woman's interview is published on an Iranian online channel, entitled 'The heart-breaking words of this mother who became the murderer of her two daughters aged one year and two months'.[4] The caption of the video starts with: 'I killed my children with too much love, I never thought I would become a murderer'.[5] The woman is dressed in black and shown in profile, hidden by her veil. Throughout the video, the interviewer's face is also shown sympathizing with the woman apparently held in a psychiatric prison. Moreover, we arrive at the heart of the performance, in this case by exploiting theatricality that creates a fourth wall between the mother and the criminal; the mother is given a role and so 'becomes' a murderer, without really being one. Here, this mother upsets her audience, touches their hearts, the adjective used in Persian in the title, meaning rather 'that tears out the heart'. She tells of her life and her suffering and speaks honestly about her backwardness at school, her family difficulties, and the life she did not want for her daughters. The second sentence of the video caption also speaks of a woman who as a child played mummy with her dolls and who, during her pregnancy, took her vitamins and never thought she would become a murderer. While she is being interviewed, another frame appears on the screen next to the interview image. It shows a well-dressed little girl in pink with long, curly black hair playing with a doll; one can imagine that it is her daughter and that the image comes from her phone, for example. One can also imagine that the girl playing with her doll is there as an illustration to influence the audience as much as possible. The role is still emphasized: playing mother, then becoming a killer. It is therefore difficult to connect this mother with an infanticide. The notion of playing or performing is constantly recalled, and the representation remains. In this way, a distance is created between the presupposed nature of a mother and the real thing. In this example, we are also in 'The Medea Complex' that Robert Tyminski develops in his article (Tyminski 2014).

S'econdly, on the website Wikifeqh.ir devoted to religion, law and jurisprudence in Iran, there is an answer explaining the reason for the talion or '*qiṣāṣ*' of the mother in the event of infanticide, while the father or paternal grandfather only risks a more or less heavy fine: The mother is the one who naturally sacrifices herself for her child and if a mother reaches such a level of ferocity leading her to infanticide, she becomes harmful for her family and society. She must therefore be annihilated. It also imposes a so-called natural behaviour on the mother-woman: a mother who kills, without taking into consideration the reasons that led her to commit this act, is no longer a mother but a dangerous psychopath and a monster to be annihilated, while the father remains the vital pillar of his family and is therefore protected by the law.

Thirdly, the slogan or expression inspired by the *ḥadīth* 'paradise is under the feet of mothers', apart from being heard everywhere, in schools, on the radio, on television or in conversations, also adorns the huge urban murals in the different cities of Iran, paying tribute to mothers. These words are often illustrated with a woman in a chador climbing the steps to heaven. In each of these three 'images' of varying nature, we find ourselves in a process of representation, in a kind of paradigm that assigns a fixed role to a woman who is now a mother, and in a framework in which this woman-mother remains fixed. Being a mother is therefore a fable to be lived and a tailor-made identity that Iranian society, like other societies, imposes on women (Khajehi 2018). The picture places the mother-woman in the sphere of the sacred. She remains an ideal being with divine characteristics, destined for paradise. In Tehran's metro stations, as everywhere in the city, there is a set of posters paying tribute to women and mothers, but also criticizing certain social appearances of women. In 2016, a poster was shown depicting a schema of a woman's body in an executive outfit, i.e., in a long coat and official veil, but made up of office equipment such as computers, files, etc. (The Tehran City Council denied any responsibility for the poster.) Mircea Eliade, in his book *The Sacred and the Profane*, speaks of the necessity of sacred space for the stability of religious man. This centre of gravity plays the role of a compass to hold society together. The woman-mother acts as a compass: to hold Iranian society together, she must stay at home, away from the professional world, to ensure, as they say in Iran, the structure of the family. However let us not forget that, in this society, more than 50 per cent of university students are women,[6] and that they are taking on more and more responsibilities within the country's official bodies.

If society imposes a role on women, who are constantly presented with a halo veil and within their family, the *real woman* finds an escape route in the theatre to paradoxically distance herself from the idea of representation. She creates her new fable, she 're-tells' her story and gives life to a new social history, as she would like it to be.

Euripides' *Medea* has been translated several times from English into Persian and each time with success. For example, it was re-translated[7] in 2013 and it has been re-published a dozen times[8] (Nedaei 2013; Shahbazi 2022), which is very significant compared to the average publication of works in Iran. The online press *khabaronline.ir* announced the third edition of the play with the headline: 'Tragedy of a woman who murdered her children is reissued'.[9] The article begins as follows: 'The play of *Medea* is a sad and fascinating story of a woman's revenge against her husband and children, written by Euripides . . .'[10] The title and tagline of the article emphasize the moving aspect and accentuate the maternal dimension of the play in order to attract the attention of internet users. As a result, these unusual facts are bound to capture the audience's attention: this woman-mother with an exceptional story attracts viewers like a news item or a 'fairground animal' to be watched. However, Iranian artists are moving beyond this strangeness, which is not at first sight compatible with Iranian society, and are focusing on the narrative of women in certain social circumstances. By studying recent creations inspired by *Medea*, we will examine the expressive potentials that the text offers to the performance.

Hanane Hajj Ali (Ḥanān al-Ḥājj 'Alī) evokes the current Lebanese situation in the creation of her play *Jogging* (Hajj Ali 2018).[11] Indeed, the show changes and completes itself over time, which is why some of the latest performances do not exist in the published version of the play. It continues to evolve during each live performance and thereby surpasses the written version of the text. This dramatic dynamic reflects what she says about Medea: 'a very current myth that has crossed several centuries, a myth that moves like the world that moves'.[12] She also talks about her paradigm shift and understanding of this text. When she was an art student, although fascinated by the character, Hajj Ali refused to play Medea, she talks about getting a 0 and with a lot of pride because she was not at all convinced that a mother could kill her children whatever the reason. However, all that was changed during the period of her son's illness and that waking dream moment during her jogging session when she saw herself killing her child to relieve his pain. She says that there are times in life when we have tried everything and cannot do it anymore, like when a child is sick and suffering or when a mother in an extremely difficult economic situation cannot give her child a drop of milk. In this way she evokes her deep understanding of wanting to protect her child by freeing it from life. According to the director, we have seen so much catastrophe in these societies that we are forced to open our eyes and that it is no longer possible to lie. She points out that today the die is cast and there will be more infanticide, because these societies no longer work politically and there appears to be no escape.

Experiencing *Medea* in Iran

In August 2017, together with my colleagues in the House of Art and Culture of Fanous of Tehran, we organized a meeting session between young artists working on *Medea*. At this event, each participant introduced their dramaturgical and social view of the text. This analysis is also interesting because it can partly demonstrate how the status of women in Iran has already been reflected upon in a very young artistic milieu. The case studies demonstrate the expressive potential still alive in Euripides' *Medea*. Although Anouilh's play is translated into Persian, Iranian artists prefer to draw inspiration from the Greek tragedy that lets the character free herself and not be condemned to death. These creations are like an artistic and social manifestation delivering a real image of women, far from the idealized and divinized connotations prevailing in society. These staging projects can also explain how and to what extent Iran experienced the emergence of the Women, Life, Freedom movement in September 2022.

The young director Shahrzad Nazarpour staged *Medea* in 2017. According to her, the text is not a feminist play, but tells the story of a woman in revolt against a patriarchal society. She finds the world of the play very close to the lives of the women around her: battered women who did not stop loving their husbands, women who constantly forgave their partners' infidelity, and women who lived in sadness. In her project, she presents an evolution of the character throughout her play: the evolution from a passive Medea resembling these submissive women, to a Medea embodying the new generation of Iranian women, women who want to advance like men and want less constrained relationships. However this new generation is not immune either, for a relationship outside marriage, even a hidden one, can be disrupted by a pregnancy. In Iran, abortion, except in special medical situations before the fourth month for married women, is illegal. In such a case, the woman is as strongly condemned by her family as by society. Nazarpour makes a comparison between *Medea* and her family's position following her departure with Jason: she portrays a young woman breaking the family and social law.

In her adaptation, two female characters linked by their braided hair interpret, one, a mother waiting for her husband and the other, her foetus talking about their present life and her future as a woman. The woman-foetus embodies both Medea child and nurse. These two no longer want to continue in the circle of this life, but rather to free themselves from male domination. The foetus reasons Medea into forgetting her love and keeping her so that they can continue together; but at the end of the ninth month, the father returns, and Medea kills her daughter, her nurse, the alter ego with whom she could wage a social struggle. She then kills herself, but the circle continues: she lives again, falls in love, and then becomes pregnant. The man leaves her and returns to destroy everything. The young director evokes this cycle by referring to the fact that in Iran, as in other countries no doubt, women are still forced to wait for a man to fill their lives. A brief look at popular and oral literature is enough to demonstrate the omnipresence of this state of waiting for women. Medea thus speaks of two generations of Iranian women and some of their concerns, but this character and her story can also be relevant to other issues, such as immigration and professional independence for women.

These topics were addressed in Fariborz Karimi's 2015 creation. The young director goes back to his childhood memories and the story of his mother and her professional life choices. Inspired by friends thinking of leaving the country, or friends who have already left and are suffering from loneliness, he decides to present a Medea telling all these stories. He stages the life of a young actress at the very beginning of a brilliant career, playing Medea, the role every actress dreams of, but who falls in love and then gets married and emigrates to Poland. Far from her country and her family, while trying to find her place as an actress and to integrate into this new society, she becomes pregnant, and her husband leaves her a few months later. The language barrier, isolation, loneliness and the burden of a child bring her to the lowest point. The show tells her story by going back in time, from her fortieth birthday to her twenty-third birthday, when she plays Medea on stage. By commemorating the life of an adult woman, beyond the strictly female subjects, it creates a reflection on emigration, the artist's profession, autonomy, and the will of a generation that tries in vain to change the situation. Here Medea drowns her child in a lake in the moonlight, in a country far from her native land. The scene also evokes Ophelia's death and the end of a love story. Nevertheless, in Karimi's *Medea*, this disastrous love remains ambiguous: love for her child, her husband, her work and her country. This Medea, by killing her child, 'buries' her dreams in water, the symbol of purity and light in Iran. She thus puts an end to her struggle, which is today that of a large part of Iranian youth. Here, *Medea*'s canon forms a perfect setting for a *mise en abyme* through which the life of an individual dramatizes the life of a new generation that is fighting body and soul. Today Karimi has moved to the Netherlands to continue his studies and theatrical experiences.

Neda Shahrokhi, an Iranian director, was also interested in *Medea* in 2015.[13] For her, the character's peculiarity lies in its pragmatic and multifaceted aspect. Medea jumps into action and opposes female passivity, criticized by Shahrokhi, although she goes through different states of mind: depression, doubt, love, revolt and murder. This play, before being performed in Iran and then in Greece, was presented in Arcueil in the Parisian suburbs in France and took place in three parts: a culinary workshop/show at the *Maison des Solidarités*, an urban stroll and finally the performance of Euripides' text at the Anis Gras space.

Seven Medeas are present on stage. Each one represents one of the character's evolving stages. At the beginning, as a prologue, she recounts the imaginary continuation of Euripides' play and brings the audience into the mourning ceremony of her children. She cooks *halva*, a sweet Iranian dish made of flour, sugar, oil, rose water and saffron, which is traditionally distributed and offered during mourning ceremonies. During the cooking workshop, everything seems ritualistic, but also on the borderline between reality and performance. The audience is seated around large tables covered with black and green tablecloths on which lit candles recall the atmosphere of mourning. Medea cooks the halva, talking about the recipe and the symbolic and culinary value of the ingredients, while evoking their connection to Euripides' text. Medea explains that, thanks to this mixture of ingredients, the halva soothes the mind, while the scent of cooked flour, rose water and saffron fills the space. They invite the audience to participate in this ritual act and then to share the pastry. Medea refuses to take it, since she does not want to console herself and decides to embrace or immerse herself in sadness. This shows an assumed state of consciousness, a self-confident Medea as a strong female figure, who I think in those years was present as an inner fantasy of Iranian women: a woman who can act and enter into action without

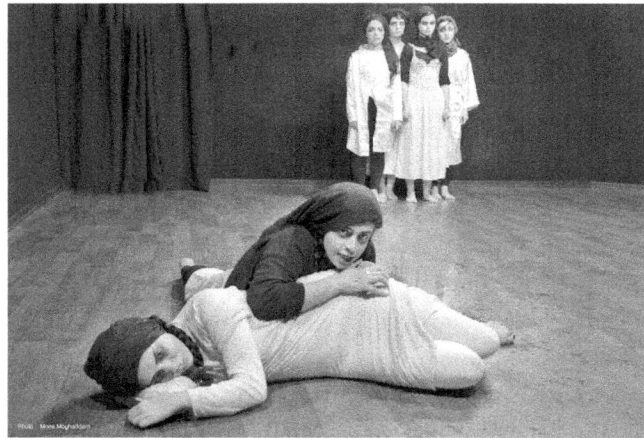

Figure 5 *Medea*, Euripides, directed by Neda Shahrokhi. Rehearsal session in Tehran, 2016. Credit: Mona Moghadam.

Figure 6 *Medea*, Euripides, directed by Neda Shahrokhi. Arcueil (France), 2016. Credit: Farideh Abtahi.

any regrets. After this cooking sequence, she leads the audience along an urban road to the place of the performance: Medea's fate. On the way, Medea's lyrical songs and traditional mourning music transform the city's atmosphere and create a kind of dialogue between the participating audience and the curious audience of passers-by to whom Medea offers halva. Along the way, a woman with a red suitcase on wheels follows the crowd; she can be seen by the audience.

She is the character of the 'contemporary woman' that Shahrokhi adds to Euripides' play, whom the audience discovers in the performance section.

The director makes few changes to Euripides' text, deleting some passages and creating a parallel world in some scenes where the thoughts of the contemporary woman can be heard. She helps with the scene changes and at the end, cleans the floor and puts away the props. She is betrayed by her husband but does not protest. She just decides to change the curtains to thicker ones to avoid daylight; she symbolizes the passivity that the director questions. According to her: 'We, contemporary people, no longer create tragedy, we are passive, we watch and give up, the great acts belong to the world of tragedy'. She also points out the connection of the text with contemporary events, for example the infanticide caused by social conditions: if she does not kill her children, they will suffer. Medea therefore decides to control the situation and 'protect' her children beyond her revenge. This idea reminds us of the video interview mentioned above, where the mother insists that she did not want 'this life' for her daughters. Shahrokhi's play questions a woman's actions, but far from being judgemental or biased. She illustrates a group of women, potential Medeas who, as they enter the stage, rinse their faces with water, deciding to wake up and see the world. The contemporary woman, on the other hand, is content to clean up the water that flows all over the stage, as this source of awakening can be harmful to her.

> Contemporary woman: This house ... these curtains ... I have to change these curtains; I have to buy new thick curtains so that the light doesn't get in.[14]

In 2023, when I ask Neda Shahrokhi about this project and a possible new adaptation of *Medea*, I see that her part has completely evolved. She says that in 2015 – as she also mentions Nazarpour – she was surrounded by rather passive women. She insists on her activities in the associative field with underprivileged women (homeless, drug addicts, prostitutes, etc.) and says that these women were there rather as a result of family problems caused by a mythogenic world where men control everything. These women were mostly married at a very young age, became mothers at a very young age and were often abandoned by their husbands. They had no resources and no support from their respective families. For Shahrokhi these women, like the middle-class women with their own but less visible problems, were wounded women who did not act, they were in a state of total self-destruction and in a world with no way out. That is why she created the character of the contemporary woman. She represented women of that time, caught up in the superficial aspect of life without any conviction. Even though at the time there were feminist movements by some women in Iran and abroad, the majority of women looked like this character.

In contrast, today she sees a completely different Iranian society. She finds herself in demonstrations among 'normal' women: housewives who until yesterday thought they were subject to the law of this country in a restricted setting without freedom. While these women were already doubly subject, both to the law of the home and the law of society, they are now present on the front lines ahead of men. They are no longer afraid and free themselves from internal and external patriarchal power. They are increasingly distancing themselves from the controlling male gaze on their bodies and thoughts. Shahrokhi therefore specifies that her Medea of today is inspired by those women who give everything, even their children and relatives, to keep their freedom intact. This is indeed visible through videos of mothers who lost their children, young and old, in the demonstrations. Instead of being isolated and bereaved, they are in direct confrontation and make very constructed speeches devoid of any sentimental or emotional dimension. They call for resistance and continuity of the movement.

Medea in Lebanon, a different face

The feedback is not the same when we talk about *Medea* in Lebanon. If this play in Iran has found its place in the repertoire of ancient plays and contemporary performances, its presence in Lebanon is more modest. Today, the main reference for *Medea* is Hanane Hajj Ali's play *Jogging*, but there are other creative projects or performances inspired by Euripides' play and the character of Medea. However, as in the *Jogging* show, she is shown through other characters that have been adapted in order to resemble the myth. Sometimes there is also a form of resistance to *Medea* in Lebanon, because the murderous aspect, as mentioned above, is often in the foreground. This was perceived when I interviewed several young artists and other more established directors. For example, for Caroline Hatem,[15] a Lebanese actress and director, Medea does not seem interesting; for her the character is capable of doing harm to the point of killing her children for love of Jason. Medea seems to her too revengeful. She describes the play as psychologically primitive, emphasizing that she is neither judgemental nor contemptuous, but she does not find political value in the play. However, she mentions the fact that this text has attracted the attention of several female actresses and directors in Lebanon, because according to her, *Medea*'s play allows female actors to showcase themselves and to sublimate their acting. The text thus becomes a dramatic tool.[16]

Nevertheless, for those who are inspired by this character, the socio-political situation is *ultimately* introduced in the conception of the play, even if it is an adaptation or an inspiration. Lebanon, like Iran, remains a society in which abandoned and neglected women are stigmatized and rejected. They often find it difficult to take their destiny into their own hands and sometimes, out of obligation, they return to live with their parents. Medea, however, does not fit this image. She decides to leave her country and this time stays put in the new one, without letting herself be defeated. *Medea* thus remains fascinating for Lebanese women artists but is not the object of hyper-representation as in Iran. Valérie Cachard, Lebanese author and playwright, evokes her experience in a work that approaches the character of Medea.[17] For her, Lebanese society in general is not ready to hear the responsibility of men in the various crimes committed. Society is not yet open enough to this story without falling into a moralistic way of blaming Medea. Her play *Bloody Mary* is in fact partly inspired by the myth of La Ilorona, which for her is an incarnation of Medea.[18] La Ilorona, in the folklore culture of Hispanic America, is a ghost representing the grieving soul of a woman who has lost or killed her children. In this play she wanted to explore the attempt to harm her child more than the act itself. It is the story of a mother who attempts to stop her daughter from growing up while telling terrible stories to prevent her from falling asleep and therefore from growing up. Cachard said that she did not know the myth of Medea very well and that the desire to work on this character came from Chantal Mailhac, a Lebanese storyteller with whom she had often worked. The project was also carried out with Nadine Sures,[19] who is a performer. They started to work in a 'stage writing' approach in 2019, but eventually both left the country or moved on to another professional area. Then Cachard took two years to produce several versions of this story: first the elaboration of the collective writing, then a monodrama play and after that a play with the presence of several characters like the mother and the grandmother, and finally a version that I was able to study for the writing of this chapter. Cachard says that from the beginning she was more sensitive to the myth of La Llorona than to that of Medea. She based her adaptation on the character of the abusive mother and the transmission of fear.

In this play she moves away from *Medea*, but she does not know her real reasons. She mentions that she did not really feel able to deal with the infanticide or that she wanted to show the act without a passage to the act, which according to her put her under more stress. She also points out that the infanticide could probably have taken up all the space and that she would not have known how to handle the different fragments of the story. She also asks about Medea's maternal relationship with her children before the murder, her future and her daily life after the act. This effectively emphasizes Medea as a mother more than Medea as a woman fighting against an unjust power. This aspect of the character is very present when I interview young Lebanese artists who generally avoid staging Medea, although they show a particular interest in the character of Antigone.

MARY
...Water and fire don't mix. It's odourless, colourless, it transforms the air, it brings a white van. You have to get out, jump out of the window. You have to believe that there is really someone behind the door. You have to open the door and accept going out. You have to agree to get out and close the door. The chair no longer swings.

In her statement of intent for the second version of her play she evokes a selfish female character wishing to free herself from all constraints, a lucid woman wishing to save her children from the slavery that arrives with the colonizers. So, La Llorona drowns her children for different reasons depending on the version of her story. According to her, people today say that she wanders around the rivers, wearing a white dress and that she takes the children she meets and makes them her own. Here, then, there is a female figure who is always looking for her motherhood as a form of nostalgia or going back. Cachard refers to the events of October 2019 in Lebanon, where the country was hit by an unprecedented economic crisis and that the unstable situation led her two collaborators to suspend the project in December. Nevertheless their encouragement has always accompanied the author and her writing career.

During the adaptation process, Cachard extensively questions the parental bond. The themes of mother–daughter relationships or transmission between women are often present in her texts, but according to her, these themes have never been approached from an obscure angle. The idea of infanticide allowed her to explore the ambivalence of the bond between mother and daughter and vice versa. However, she hesitated a lot with this approach, she told herself from the start that the main character would not have a child, for example. So, she was faced with a series of questions:

What makes a mother say to her daughter 'I want to kill you'? What makes her do it? Who is responsible for the death of La Llorona's children? She herself or the handsome hidalgo who leaves her?

Then, beyond the questions directly linked to the legend, she addressed other questions: How to avoid being abandoned? How to avoid suffering? What are tears for? What haunts us without our knowledge? How are fears and anger suppressed? How are fears and anger transmitted? Are there typically feminine fears? What happens to our archaic childhood fears when we grow up? What makes us grow up? What stifles our growth?

THE HOARSE VOICES
Yes, you have to taste it
Yes, it's the cocktail that helps the girl to
relax So be sure to prepare it well
Yes, prepare it.
Need lemon,
tabasco
Tomato juice and
vodka Salt, pepper
and ice cubes Fish-
shaped
Bloody Mary tasty cocktail
Bloody Mary you sting our
eyes You have to resist and
not cry No crying[20]

Why shouldn't a little girl grow up in this world and in the current Lebanese situation? Cachard answers this question by pointing to her reformulation. She hesitates between being able to grow up and having to grow up. She thinks that in today's world, we talk about 'women's rights' when it is convenient. In this regard she talks about the episode at Qatar airport in October 2020 where female passengers were forced to undergo gynaecological tests to make sure they had not given birth and abandoned a baby in the toilet. For her, this type of event, which should raise more outrage in the long term, just turns into a news item. This leads one to believe that current societies do not really accommodate the female presence or the 'female rhythm' as she puts it. In this scenario, the female body becomes a space to be framed or controlled so that it can enter unnoticed into a 'male world'. Thus, the character of Medea and her story opposes this arrangement and demonstrates the boundaries that become problematic. In other words, in these circumstances Medea overturns the established order and shows that truth does not necessarily apply to the illusion of reality in a male world. After all, the author questions the veracity of Medea's desire to become a mother or a wife. Indeed, the couple is formed so that she changes 'home', so that she escapes her father, but ultimately her body is possessed differently. Being abandoned in the land of exile excludes her completely from this world, even the male world.

How can we juxtapose this fascination for the Llorona and/or Medea in the contemporary Lebanese context? Cachard mentions that in the current Lebanese situation it is not good to be a little girl, a little boy or a teenager. Since a survival mode has been in place since 2019, young people are not given what they need: love, the necessary attention, spaces to let off steam, places to feed their imagination. She says that most parents focus on basic needs. According to her, there was already a lot lacking before the crisis and the middle class, from which artists and intellectuals often came, acted as a buffer between the other classes. Today these people have left the country or are suffering from the crisis. For example, access to quality school education is becoming very complicated and expensive. For her, it is difficult to grow up with a permanent fear in our stomach. Here we come close once again to the questions of Iranian artists. Not seeing a future to offer the next generation also leads to the notion of genocide, but a rather 'protective' and 'saving' genocide to protect one's children from the harshness of social, political and economic life.

Finally, for Cachard, there is the foreigner who wanders from land to land and always has to leave again, the one who in the end has difficulty finding her place. There are also women who do not accept what their father or husband or any male authority figure imposes on them. She also makes the link with the revolutionary movements in Lebanon and Iran and says that we just have to look at what is happening in these countries. Indeed, the image of the woman in revolt is first and foremost. Women who even fight physically with armed men. For her, this is happening in Western society with the wave of denunciations in artistic, literary circles, etc. The Medeas of today are then the women who are not afraid to speak out and act.

For Jessy Khalil,[21] a Lebanese director who has been living in France for five years, the encounter with *Medea* goes back to 2008 during a workshop on Greek tragedy in Cyprus. She chose *Medea* because she was interested in the psychological aspect of the character. Nevertheless, this interest went beyond the question of violence and murder, but rather into a dialogue between her and Jason, which founded the structure of her staging of Medea. This idea of a conversation between the couple in fact explores the emotional and passionate aspect of the text. It spontaneously establishes a dialogue between the two male and female characters, which is quite rare in contemporary Medea productions. For Jessy Khalil, Medea is brave and whole, and I think that the process of verbalizing this state of mind was very important for her: that Medea be heard and understood. In Middle Eastern societies in a state of flux and turbulence, this need to be heard becomes a necessity and makes women active. For Khalil too: there are many Medeas in Lebanon, those who took to the streets in 2019, those revolutionaries who demanded justice and this time without any violence. Khalil thinks that things are moving slowly in Lebanon, and that there is still a lot to achieve for women. She says that despite the social façade that seeks to show women as free, the law is still outdated and favours men. It is therefore necessary for all the Medeas to come together to change things but also to close the wound that Lebanon has carried since the war, and which is worsening with the current crisis.

Thus, almost two and a half thousand years after the creation of *Medea*, artists from another geographical area still take Euripides' side in talking about the place of women in action. Even if the vision of the character is not totally identical in Iran and Lebanon, *Medea* becomes important tragic material in understanding these societies. This can be compared to the place that Antigone occupies in the studies of Judith Butler (Butler, 2000) for example. The evolution of the artists' focus from the maternal to the resistant-feminist aspect through time also indicates the sensitivity of contemporary social concerns. The play and the character on the contemporary Iranian and Lebanese stage are thus transformed into a matrix of fable that renews itself to narrate and criticize contemporary society. With so many Medeas everywhere these societies seem to hold out hope for change, life and freedom.

Notes

1   See www.orientale.fr/page_1269_fr_11707_Alexandra-se-revait-en-princesse-a-declare-Paul.htm [2022].
2   Some of the iconographic productions are distributed via the Instagram page: www.instagram.com/freeiranianwomen2022. But it should also be noted that the pages relaying the Femme, Vie, Liberté movement have been victims of several cyber attacks. We are not sure about their longevity. There are also now several murals and pieces of street art dedicated to this movement in many cities around the world. See Cloe Hakakian's work in Los Angeles, or the website of https://streetartutopia.com/tag/mahsa-amini.
3   See: Khajehi, Yassaman, Mohammad Amin Zamani and Richard Schechner, 'Fragments of a Revolution: Performativity vs. Theatricality in Iran, September 2022–January 2023'. TDR, 2023, 1–9. doi:10.1017/S1054204323000163.
4   See www.aparat.com/v/WV64R [accessed in 2022].
5   Idem.
6   The percentages are different depending on the source, but they vary between 45 and 60 per cent in 2022.
7   Already translated in 1970 by Abolhassan Vandeh var, Amir Kabir editions.
8   Example: www.bidgolpublishing.com/Book.aspx?Id=156 [2022].

9　See www.khabaronline.ir/detail/262821/culture/book. The link was available, but is no longer accessible in 2023.

10　Idem.

11　Daniela Potenza discusses this show in Chapter 4 of this book.

12　Interview with the artist, November 2022 – Beirut.

13　I participated in this project as a playwright: http://fanousehonar.com/en/index.php/products/38-medea.

14　Final scene of the play, written in Persian and translated by myself into English.

15　Interview with the artist, May 2022 – Beirut.

16　Interview with the artist, November 2022 – Beirut.

17　Interviews and exchanges with the artist between September 2022 and January 2023.

18　Unpublished play for the moment.

19　See https://nadinesures.fr.

20　Extract from the play written in French and translated by myself into English.

21　Interview with the artist, January 2023 – Clermont-Ferrand.

References

Bungard, C. and V. Deno (2021), 'Medea Barbarosa?: Marriage, Betrayal, Alterity and the Woman from Colchis', *International Journal of the Classical Tradition*, 28: 1–22. https://doi.org/10.1007/s12138-019-00532-4.

Butler, J. (2000), *Antigone's Claim: Kinship Between Life & Death*, New York: Columbia University Press.

Euripides (2022), *Medea*, English trans. Gh. Shahbazi, Tehran: Gh. Ed. Bidgol.

Euripides (2013), *Medea*, trans. A. Nedaei, Tehran: Afraz.

Euripides (1970), *Medea*, trans. A. Vandeh var, Tehran: Amir Kabir.

Hajj Ali, H. (2018), *Jogging: Theatre in Progress* [*Jogging, Masraḥ qayd al-Taṭwīr*], trans. H. Abdulrazzak.

Khajehi, Y, M.-A. Zamani and R. Schechner (2023), 'Fragments of a Revolution: Performativity vs. Theatricality in Iran, September 2022–January 2023', *TDR*, 2023: 1–9.

Mendelsohn, D. (2002), *Reading Greek Tragedy*, Oxford: Oxford University Press.

Saxonhouse, W. (2005), 'Another Antigone: The Emergence of the Female Political Actor in Euripides' Phoenician Women', *Political Theory*, 33(4): 472–94.

Tyminski, R. (2014), 'The Medea Complex – Myth and Modern Manifestation', *Jung Journal: Culture & Psyche*, 8(1): 28–40.

6

Antigone in Iran

Towards a Political Subject of Resistance

Rezvan Zandieh

Antigone is the 'feminine figure who defies the state through a powerful set of physical and linguistic acts' (Butler 2002: 2), or who 'unmasks power and steps aside in the name of the justice of the gesture' (Bantigny 2015: 17), or defines 'the transition from the rule of law based on maternity, a rule of law based in kinship, to a rule of law based on paternity' (Irigaray in Butler 1893: 4). Some exemplify this to give an ethical conception of subjectivity (Doré and Lambert 2015). For others, the play is about Creon and his victory (Bernard-Henry Levi in Lussier 2005: 45). Today in Iran, we observe an *antigonian* situation: the Creonian punishment of the state, which is supposed to restore order, which in turn, actually generates disorder. Crushing the popular uprising was supposed to be an act of counter-insurgency discourse, a demonstration of the state's absolute power, and a reminder of the fragility of oppressed bodies. But as the state is confronted with the resistance of women revaluing their collective power and spreading it to other oppressed bodies, the opposite happens, and the state itself is caught by the spectre of its own powerlessness. In 2022, the 'Women, Life, Freedom' movement manifested an inspiring example of this situation.

The examination of various interpretations of Antigone in Iran highlights this question of *antigonian resistance*: *Antigone in Wonderland*[1] (Popak Hidji, 2010), *Antigone* (Homayoun Ghani-Zadeh, 2011) and *Antigone* (Ali Razi, 2018). I therefore propose an analysis of the character of Antigone who, in her double act of resistance through disobedience to the Creonian law as well as her public claim, politically subjectivizes herself. This subjectivation in the face of totalitarian power is a burning issue in the authoritarian context of the Islamic Republic of Iran and so many other contexts globally. The question that arises is: what does Antigone represent in these performances?

Fighter Antigone in the land of patriarchy

Antigone in Wonderland is a rewriting that 'realizes scenically and symbolically what could not be done in reality.'

Blin 2014

Antigone in Wonderland is a staging by Popak Hidji (Tehran, 2011), which was chosen as the winner of the Eleventh International Festival of Puppet Shows. In this show, Sophocles' play is completely rewritten. The stage director applies traditional Iranian theatre techniques such as *Naghali, Siah Bazi*, and shadow theatre. Punctuated by the use of folk songs, the show is also an adaptation of *Shahr Gheseh* (City of Tales), an Iranian cult play from the 1960s.[2] First, on stage, we see a castelet with a narrator and a chorus of musicians. The characters of Creon, Hemon and Ismene appear in the form of childlike girdle puppets in the guise of animals. Only Antigone, played by the director, is represented by an anthropomorphic puppet. During the performance the actors appear and call out to the puppets. The whole staging has a comical aspect while the language used is popular and parodic.

In the tragi-comic genre and the style of artistic fusionism, the artist in this show denounces the economic, social and political problems of the Iranian middle class rather than the wealthy elite. Antigone is a young theatre student from this class who becomes pregnant as a result of being raped by her boyfriend, Hemon, who is an actor from the bourgeoisie. Despite her best efforts, she is unable to have an abortion and this seals her tragic fate. The *fatum* is then embodied by the double action of intrafamilial patriarchy (Creon's anger and almighty power) and state patriarchy (the legal prohibition of abortion, the high costs of illegal abortion), the articulation of which entrenches the tragic life of women. To punish Antigone, Creon forces her to marry Hemon, exacerbating the tragedy because the costs of marriage and living together are high in Thebes (but this in fact references conditions in Tehran). After unfavourable predictions, Creon wants to have the child murdered. To protect the baby, Antigone and Hemon emigrate abroad. After Creon's murder by their son many years later, Antigone and Hemon return to Thebes (i.e. Tehran). However, Hemon then succeeds his father only to become a tyrant himself. Antigone rebels against her husband and is killed during the popular protests against the tyrannical power.

Hidji updates the social condition of this social class by linking it to more recent political circumstances in 2009, the Green Movement.[3] This actualization offers a range of possibilities for concretizing the issue of Iranian women through the image of Antigone. On the one hand, it allows Antigone to be politicized and removed from the image of the female victim of patriarchy. On the other hand, Antigone, by joining the demonstrations of this movement, implicitly represents one of the symbols of this movement (i.e. Neda Agha Soltan).[4] Finally, this historical contextualization promotes a redefining of women's resistance in relation to this defining event.

Through Antigone, the theatre student, and her confrontation with Creon and Hemon the recurring patriarchal powers, we become aware of the immense socio-political problems facing women in this social sphere: abortion, unwanted and unmarried pregnancy, rape, forced marriage, immigration, an unequal education system, economic dependence, male domination in intimate and social relationships, and in particular, the economic and material challenges, the precariousness and unemployment of students and cultural workers (i.e. theatre artists), as well as censorship and political restrictions on artistic productions.

In this production, three forms of patriarchal power, familial, legal and political, are intended to be revealed through the character of Creon. The first is the manifestation of patriarchy in the familial sphere, through the figure of a patriarch (i.e. Antigone's father-in-law, Creon), who imposes his decisions on Antigone (and Hémon), which are hers to bear: Creon does not accept, at the beginning, the emotional relationship between Hemon and Antigone; he then prevents Antigone from aborting an unwanted child; he forces her to marry his son and to immigrate; and Creon humiliates Antigone because of her extramarital pregnancy and her desire to abort. The image of Hemon, on the other hand, does not fare better: despite his love affair with Antigone, he forces her into a sexual relationship and threatens to abandon her for other women. Hemon is also clumsy and weak and becomes an alcoholic and homesick when he cannot find employment. Finally, he becomes despotic and manifests patriarchal violence when he assumes power after the death of his father. As for the legal form of patriarchal power, it is as much about the law restricting women's rights to control their bodies as it is about Creon's infiltration of the court and his influence in changing the judge's decision. Finally, the dictatorial and oppressive image of Creon (and Hemon) underlines the political form of this power.

In this work, we can see through the story line and also the use of local vernacular and folk songs, a direct reflection of the oppressive socio-political conditions imposed by the established power structures in Iran on these characters: forcing Antigone to be silent by beating, torturing, and determining her reproductive labour, the protests against the injustice of the power, etc. The vehement criticism of patriarchal power in this play is revealed thanks to the use of tragic material from Antigone, popular language, the comic genre and folk tales.

Homayoun Ghani-Zadeh and her misogynistic Creon

Whereas in the first adaptation the problems, role and place of a particular class of women in Iranian society are explicitly revealed, in the second these problems remain implicit or even erased in favour of the aesthetic genre and the emphasis on the role of power. In Homayoun Ghani-Zadeh's 2011 adaptation, presented in Tehran and Estonia, Creon is played by an Iranian actor and the rest of the cast is Slovenian. This staging offers an accurate interpretation of the tragic plot while hybridizing Sophocles' play with a grotesque and Beckettian atmosphere. This distinguishes it, through the aesthetic genre, from the first adaptation by Popak Hidji.

In this play, which takes Creon as the main character, Ghani-Zadeh draws upon the insignificant and absurd world of politicians. The seriousness of the plot, the actions and the dramatic knot are reduced to absurd and banal acts: eating rotten eggs, ordering milk, looking for a golf ball, committing suicide due to a lack of fried eggs, or the ban on eating eggs as a punitive measure, etc.

Against the bright red background of the stage, the actors wander around in white pyjamas that are reminiscent of the outfits of psychiatric patients. They look as unreal as living corpses and as pale as ghosts. Their movements follow geometric and repetitive logics, and all expressions and emotions are roboticized. To give a few examples: the actress playing Antigone frantically shakes her hands; Tiresias walks holding his shoes in his hand or the anguished Ismene hysterically walks back and forth across the stage. The absurd and distressing atmosphere of this world is reinforced by the sense of stagnation and decay that haunts the stage: the bright red wall, the incessant ticking of the clock, the flies that infest the city, the terrible smell of rotting corpses, and the discussions of the characters obsessed with their meals. The meal scene is haunted by the memory of death, and the lack of water to for personal hygiene further immerse the spectator in this atmosphere. In other words, it seems that the actors, apart from Creon, are stripped of their humanity, made numb like automatons, made abject like insects. It seems as if only time passes while the people are stuck in the absurd repetition of powerless actions.

In this general atmosphere, Creon stands out from the other characters. It seems that the stage director attributes the possibility of action only to the character of Creon, so much so that the difference between the freedom of movement of the actor who plays Creon contrasts with the corseting of all the other actors. Indeed, in all the other roles the actors are reduced to mere moving bodies. The question of the *antigonian resistance* seems to be put aside in favour of highlighting the almighty power of the tyrant. And this, it seems, is done to question his essence.

We can hardly distinguish Antigone in the hierarchy of characters, whether it be in visual codes, her presence, or even her dialogue. She is ridiculed like Creon and the other characters; her act of resistance is trivialized[5] like her death. Unlike the first play, in this one, moving away from realism, it is not made clear to which social class the two sisters belong. Nevertheless, it can be assumed that they come from a wealthy family. We can also imagine that Ismene has connections with the world of theatre, since at the end of the performance she leaves for New York with Antigone's corpse in order to become an actress.

With regard to the issue of power, the artist highlights the character of Creon to relate him to Iranian politicians. This is particularly emphasized by the fact that Creon is the only character to speak Persian, which can be seen as a direct allusion to the political authorities in Iran. It seems that the aim of this aesthetic effort is to highlight the issue of power. By showing more of the human dimension (as opposed to the 'robotization' of the other characters) of Creon, especially in his gestures, stage manners and acting, Ghani-Zadeh seeks to give a more realistic image of power. In doing so, he aims to avoid misinterpreting the target of the message and to emphasize a negative dimension of the message. In the torture scenes, for example, where Creon violently beats his wife, the actor acts in a realistic way and moves naturally on stage. These long scenes of violence are clearly different from others in which the actors act more like robots and follow geometric placements.

The accentuation of the character of Creon, it seems, is intended to point out the misogynistic and authoritarian character of political power: Creon furiously whips his wife as a prisoner whose hands are handcuffed, dragging her down the stairs, he ignores Ismene and mocks her cruelly when Ismene wishes to support her sister, he humiliates his wife by accusing her of having given birth to a son who ate rotten eggs, he berates Antigone by shouting at her aggressively not to move. These actions, repeated as a daily ritual, take on a natural, even intrinsic, dimension to power.

This misogynistic representation of Creon – as much through scenic and dramaturgical elements as through semantic and narrative ones – then produces a devalued, even domesticated, image of female characters. In a reciprocal mechanism, this image and the misogynistic character of power is reinforced. Furthermore, there is a tendency to reduce the role and place of women to essential and natural tasks, such as being associated with the obsessively presented meal scenes. One might speculate as to whether this way of representing these scenes might contain undertones relating to sexual relations which are forbidden to be represented in Iran. The fact that the motive for Hemon's suicide is linked to Antigone's failure to prepare fried eggs for him (among other examples) leads us to consider this hypothesis as plausible.

Finally, a legitimate question to ask is whether this contrast between the representation of power and that of the other characters is intended to highlight the state of alienation of individuals in power relationships? Or whether the dehumanization of the characters in this show highlights their animalization and their Kafkaesque transformation into insect-men?

Antigone confronts Creon of the Islamic Republic

The emphasis on the character of Creon is modified in the third adaptation. Staged in 2018 in Tehran, the *Antigone* by Ali Razi, an Iranian stage director living in Paris, has a more realistic staging style than the adaptation by Ghani Zadeh or Popak Hidji. Intensifying the dramatic actions, this realism favours the main plot, the conflict between Antigone and Creon (i.e. woman and power). In this show, the update of the tragic material is carried out in a subtle and indirect way. The references to the socio-political situations of the artist's country of origin are more tacit and are part of the 'rhetoric of circumvention', a particular kind of term coined by Farzan Sojoudi:

> This substitution of signifiers is done in different ways. By metaphor; by metonymy; by gestural, bodily and behavioural signifiers and by figures of speech such as euphemism, allusions, connotations, etc. It must be said that our history is haunted by allusions, connotations, metaphors and this kind of stratagem. This has given rise to a kind of rhetoric that I call the rhetoric of circumvention.
>
> Sojoodi 2017: 52

The fidelity to the original story, the course of events and dramatic actions is more or less respected. However, there are two points that make this relative. On the one hand, the reference to immigration updates the tragic material. Ismene, played by a French actress, has emigrated to France, and on her return to her native country she becomes aware of the conflict between her sister and her uncle. The play opens with a long monologue by Ismene, describing the crisis of uprooting and belonging of immigrants. Autobiographical in nature, this monologue seems to be a personal statement by the stage director. On the other hand, this is a kind of distancing linked to the fact that the characters step out of their roles and recite dialogues that evoke this updating.

In this third show, the social contextualization of Antigone is not as concrete as in the first show and not as abstract as the second adaptation by Homayoun Ghani-Zadeh. In other words, the direct references to present a particular social layer through the character of Antigone (in the first show) are replaced by a mode of expression in which connotations play an important role:

> The apparatus of control in Iran, in this case the apparatus of control in the theatre, is not concerned with the signified or the content . . . What matters to it is the signifier or the form of expression. The forbidden content must be expressed through layers of complex meanings. This is due to the nature of surveillance, which is the exercise of the omnipotence of power. It constantly reminds the artist and the audience of its omnipotence so that they never forget to see themselves as subjugated. Therefore, what matters is the exercise of surveillance itself rather than the prohibited content.
>
> Sojoodi 2017: 52

Realizing operationalization of the censorship apparatus in Iran, Razi employs the codes which circumvent the prohibitions on identifying the mythical characters with the issue of patriarchy and women's resistance in Iran.

In terms of the question of particularizing the universal, the character of Ismene plays a functional role. Her initial monologue on immigration tells us that this is the middle class, a class with the financial means to send their children abroad, with a common discourse on the marginalization of Iranians who have immigrated:

> ISMENE
> Every year I come back here at least once and every time I feel more like a stranger, ... I have been told several times that I am lucky not to grow up here. . . . I would have liked to tell them: don't think of me as a stranger, I am one of you. But they just said, you don't live here and you don't know what's going on here.
>
> Ali Razi 2018

The stage director does not develop the social background of the two sisters further. Nevertheless, by choosing a French actress to play Ismene, he makes the marginalization of this social layer in their own country more tangible. The dramatic use of Ismene's role, by exposing a paradox between herself and Antigone, thus serves to reinforce the powerful and active image of Antigone: Ismene's anxieties, worries and fears that highlight Antigone's certainty and courage and determination to rebel against Creon. While Ismene cries, exposing her fears, and tries to dissuade her sister from disobeying, Antigone acts decisively without justification or speech. The way she manages time in her acting performance puts her in a position of power, not only in relation to her sister, but also in terms of her uncle. Thus, the character of Antigone is built on a solid foundation with incisive, disobedient and transgressive character traits.

By activating the semiotics of 'rhetoric of circumvention' explained above, the actor (and stage director) draws a parallel between the character of Creon and the political leaders of the Iranian regime from the very beginning of the performance in the scene of Creon's throne speech. The type of speech and language, the acting, the 'gestural, bodily and behavioural signs' of Saber Abar in this scene undoubtedly evoke the ideological speeches of Iranian politicians. In this case, Creon's cloak plays an important symbolic and practical role.

The cape allows the actor to realize his gestures and movements to make this parallel more credible. It also serves to distinguish not only the role of Creon-father from that of Creon-king, but also the role of Creon from that of Hemon, both characters played by the same actor. Referring to the special costumes worn by Iranian religious and political authorities, the cloak can be seen as a means of marking the distinction of power – place and position of dominance – from the individual himself. This use of Creon's cloak as a symbol of power can be seen as a form of aestheticization of a popular belief that the exercise of power corrupts man:

ISMENE
when he puts on that red coat, he changes, he wasn't that bad before he became the king.
ANTIGONE
I would have liked to say to him, Creon do not show yourself in this square, do not put on this coat.

Ali Razi 2018

By using the cloak judiciously, the actor helps the audience to better understand the different facets of the character, in this case being Creon-father versus Creon-king.

Antigonian resistance and the announcement of political subjectivity

The Antigonian resistance is about the double act of opposing Creon's decision and his public claim. This is what allows her to subjectivize herself. In other words, Antigone, by pronouncing two statements, one performative and the other declarative, passes from the status of an individual to a status of political subject. Here, the subject rejects the identity of the powerless woman-victim, refuses to be objectified in the figure of the dominated, and instead asserts her *agency*, that is to say, her irreducible capacity to act whatever her social circumstances. Antigone's resistance shows the strength of both *fatum* and its exact opposite as she subverts the status of victim to become a political subject. What embodies *fatum* here is the almighty power of Creon, whose tyrannical power aims to reduce individuals to silent and governable objects. By *consciously* refusing to be silenced, Antigone grasps power through the imprint of its very hold: since the tyrant's territory has as its object the perfect domestication of bodies, showing the limits of this power is within the reach of my body, my voice. Paradoxically, it is Creon's immense power that constitutes his point of weakness. Indeed, Antigone's speech, emerging from the required silence, instantly becomes an act of resistance that overrides fear as the essential means of subjection and the very object of the tyrant's satisfaction.

Faced with a power that is not so much interested in being obeyed as in being feared, and that sees in the strategies of circumvention put in place by its agents, to claim its act head on is then the necessary achievement of the act of resistance. It is this act that makes Antigone a political subject and elevates the Antigonian gesture of resistance so special. Hence, the *principle of Antigone* (Bantigny 2015: 17), which distinguishes the individual dimension of a transgressive act from its political dimension, makes disobedience an unveiling or a public performance of disobedience:

> 'Yes, I did it,' is to claim the act, but it is also to commit another deed in the very claiming, the act of publishing one's deed, a new criminal venture that redoubles and takes the place of the old.
>
> Butler 1893: 8

More precisely, this word is what makes it possible to distinguish, according to Aristotelian teaching (1991), the Zōé from the bios, the natural life from social life, or to use Agamben's words (1997, 1999), *bare life* (survival) from good life (life of justice). Thus, while honouring human dignity, it allows the rupture between Antigone's dignified death, assumed and transcended, and Creon's unworthy life to be revealed. It is indeed through this word that the particularity of the resistance falls within a positive affirmation, instead of being limited to a simple negation of a contested authority.

The question that now arises is whether the character of Antigone in her adaptations conforms to this interpretation, that is to say, the political subject of resistance? How do these productions show both sides of the act of Antigonian resistance by resonating with the resistance of Iranian *women*? Finally, does this resonance offer a subjective image of the Iranian woman as victim? The first image, which represents the Immortal man asserting 'the rights of the Infinite exercising their sovereignty over the contingency of suffering and death' (Badiou 2003: 33), contrasts with 'the state of victim, of suffering beast, of emaciated dying, assimilating man to his animal sub-stance, to his pure and simple identity as a living being' (31).

It should be noted that the category of *Iranian woman* is an illusory entity. As a matter of fact, it carries with it the idea of a false homogeneity and essentializes a group of women who have lived in Iran, but who are different from each other in terms of social class and social layer, ethnic and religious affiliation. It is therefore more about Iranian women from different classes, ethnic groups and social layers. This diversity is then observable in the three performances analysed through the images of Antigone and Ismene: Antigone, a theatre student from the underprivileged class who comes from the provinces in Hidji's adaptation; Antigone from the bourgeois class in Ghani-Zadeh's adaptation; and Antigone from the wealthy middle class in Razi's work.

As for the issue of power, represented by the figure of Creon, it seems that the main target of the three analysed shows is more the exposure of patriarchy inherent in a form of 'macrophysics of sovereignty' (Fernanda Canavêz 2011: 154) than biopower that is exercised over the human body and life.[6] That is, 'in the idea of a power rooted . . . in a general system of domination promoted by an element or group' (ibid.: 152).

Since resistance is organized in an active dialectic and in coexistence with power, the three performances are about aesthetisizing a form of resistance that manifests itself in the struggle against the order and law of a tyrannically sovereign state. Drawing a parallel between the character of Creon and Iranian politicians, these adaptations deal primarily with resistance in this form and reveal the oppressive effects of established power in Iran. It is the implementation of a form of aesthetic strategy of resistance while being part of the 'rhetoric of circumvention'. However, this form of resistance does not address the particularity of the Antigonian resistance, which is the question of political subjectivation. For this, it is necessary to see how each production shows both sides of the act of Antigonian resistance.

In Popak Hidji's adaptation, the act of covering the body is deferred to a series of actions relating to the material condition of the student's life. The dramaturgical work situates the ancient character in a series of conflicts whose references are directly related to the social and political conditions of women and their relationship with patriarchy in Iranian society. These conflicts, between her and Creon-father-in-law, Creon-patriarchal law, Creon-political power, Hemon-husband and Hemon-tyrannical power, are clearly recognizable to the Iranian audience. This series allows us to see the specific path that Antigone has gradually taken to become a political subject. The confrontation with these conflicts builds the character from a simple student to a political subject of resistance who actively participates in protests, while passing through acts of civil disobedience. Antigone's journey is well humanized in the sense that her human defects are not concealed or essentialized, but are instead socialized. The cause and effect of becoming a subject are also specified and nuanced: at the beginning, Antigone is unable to choose criminalized abortion. She is therefore forced to comply with her father-in-law's decision. The reason for this capitulation is not abstract, but rather it is subordinated to the examination of social and political situations: the patriarchal and capitalist appropriation of women's bodies, the family, social and cultural pressures exerted on them, and the significant obstacles for women from the underprivileged classes (financial problems). Finally, Antigone's (i.e. Neda's) active participation in the protests against the unjust authority that costs her life can be seen as a political and final affirmation of the act of resistance, that is to say, its claim. By beginning and ending the show with her death in the context of these protests, the director emphasizes Antigone's subjectivity.

As for the character of Ismene, she contributes, paradoxically, to refining the subjective image of Antigone and to nuancing and de-essentializing the resistance of women. Her opportunistic portrayal, which seeks to take advantage of the situation and gain the upper hand in various circumstances, and which ultimately becomes an accomplice of patriarchal power, suggests that the condition of women must be approached in an intersectional rather than essentialist manner.

In Ghani-Zadeh's adaptation, on the other hand, there is no effort to contextualize or particularize the act of burial, nor the subject of resistance. The act remains abstract and without practical or recognizable reference beyond the theatre. Impacted by the aesthetic genre and lightened accordingly, it is reduced to a simple narration of the dramatic action like the others, without any particular distinction or precise value. It seems that it serves to highlight Creon's misogynistic and authoritarian character, rather than to stage the Antigonian resistance. The same applies to the subject of the act, Antigone. Neither in the scenic elements, nor in the acting and staging, as we have already noted, is the character of Antigone singularized or highlighted. At times, some of her gestures, such as that of lowering her head before Creon's orders, create a mostly obedient posture. Finally, she is barely distinguishable from Ismene, who is supposed to have a character contrary to hers, as they are dressed and made up identically, and act, behave and move in the same manner. In this staging, the word is thus taken away from the actors, who can only speak through their roles. It seems they are stripped of their autonomous poetry to submit their bodies entirely to its own symbolic language.

The third adaptation by Ali Razi is the only one of the three in which the act of throwing the ritual dust on the corpse is not narrated, but is performed on stage. In contrast to the second adaptation, this one attributes importance to this act by devoting part of the stage design to a large tray of earth where part of Antigone's play takes place. One wonders whether this earth does not refer, in a sense, to exile, and whether Antigone is not an exile in her own land?

Naval Sharif's acting in this play singularizes the determined character of Antigone. In contrast to the tragic antagonists, she represents a humanized Antigone, both caring for her life and decisively prevailing over fear. The dramatic function of Ismene's role – to reinforce Antigone's subjective image – is well taken into account in this show. There is a continuity of dramaturgy in the staging of this contradiction between the two sisters here: Antigone's choice of resistance and dignified death versus Ismene's choice of obedience and an undignified life. This contradiction (dignified death vs an undignified life) is presented not only in the dramaturgy, but also in the staging: in an icy, cold space dominated by metal kitchen equipment, Ismene is only concerned with food, a vital element symbolizing survival. In contrast, Antigone's entrance is elaborated with a pot of red pelargonium, the only life-giving element in this icy atmosphere symbolizing (good) life. By taking care of this flower (Antigone) while talking about the need to transgress Creon's order, the play asks the existential question: who finally honours life?

The second part of the Antigonian resistance takes on a special significance in this show. Razi transposes this part of Sophocles' play – the public claim of the act of resistance – into two scenes: one, when Hemon proposes to pretend that Antigone is insane to save her life, and again, when Creon grants Antigone leniency by offering to conceal her act. In both cases, Antigone asserts her act in a determined way, while refusing the proposal of life (i.e. survival). By applying the technique of Brechtian distancing in the scene of the refusal of Creon's proposal, Razi gives an additional political dimension to the Antigonian resistance. Finally, the subjective image of Antigone reaches its climax just before her death. By taking Creon's place, where he delivers his speeches of power, Antigone reverses the relationship of dominated-dominant.

Conclusion

In the context of post-revolutionary Iranian society, the figure of Antigone is particularly fertile, as she resists power and the state, beyond her own death and even through it. As we have seen, through the ancient figures of Antigone and Creon, and behind the alibi of the apparent political neutrality of the tragic material, Iranian artists find a way to circumvent censorship and express criticism of the totalitarian power of the state. The adaptation of the tragic work is thus employed as an artistic strategy.

In Homayoun Ghani-Zadeh's adaptation, this strategy focuses only on exposing the misogynistic and authoritarian nature of power, and the absurdity of its relations. The antigonian resistance thus becomes a kind of desperate and sterile political statement. On the contrary, in the adaptations of Poupak Hidji and Ali Razi, the aestheticization of these two aspects of the antigonian resistance, offers a subjective and political image of the resistance of women in Iran, who succeed in appropriating the absolute right of word and action from the power, as the very recent movement of 'Woman, life, freedom' testifies.

Notes

1 Winner of the best direction award at the International Puppet Theatre Festival.
2 *Shahré Gheseh was* first written and directed in 1966 by Bijan Mofid. Inspired by old Iranian songs, anecdotes and proverbs, applying irony, symbolism and expressions of slang culture, this play is a story of the metamorphosis of men and the loss of their identity.
3 The uprising against the outcome of the presidential election.
4 A young girl killed during this movement and who has become one of its symbols.
5 It should be noted that this trivialization concerns not just the character of Antigone, it predominates over all the elements of staging, acting and tragic material.

6 The Foucauldian formula that characterizes biopolitics today is: 'to make live and let die'. If in the old regimes, power was exercised through the right of life and death, biopolitics functions on the one hand by discrediting death and making it taboo, and on the other hand by emphasizing life and its regularization. It is then exercised through the right to make people live (Foucault 1997: 159).

References

Agamben, G. (1997), *Homo sacer I: Le pouvoir souverain et la vie nue*, trans. Marilène Raiola, Paris: Seuil.

Agamben, G. (1999), *Ce qui reste d'Auschwitz: l'archive et le témoin*, trans. Pierre Alféri, Paris: Payot and Rivages.

Aristotle (1991), *Politique, Tome 1: Livres I et II*, trans. Jean Aubonnet, Paris: les Belles lettres.

Badiou, A. (2003), *L'éthique, essai sur la conscience du mal*, Paris: Nous.

Bantigny, L. (2015), 'Le principe d'Antigone: Pour une histoire de la désobéissance en démocratie', *Pouvoirs*, 155: 17–28.

Blin, F. (2014), 'Antigone ou les masques de la marginalité au cœur du pouvoir', *Les chantiers de la création: Revue pluridisciplinaire en Lettres, Langues, Arts et Civilisations*, 15 Octobre. Available online: http://journals.openedition.org/lcc/702 (accessed 1 septembre 2014).

Butler, J. (2002), *Antigone's Claim*, New York: Columbia University Press.

Doré, C. and C. Lambert (2015), 'Antigone: emblème de la voix des femmes en éthique', *Recherches féministes*, 28(1): 1–10.

Duroux, R. and S. Urdician (2010), 'Antigone, retours sur une fascination', in R. Duroux and S. Urdician (eds), *Les Antigones contemporaines (de 1945 à nos jours)*, 13–32, Clermont-Ferrand: Presses Universitaires Blaise Pascal.

Estellon, V. (2010), 'Mémoire, genre, identité et lien social: le cri d'Antigone', *L'Esprit du temps, 'Champ psy'*, 58: 141–59.

Fernanda Canavêz, H. M. (2011), 'Sur la résistance chez Freud et Foucault', *Recherches en psychanalyse*, 12: 149–57.

Foucault, M. (1997), *Il faut défendre la société: cours au Collège de France, 1975–1976*, Paris: Seuil.

Lussier, A. (2005), *Le projet d'Antigone: Parcours vers la mort d'une Fille d'Œdipe*, Montréal: Liber.

Pinçonnat, C. (2012), 'Le Complexe d'Antigone: Relectures féministes et postcoloniales du scénario œdipien', *Klincksieck, Revue de littérature comparée*, 344: 495–509.

Raymond, T. (1964), 'La philosophie du pouvoir dans l'Antigone de Sophocle', *Revue des Études Grecques*, 77: 364–5.

Sojoodi, S, entretiens par Zamani, M. (2017), 'Les codes de la représentation dans le théâtre iranien, et le spectateur occidental: entente ou malentendu?', *Alternatives théâtrales revue des arts de la scène*, 132: 50–3.

Steiner, G. (1992), *Les Antigones,* trans. Philippe Blanchard, Paris: Gallimard.

Vernant, J. P. and P. Vidal-Naquet (2001), *Mythe et tragédie en Grèce ancienne*, Paris: La Découverte.

7

When Iraqi Theatre Met the World Again

Haythem Abderrazak and His *Looking for Oresteia*

Antonio Pacifico

In September 2018, a Franco-Iraqi adaptation of the *Oresteia*, the famous trilogy of Greek tragedies written by Aeschylus in the fifth century BCE, was performed at the Centre Dramatique National (CDN) in Besançon (France). The adaptation, entitled *Looking for Oresteia*, was the result of a project of common experimentation that was carried out for almost five years between France and Iraq by two stage directors, Haythem Abderrazak (Hayt̲am ʿAbd al-Razzāq) and Célie Pauthe. These directors knew each other through the mediation of Siwa, a cultural platform created in 2007 to encourage exchanges between artists, intellectuals and citizens from both Arab and European countries. Their project was coproduced by the CDN, which Pauthe has directed since 2013, and LaFonderie, another theatrical institution based in Le Mans (France). Moreover, the project saw the participation of the Continuing Training Space Workshop (Waršat faḍāʾ al-tamrīn al-mustamirr) founded by Abderrazak in Baghdad in 1998, several French actors and Yagoutha Belgacem, one of the founders and current director of Siwa.

The primary purpose of the present chapter is to elaborate on the case study of this adaptation and shed light on the current state of the Iraqi theatrical 'field' and its main challenges (Bourdieu 1996). Indeed, this case study, allows us to identify the multiple obstacles Iraqi stage directors face today in their country and, simultaneously, examine the uneven and often complicated relations existing between a 'peripheral' field, such as the Iraqi one, and the main 'centres' of international theatre, especially after 2003 (Casanova 2004).

The Iraqi theatrical field has scarcely been investigated since its inception during the 1940s when it emerged due mainly to government economic support. This was all the more true after the Baath party seized power in 1963.[1] As soon as the regime tried to silence most Iraqi artists and playwrights by promoting a theatre that glorified the war against Iran or a specific kind of light comedy that merely featured dancing, singing and joke-telling, scholars found no interest in studying it. This lack of interest in Iraqi production also emerged during the 1990s when the country witnessed severe political, social and economic unrest due to the invasion of Kuwait (1990), the Gulf War (1990–1), the Shiite uprising (1991) and the imposition of harsh economic sanctions (1990–2003). Moreover, after the American invasion and the fall of the Baathist regime (2003), the bloody ethno-sectarian conflict (2006–7) and all the other forms of endemic violence that hit Iraq seriously prevented scholars from stepping foot in the country, thus contributing even more to the segregation of its theatrical field and cultural figures.

Therefore, in order to explore this work by Abderrazak and Pauthe and propose some hypotheses on the current state of Iraqi theatre, we will look above all at the 'trajectory' and current 'position' occupied by the Iraqi stage director in the theatrical field (Bourdieu 1996). In addition, we will explore the trajectory and impact of all the other actors who contributed with him to the staging of this adaptation. Finally, in the third section of this chapter, we will examine the concrete work carried out by Abderrazak and Pauthe, focusing on some moments of conflict and 'crisis' that the two directors faced on the stage.[2] An accurate analysis of these moments will help us shed light on Abderrazak's positioning in the Iraqi field and the international one field, complementing our reflections our reflections on the material contingencies in which this project has been conceived.[3]

Haythem Abderrazak's trajectory as an actor, academic and stage director

Haythem Abderrazak is an actor, academic and stage director, born in Iraq in 1953. He began his artistic trajectory in Baghdad while he was only a student at the College of Fine Arts (Kulliyyat al-funūn al-ǧamīla). In 1974, he acted in the adaptation of the *Epic of Gilgamesh*, produced by one of the most significant directors of modern Iraqi theatre, Sami Abdul-Hamid (Samī ʿAbd al- Ḥamīd, 1928–2019). In 1977, he graduated from the College of Fine Arts, from which he also obtained a MA in 1997 and a PhD in 2003.

In the following years, he continued acting in theatre and on television, participating in many plays and TV series, such as *Love Heights* (*Fī aʿālī al-ḥubb*, 1997), *Sidra* (Sīdrā, 2000) or *The Case 238* (*al-Qaḍiyya 238*, 2001). He also founded in Kirkuk the so-called Troupe for Experimental Theatre (Firqat al-masraḥ al-taġrībī) (Ḥasan Mūsā 2012).

After graduating, he acted in significant plays directed by Ṣalāḥ al-Qaṣab (1945), Fāḍil Ḥalīl (1946–2017), Mohsen Al-Azzawi (Muḥsin al-ʿAzzāwī, 1939) and Qasim Muhammad (Qāsim Muḥammad, 1936–2009), another prominent stage director of the Iraqi theatrical field.[4] In 1984, Abderrazak began his academic career as a professor in the Acting Department of the College of Fine Arts, always in Baghdad. And in 1988, he founded the Continuing Training Space Workshop with other Iraqi actors and performing artists, such as Iqbal Naeem (Iqbāl Naʿīm, 1958) and Maymoon al-Khaldi (Maymūn al-Ḫālidī, 1950).

As for his career as a stage director, Abderrazak directed his first play, titled *Sorry Sir, I Didn't Mean That* (*Aʿtaḏir ustāḏī lam akun aqṣid ḏālika*), in 1998. He then continued to direct plays mainly in Iraq until 2004 when, during his participation in the Cairo International Festival for Experimental Theatre (Mahraǧān al-Qāhira al-duwalī li-l-masraḥ al-taġrībī), not only did he win the prize for the staging of the best university work (Hādī 2004), but he also attained a certain degree of symbolic 'capital' (see Bourdieu 1996) that allowed him to travel in various Western countries, including the United States, France and Germany where he also enjoyed an artist residency for three months (al-Šarqī 2021).

Furthermore, as stated by Abderrazak himself in one of his articles, 'Reading the Difference' ('Lecture de la différence/Qirāʾat al-iḫtilāf' 2020), such traumatic events as the American invasion and the fall of the Baathist regime, which occurred in the same period, had a considerable impact not only on Iraqi society as a whole but also on the country's theatrical field. According to the stage director, for instance, they forced many artists of the Iraqi field of theatre – and especially those who stayed in the country like him – to cope with 'new' symbolic difficulties and issues that had been much sidelined during the previous years of lockdown:

> ['Reading the difference'.] This expression has become an obsession for me since we opened up to the world and engaged in the path of dialogue, exchange and mutual differentiation to re-read the complete lockdown we lived in before 2003. This does not mean that I am with the post-2003 years of chaos (or the American invasion of Iraq and the fall of Saddam Hussein). The fall of the wall between us and the world was a crucial event … Far or near from any form of political commitment, we began staying on the theatrical stage as if we were on the stage of dialogue. A dialogue we began carrying out with the other and the self because the other, in this new world, became essential to read the self and question or reject our ego and its harmful hormones.
>
> 78–9[5]

These events, moreover, also affected the material dimension of his work as an actor and a stage director, as we will shortly see below.

During the last twenty years, Abderrazak has acquired more symbolic capital and won other crucial prizes, such as the Honour of the Tuesday Forum of the Iraqi Writers and Intellectuals Union (Takrīm li-l-multaqā al-ṯulāṯā' li-ittiḥād al-udabā' wa-l-kuttāb al-ʿiraqiyyin) which he received in 2019 (Ǧāsim 2019). He also continued to direct multiple theatrical works, such as *Shadows* (*Ẓilāl*, 2011), *The Democratic East Disease* (*Maraḍ al-šarq al-dīmuqrāṭī*, 2012), *The Death of a Stubborn Citizen* (*Mawt muwāṭin ʿanīd*, 2013), both inside and outside Iraq. Moreover, he continued teaching and training new generations of young performing artists in the space he created in 1998 with Iqbal Naeem and other Iraqi actors, which has become one of the major learning institutions of the Iraqi theatrical field since then.

In this phase, Abderrazak overtly deplored the state of Iraqi theatre and, despite the solid relationships he established with almost all the people who directed the Department of Theatre and Cinema at the Iraqi Ministry of Culture or the Iraqi National Theatre (al-Masraḥ al-waṭanī al-ʿirāqi),[6] with whom he still collaborates, he continued earning his living mainly from his two other jobs as a Professor at the College of Fine Arts and an actor in multiple TV series and films, such *as The Girls' House* (*Bayt al-banāt*, 2008), *Naima's Road* (*Ṭarīq Naʿīma*, 2012), *The Red Violet* (*al-Banafsaǧ al-aḥmar*, 2014) or *Baghdad in My Shadow* (*Baġdād fī ḥayyālī*, 2019). In addition, Abderrazak often criticized Iraqi government institutions for ignoring the artistic productions of their country, despite the absence of censorship and other forms of significant political interference in his work (Ḥasan Mūsā 2012).

In an interview with Pauline Donizeau and Laetitia Dumont-Lewi (2019), he was even more explicit. He accused the Iraqi institutions of total disengagement from the country's cultural field and clearly pointed out the lack of strategies in the management of their resources:

> [Iraqi] current leaders do not know anything about culture and are not interested in it. The only thing that is important for them is to open religious schools! The city of Baghdad was once an important cultural centre. Parliament members know and praise this prestigious past, but do not implement any cultural policy, there is no cultural strategy. Everything that exists from the point of view of culture results from individual initiatives.

99

Concerning his first encounter with Siwa, Abderrazak met Belgacem and Jean-Pierre Han, a professional journalist, a theatre and literary critic, and one of the leading platform members, at the Amman International Theatre Festival, initially in 2005 and then again in 2006. In 2007, Abderrazak participated in a workshop organized by Siwa at the Théâtre de la Cité Internationale in Paris, where he worked with the French director Michel Cerda on a text entitled *Hamlet without Hamlet* (*Hāmlit bi-lā Hāmlit*, 2005), written by the Iraqi poet and playwright Ḥazʿal al-Māǧidī (1951). In 2008, he participated again in a residency organized by Siwa in France, this time at the Odéon-Théâtre de l'Europe, where, among other things, he had the opportunity to talk about acting and its specific style in the Iraqi dramatic tradition.

In the following years, Abderrazak continued to frequent Belgacem, Han and all the other platform members in a series of residencies and events that took place in both France and Iraq. Meanwhile, Belgacem visited Abderrazak, Naeem and their Continuing Training Space Workshop in Baghdad with other French artists and cultural protagonists in 2009 and 2010, thus paving the way for a Franco-Iraqi adaptation of the *Oresteia*.

The trajectories and impact of the other cultural actors involved in the project

The idea of working together with Pauthe on an adaptation of the *Oresteia* materialized for the first time in 2014 when Abderrazak met with her and another Iraqi actor and stage director living in Europe, Mokhallad Rasem. However, the latter abandoned the project shortly after.[7] As stated above, their meeting was supported and organized by Siwa, a cultural platform officially founded by Belgacem, a Franco-Tunisian, in 2011.

The platform was initially set up in Redeyef, a small city located in Southeastern Tunisia, although some of its members were already active in various Arab countries at the moment of its foundation. In Redeyef, the platform contributed to creating a local cultural centre in a building belonging to the Gafsa Phosphate Company (www.arabculturefund.org/Projects/6772). It also organized several cultural events, artistic experiments, workshops and residencies to liberate the city from its isolation (Han and Belgacem 2020: 30–4). Moreover, as can be seen in the description of the platform available on the website of the CDN, since 2007, Siwa has set itself ambitious goals that involved the whole field of Arab contemporary culture(s), including allowing experimental artistic works produced in the Arab countries to reach Europe and vice versa:

Siwa Platform, created in 2007, is an itinerant artistic laboratory of the contemporary Arab worlds. Designed to encourage exchanges between artists, intellectuals and citizens of the Arab and European worlds, Siwa Platform produces spaces for reflection based on artistic experimentation. The platform shows in Europe the most experimental cultural productions of these countries. In reciprocity, it promotes European artistic experiences in Tunisia and Iraq. Siwa is also and above all a place of rejoicing where one can exhibit and debate in complete freedom, conduct long-term research and capture the symptoms and tensions that affect these worlds. Conducive to ruptures and fractures, Siwa is resolutely open to any experience of freedom (www.cdn-besancon.fr/siwa-plateforme).

In 2010, in Baghdad, the platform also met the Iraqi photographer Latif Al Ani (Laṭīf al-ʿĀnī, 1932–2021), with whom it tried to launch several activities on his artistic works and personal archive. At the same time, in 2014, Belgacem tried to organize with the support of Catherine David (1954), a French curator who had already worked on contemporary Iraqi arts, and Anas Abdul Samad (Anas ʿAbd al-Ṣamad, 1974), an actor and a stage director, a series of exhibitions in key places of the city of Baghdad, even though the project never saw the light of day and was finally postponed (Han and Belgacem 2020: 28–9).

As for the role of Siwa in *Looking for Oresteia*, it seems that the platform played a crucial role in this project well before the stage directors chose the text to adapt. Indeed, Belgacem and the other platform members met with the Iraqi stage director and some of the actors who used to work with him for the first time in Jordan in 2005 and 2006. The platform also discussed with him the idea of a joint project between France and Iraq much earlier (Pacifico, Abderrazak 2022). Moreover, Siwa accompanied Abderrazak and Pauthe during their first conversations regarding the text of the Greek trilogy in 2014 and, at the moment of the staging of the adaptation, Belgacem took on the role of artistic director of the project.

After 2014, Siwa continued to organize for Abderrazak and Pauthe residencies and other opportunities for discussion on the text of the *Oresteia* in both France and Iraq. This gave impetus and supported the production of a new Arabic translation of the Greek trilogy in order to facilitate Abderrazak and his actors in their dramatic work (Donizeau and Dumont-Lewi 2019: 96–7). To do that, the platform also organized two residencies for the translators involved in the project in Saline d'Arc and Senans (France), putting the translation issue at the very core of *Looking for Oresteia* (Seddik 2020).

During their first residency in Baghdad, Belgacem and her cultural platform also tried to support Abderrazak in his request for financial help from the Iraqi

Ministry of Culture. The platform, in addition, concretely helped him, Naeem and the other Iraqi actors who participated in the project obtain a space for their rehearsals from the branch of the TotalEnergies Foundation located in Baghdad (Donizeau and Dumont-Lewi 2019: 99). At the same time, Siwa received for them the support of the French Embassy in Iraq, the French Institute (Institut français) in Paris and the Office for Contemporary Performing Arts Circulation (Office national de diffusion artistique – ONDA) in France.

Nevertheless, despite all the efforts implemented by the platform, this project would have never seen the light of day without the decision of Pauthe, the current director of the CDN, to associate Siwa with her institution for the entire duration of her mandate:

> When taking office, one of my first decisions was to associate Siwa Platform with the CDN for the entire duration of my mandate. The reason was that the work carried out by Yagoutha Belgacem seemed to me to be exemplary in all respects: on the one hand, in the audacity and inventiveness with which she builds bridges between artists, languages, cultures and aesthetics from the Arab world to France, from France to the Arab world; on the other hand, by the depth of the links she maintains with the artists she surrounds herself with. Moreover, the inclusion in time of a project such as *Looking for Oresteia* was absolutely necessary if we wanted it to have the chance to see the light of day.
>
> Bagdad/Besançon. Bizānsūn/Baġdād 2018: 5

As stated in the account given by Belgacem and Han on the history of Siwa, Pauthe, too, met with the platform well before 2014 (Han and Belgacem 2020: 26). She also accompanied Belgacem and the other platform members in their travel to Iraq in 2010, in addition to being a well-established stage director and an educator in significant French institutions, such as the École Nationale Supérieure des Arts et Techniques du Théâtre (ENSATT) in Lyon and the École Supérieure d'Art Dramatique (ESAD) in Paris. Moreover, at the time she started working with Abderrazak on the adaptation of the *Oresteia*, Pauthe had already adapted the texts of prominent Western writers and intellectuals, such as Ingmar Bergman, Thomas Bernhard, Sarah Berthiaume, Maurice Maeterlinck, Heiner Müller and Eugene O'Neill (www.lesarchivesduspectacle.net/?IDX_ Personne=167). Through her previous works, she also distinguished herself for the prominence of the written text and the peculiar adherence she implemented towards it.[8]

The same decision adopted by Pauthe was taken a little later by François Tanguy, the Director of LaFonderie, who also hosted Abderrazak, Pauthe and their respective actors for two residencies in Le Mans. These residencies took place, in the first place, in September 2016 and, later, in September 2018, just some days before the final staging of the adaptation at the CDN in Besançon. Indeed, in 2018, the institution directed by Pauthe decided to host the first official representation of *Looking for Oresteia*. The play was scheduled during a week devoted to Iraq and its contemporary cultural production, which saw the participation of other Arab artists and intellectuals, such as Youssef Seddik, a philosopher, an anthropologist and the translator of the new Arabic translation of the Greek trilogy, supported by Siwa.

In 2019, this week devoted to Iraq and its contemporary culture was also followed by two other editions of the same event, significantly titled the *Baghdad Festival*. The latter revolved around another work produced and directed by Abderrazak and his group of actors, *The Democratic East Disease*. However, it also revolved around the work of other Iraqi artists quoted above, such as photographer Latif Al Ani and stage director Anas Abdul Samad.

Looking for Oresteia: a Franco-Iraqi adaptation of the Greek trilogy?

As for the concrete work carried out on the stage, Abderrazak directed the adaptation of *Agamemnon*, the first part of the trilogy, while Pauthe worked on its second part, *The Libation Bearers*. The adaptation of *The Eumenides*, the third and conclusive part, was instead directed by both directors. The play was staged in French, Modern Standard Arabic and Iraqi Colloquial Arabic to allow each actor to use the language they felt most natural. The music was performed live by artists Sari Al Bayati and Khaled Al Khafaji, while Arafat Sadallah and Hajer Bouden worked on translating the text. The other creative roles, including lighting, videos, music and costumes, were assigned to French artists.

From a thematic perspective, the adaptation addressed several crucial questions for our contemporary societies, such as violence, revenge, democracy and transitional justice, which also represent some of the main topics covered by the original text. However, from the beginning of their collaboration, Abderrazak and Pauthe saw *Looking for Oresteia* as a project of common experimentation and, at least partly, as a project of emancipation from the text of the Greek trilogy.[9] For this reason, they used the *Oresteia* more as a material or a tool to rely on rather than a text to reproduce on the stage faithfully. It is thus not surprising that the action of the first part of the play takes place in a Baghdadi hospital overwhelmed by the number of injured people caused by recent ethno-sectarian conflicts or that the whole adaptation is full of references to contemporary Arab and European cultures.

Furthermore, both directors saw their adaptation as a work *in fieri*, i.e. a work that had no aim of being terminated once and for all, but was, on the contrary, endlessly open to modifications and rearrangements. In this sense, the adaptation text was repeatedly revised during the years that preceded its staging and continued to be modified until the last repetition residency occurred in Le Mans in 2018 (Pacifico, Abderrazak 2022). These modifications were often discussed during meetings and workshops moderated by Jean-Pierre Han, the same Siwa leading member Abderrazak met for the first time in Amman in 2006 ('Abd al-Razzāq 2020: 86–7).

However, despite these common 'strategies' and specific mediations (Bourdieu 1996), the two directors disagreed very early on crucial features of their project, producing several deadlocks and moments of crisis in the whole creative process.

As soon as they started adapting the text of the trilogy and, more specifically, its third part on which they worked together, some significant symbolic conflicts emerged between them. These conflicts involved, above all, two elements of the adaptation. The first of these elements was related to the visions of both stage directors of the original text. Indeed, on more than one occasion, Abderrazak complained about Pauthe's attitude towards the *Oresteia* and its written dimension. He often perceived Pauthe's vision of the original text as 'reverential' (Pacifico, Abderrazak 2022), while he and his actors could not stop drawing on other dramatic tools, even in an adaptation work such as the one they were implementing with Pauthe:

> It took a lot of time and space to renegotiate our relationship with the written text and its sacredness in French theatre. [Our] disagreement always related to the opposition between the written word and the unwritten one in relation to the dramatic space. We wanted to fill that space with the unwritten word that was nothing more than the text of the body, the text of feelings and [other] tools.
>
> 'Abd al-Razzāq 2020: 84–7

In a private interview I had with him in October 2022, Abderrazak also declared that this was one of the 'sharpest' conflicts he had with Pauthe since he had spent all his trajectory as an artist and stage director working on the body, the rhythm, and other 'languages' that looked to him more 'universal' than those of the written text proposed by the French director (Pacifico, Abderrazak 2022 and 'Abd al-Razzāq 2007). Moreover, the same problem was noticed by Belgacem, who declared in the interview with Donizeau and Dumont-Lewi quoted above that the approaches applied by the two directors toward the *Oresteia* were significantly different, despite their initial agreement on the experimental and changing character of their work (2019: 96–7). She also defined their respective visions of the original text as 'organic' – in the case of Abderrazak – and 'intellectual' – in the case of Pauthe:[10]

> During the conversations with the translator, it appeared that there was a real proximity between Arab culture and Greek culture, or in any case that there was an indisputable Greek heritage in Islamic culture. The Iraqis do not have an intellectual approach to Greek tragedy, they maintain an organic relationship with it: they recognize in it what they experience on a daily basis, and also the ancient rituals still present in some of their religious practices. It was, therefore, an important text for the two directors, but they approached it in radically different ways: Célie with a more intellectual relationship to the text, Haythem with an approach more anchored in the body.
>
> 97

The second element that the two directors had to face concerned some specific references Pauthe wanted to make to Iraq and its political crisis in the adaptation text. In this sense, one of the most significant conflicts emerged between them when Pauthe decided to rely on several Shiite rituals for the second part of the trilogy, *The Libation Bearers*. From Abderrazak's point of view, this was wholly inappropriate. He argued that that kind of element would have been perceived as 'sectarian' by the Iraqi public and would have prevented the adaptation from being staged in Iraq (Donizeau and Dumont-Lewi 2019: 99).

The same conflict also occurred during their collaboration for the third part of the play and, more specifically, for its final scene. In this case, Pauthe wanted to add at the end of the adaptation some images that portrayed Iraqi people going to vote for the legislative elections that took place in the country in 2018. However, Abderrazak firmly opposed Pauthe's decision, arguing that the topics addressed by the adaptation involved the entire world, not only Iraq. In addition, this time, the Iraqi stage director was even more transparent. According to him, the problematic aspect of such an element lay in the symbolic dimension of the adaptation that had to remain 'universal' and not anchored to a specific 'local' context, not even to the Iraqi one.[11] In other words, here, the risk was one of producing an Iraqi version of the *Oresteia*, a version which had nothing to do with the 'universal' dimension of the adaptation Abderrazak wanted to achieve, as also stated in Pauthe's terms:

On the stage, we carried out a deeply artistic act. We asked ourselves the fundamental questions of theatre in each situation of staging, while directing actors and in dramaturgy. However, the very idea of the *Oresteia* came to me because of the resonance of the text with the state of our democracies, including Iraq. The challenge was not to confine our entire reading of the *Oresteia* in the Iraqi context, a trap into which I myself could have fallen. This would have transformed the work into an Iraqi *Oresteia*, but it actually is a Franco-Iraqi *Oresteia* and, in this sense, *universal*.

98[12]

As for the resolution of this conflict, the two directors agreed to replace the images that portrayed Iraqi people going to vote with the following words used by Pier Paolo Pasolini (1922–75) in the final scene of his *Notes Towards an African Orestes* (*Appunti per un'Orestiade Africana*, 1970):

> A new nation is born; its problems are infinite. But problems are not resolved; they are experienced. And life is slow. Going towards the future cannot have its solution in continuity. The work of a people knows neither rhetoric nor delay. Its future is in its fear of the future. And its fear is a great patience.
>
> 01:08:40–01:09:12

These words met the taste of the Iraqi stage director and, in this case, at least, the conflict between Abderrazak and Pauthe was ultimately resolved. However, from a more general perspective, it remains to be understood what these symbolic conflicts that resulted in fully-fledged moments of crisis for the project may tell us about this whole experience, the current state of the Iraqi theatrical field and its relations with the main centres of contemporary international theatre, especially after 2003.

Conclusion

To answer these questions, it seems crucial to read the conflicts experienced by Abderrazak and Pauthe in light of their respective trajectories in the theatrical field and, most importantly, in light of the impact that all the other participants, such as Siwa, had on this project.

As far as this material dimension is concerned, it is evident, for instance, that through the help of an international cultural platform and the participation in the project of a prominent French director such as Pauthe, Abderrazak could avoid many difficulties he had experienced throughout his whole career, which mainly concerned the lack of economic strategies devoted to cultural production in Iraq. As stated in his declarations, these problems continued to affect the Iraqi field after the fall of the Baathist regime, even though they did not involve the political values and ideas conveyed by the plays. In other words, through this project, Abderrazak was not only able to rely on economic support from significant French institutions, including the influential Office for Contemporary Performing Arts Circulation, but he also received some help from the Iraqi Ministry of Culture, which had hardly supported him and his artistic projects in the past (Pacifico, Abderrazak 2022).[13]

At the same time, through this project, Abderrazak had the opportunity to work in one of the leading centres of the international field, acquiring more symbolic capital and visibility on a global level. In this way, the Iraqi stage director could also exploit his international experience to increase his symbolic capital at home, as was the case for his previous experiences in other Arab countries, Germany and the United States.[14]

Nevertheless, despite all these opportunities, one may also wonder about the disadvantages Abderrazak had in participating in such a project, especially considering that, after 2003, Iraq (re)integrated the international theatrical field suddenly and abruptly. These disadvantages did not limit themselves to the fact that Abderrazak had to share his directing function with Pauthe (and Belgacem), but they also included other significant issues. In this regard, the multiple conflicts and moments of crisis that brought the two directors into conflict during their collaboration are particularly illustrative.

If we go back, for instance, to the words used to describe these conflicts, we can notice that the word 'universal' recurs in the discourses of both Abderrazak and Pauthe and that both conflicts seem connected with the opposition 'local/ universal'. This was also true for the first of them, which revolved around the relationship with the original text. In that case, Abderrazak emphasized the importance of body and other forms of communication in an effort to adopt a language that was, for him, more 'universal' than that chosen by Pauthe. We may argue thus not only that the first of these conflicts was a symbolic struggle over the notion of 'universal' theatre – which Pauthe saw in a text of the Western tradition while Abderrazak in the body – but also that the Iraqi stage director showed a specific and strong desire to build a 'denationalized' dimension for his work (Casanova 2004) – one that seems strongly connected with his trajectory at the periphery of the international theatrical field and his will to acquire a form of symbolic capital that is also spendable outside Iraq and its cultural centres.[15]

Accordingly, Belgacem's attempt at defining the respective approaches of the two directors through the opposition 'intellectual/organic' appears quite naïve and simplistic. Moreover, against this background, several hypotheses concerning the questions raised in the introduction to the chapter and at the end of the previous section may come to mind.

Concerning the current state of the Iraqi field and its relations with the main centres of contemporary international theatre, we argue that Abderrazak's case seems to confirm one of the main theoretical contributions developed by Pascale Casanova in *The World Republic of Letters* (2004). Indeed, in her essay, the French sociologist identified for any peripheral field, the presence of two internal poles: one that is usually more oriented towards the national dimension of the production and reception of symbolic goods and another one, more international or 'denationalized', which is, on the contrary, more oriented towards elements that could be seen as global or 'universal'. In other words, in our chapter, we argue that the project of this adaptation seems to confirm, at least from a theoretical perspective, the presence of an international or 'denationalized' pole also in the case of the Iraqi theatrical field, despite or, better, precisely because the many years of isolation and complete lockdown experienced by most Iraqi people until 2003.

Furthermore, if this is true, we can also assume that this same pole of the Iraqi field is now experiencing, exactly as Abderrazak himself is, 'new' forms of dependence or cultural domination that, far from affecting only the material dimension of theatre production in Iraq, also have a significant impact on its symbolic aspects. Put differently, the experience of this adaptation makes it evident that, since 2003, a portion of this field has been confronted again with the role and the effects produced by specific power relations that lie inside and outside Iraq and are also rooted in the international field of cultural production.

These power relations, however, deserve to be investigated from a more systematic perspective and in greater detail as far as an understudied theatrical field such as the Iraqi one is concerned. In this sense, we would also like to stress that, in recent years, the sociology of culture has provided us with crucial theoretical tools for exploration and that these tools, precisely as in the case study of this adaptation, seem particularly appropriate for application to such a delicate and compelling work.

Notes

1　Of course, there are significant exceptions to this. Cf. Kudaiyr 1987, Sef 1995, Al-Azraki and Al-Shamma 2017. Recent articles have also been devoted to key figures of modern and contemporary Iraqi theatre, such as Yūsuf al-ʿĀnī or Jawād al-Asadī. See, for instance, Yousif 1997 and Al-Shamma 2013.

2 Indeed, in this chapter, I adopt the theoretical approach developed over the last thirty years by prominent sociologists of culture, such as Pierre Bourdieu and Pascale Casanova. This approach obliges us to explore the 'position-takings' carried out by the actors of the cultural field in light of their specific 'position' within it. Cf. Bourdieu 1996.

3 Here, I understand 'crisis' as a phenomenon that catalyzes previous social conflicts rather than triggering new ones. On this, see Dobry 2009.

4 From a private unpublished interview with Abderrazak I had with him in Baghdad in October 2022, from here on referred as 'Pacifico, Abderrazak 2022'.

5 All translations from Arabic and French into English are mine, except for the words that Pasolini wrote for the final scene of his film. The latter have been taken from the version of the film with English subtitles. On this, see *Appunti per un'Orestiade Africana* (1970).

6 One of these people was, for instance, the same Iqbal Naeem who founded with him the Continuing Training Space Workshop in 1988. Moreover, from what we have seen during the fieldwork we carried out in October 2022 on the occasion of the third edition of the Baghdad Festival for International Theatre (Mahraǧān Baġdād al-duwwalī li-l-masraḥ), Abderrazak also seemed to cultivate a solid relationship with the new head of the Department of Theatre and Cinema, Aḥmad Ḥasan Mūsā.

7 The reasons that led Rasem to abandon the project are still unknown to us.

8 This specific attitude of Pauthe towards the written text also emerges in the work she implemented with Abderrazak on the *Oresteia*. On Pauthe's attitude in her previous adaptation works, see, for instance, Suchet 2013.

9 However, from this point of view, we must stress that both directors chose to preserve not only the main themes and structure of the original text in their adaptation, but also the dialogues.

10 Here, we are using Belgacem's quote for illustrative purposes only. Indeed, as we will see in our concluding remarks, this symbolic conflict results from specific power relations rather than distinct aesthetic traditions connected with one culture or another.

11 However, this does not mean that Abderrazak refuses to talk about Iraq or Iraqi reality within his plays. On the contrary, these two elements still have an important place in his works and are also essential in his relationship with the text of the *Oresteia*. On this, see ʿAbd al-Razzāq/Abderrazak 2020 and ʿAbde 2021.

12 Emphasis added.

13 The second of these achievements, for instance, seems highly connected with the role of Siwa and, more specifically, Belgacem, who physically accompanied Abderrazak and his actors to meet the bureaucrats of the Ministry. As for the

previous forms of economic support that the Iraqi stage director received from the Iraqi Ministry of Culture, it seems that the institution only financed the production of one of his theatrical works, *The Death of a Stubborn Citizen*. On this, cf. private interview with the stage director in October 2022.

14　Indeed, according to Casanova, the accumulation of symbolic capital on a global level can produce concrete effects also in the internal struggles existing in the national fields.

15　Unfortunately, we could not deepen our analysis of Pauthe's positioning in the French theatrical field. However, compared to Abderrazak, Pauthe is clearly in a dominant position in the international field and this could explain why she feels less need to reaffirm the 'universal' dimension of her work.

References

'Bagdad/Besançon. Bizānsūn/Baġdād' (2018), [Press release]: Available online: https://cdn-besancon.fr/sites/saison18-19/files/CONTENT/SPECTACLES/DOCUMENTS/dp-bagdad-besancon-19sept2018-web.pdf (accessed 20 October 2022).

ʿAbd al-Razzāq, H. (2007), 'Farḍiyyat al-tamrīn wa-iškāliyyat al-bīʾa al-maʿmāriyyah li-tadrīs māddat fann al-mumaṯṯil: waršat faḍāʾ al-tamrīn al-mustamirr namūḏaǧan', *al-Akādīmī*, 47: 111–38.

ʿAbd al-Razzāq, H./Abderrazak H. (2020), 'Lecture de la difference/Qirāʾat al-iḫtilāf', *Frictions*, 9: 78–90.

Appunti per un'Orestiade Africana (1970), [Film] Dir. Pier Paolo Pasolini, Italy: IDI Cinematografica/I Film dell'Orso.

ʿAzīz, A. (2021), 'Hayṯam ʿAbd al-Razzāq: law istaṯmarnā wāqiʿana fa-sanaġzū al-ʿarab drāmiyyan', *al-Šabaka al-ʿirāqiyya*, 15 January. Available online: https://magazine.imn.iq/لو-الرزاق-عبد-هيثم-فنون-استثمرنا-فسن-واقعنا/ (accessed 26 October 2022).

Al-Azraki, A. and J. Al-Shamma, eds (2017), *Contemporary Plays from Iraq*, London; New York: Bloomsbury.

Al-Shamma, J. (2013), 'Staging *Baghdadi Bath* on the Western Stage: Toward a Theatre of Trauma', *Journal of Dramatic Theory and Criticism*, 27(2): 105–18.

Baghdad in My Shadow/Baġdād fī ḥayyālī (2019), [Film] Dir. Samir, Germany; Switzerland; United Kingdom; Iraq: Global Screen GmbH.

Bourdieu, P. (1996), *The Rules of Art: Genesis and Structure of the Literary Field*, trans. S. Emanuel, Stanford: Stanford University Press.

Casanova, P. (2004), *The World Republic of Letters*, trans. M. B. DeBevoise, Cambridge; London: Harvard University Press.

Dobry, M. (2009), *Sociologie des crises politiques. La dynamique des mobilisations multisectorielles*, 3rd edn, Paris: Presses de Sciences Po.

Donizeau, P. and L. Dumont-Lewi (2019), 'Une *Orestie* franco-irakienne: Autour du projet *Looking for Oresteia*. Entretien avec Haythem Abderazzak, Yagoutha Belgacem et Célie Pauthe', *Théâtre/Public*, 233: 96–9.

Ǧāsim, M. (2019), 'Taqrir. . .D. Hayṯam ʿAbd al-Razzāq: al-muǧtamaʿ afḍal madrab li-l-mumaṯṯil', *al-Madā*, 3 March. Available online: https://almadapaper.net/view. php?cat=219750د. . .ﺮﯾﺮﻘﺗ (accessed 26 October 2022).

Hādī, S. (2004), 'Masraḥiyyat (Aʿtadir ustāḏī) rasamat ḫarīṭa ǧadīda li-l-l-masraḥ al-ʿirāqī', *al-Madā al-ṯaqāfī*, 25 October. Available online: www.almadapaper.net/ sub/10-236/10.pdf (last accessed 28 October 2022).

Han, J. P. and Y. Belgacem (2020), 'Paris, Amman, Oran, Bagdad, Besançon, Le Mans, Tunis, Redeyef. . ./Bārīs, ʿAmmān, Ūhrān, Baġdād, Bīzānsūn, Lū Mān, Tūnis al-ʿāṣima, al-Radayyif. . .', *Frictions*, 9: 22–35.

Ḥasan Mūsā, S. (2012), 'Hayṯam ʿAbd al-Razzāq: laysat hunāk malāmiḥ wāḍiḥa li-l-masraḥ baʿd 2003. Maʿa uǧūd masāḥa wāsiʿa li-ḥurriyyat al-taʿbīr, al-mumaṯṯil muʾallif faḍāʾ yaktub uǧūdahu fī-l-farāǧ al-masraḥī', *al-Tāḫī*, 18 November. Available online: www.altaakhipress.com/printart.php?art=20923 (accessed 28 October 2022).

Kudayir, D. A. (1987), 'Le théâtre irakien et l'influence du théâtre européen: 1880–1980', PhD diss., Université de Provence, Marseille.

al-Šarqī, Ǧ. (2021), 'Min ḏākirat al-iḍāʿah wa-l-tilifiziyūn. . . Laday-hi taʿāwwun iḫrāǧī wa-tamṯīlī maʿa Faransā wa-Almaniyā wa-akṯar al-duwwal al-ūrūbiyya. . . al-Zawrāʾ tastaʿriḍ masīrat al-fannān wa-l-tadrīsī al-duktūr Hayṯam ʿAbd al-Razzāq', *al-Zawrāʾ*, 20 December. Available online: www.alzawraapaper.com/content. php?id=334728 (accessed 28 October 2022).

Seddik, Y. (2020), 'Eschyle chez les Arabes/Isḫīlūs ʿind al-ʿarab', *Frictions*, 9: 110–15.

Sef, M. A. K. (1995), 'Le théâtre en Irak: histoire et changements, crises, mutations', PhD diss., Université Paris Diderot – Paris 7, Paris.

Suchet, M. (2013), 'Rythmer la langue/Yukonstyle', *Liberté*, 301: 52–3. Available online: www.erudit.org/en/journals/liberte/2013-n301-liberte0821/69938ac/ (accessed 28 October 2022).

Yousif, S. (1997), 'The People's Theater of Yusuf al-Ani', *Arab Studies Quarterly Journal*, 19(4): 65–93.

Part Three

Greek Tragedy, a Shared Heritage?

8

Ambivalence of Interpretation between Israel and France in Hanoch Levin's Theatre Tragic Materials

Emmanuelle Thiébot

Hanoch Levin (1943–99) is a prolific Israeli playwright who distinguished himself by his political work, which was once censored, and especially by causing disturbances to public order in Israel. His satirical cabarets in the aftermath of the 1967 war gained him widespread recognition; he embodied the ideals of Israel's left wing, criticizing the government's annexation policy. During his lifetime, he was the most taught Israeli playwright, 'in high schools and universities … He had access to all of his country's subsidised theatres, and it was with public funds that he almost set up a production per year' (Billard, Girard, Hispard 2011: 320).[1] He is also the founder of 'the Association of Dramatic Writers, whose aim is to defend their copyright in Israel against theatrical institutions' (Yaari 2006: 7)[2] and participated in the elaboration of a review combining theory and practice, theatre and research: *Teatron*. Levin died prematurely of cancer.

Levinian theatre is remarkable in the field of contemporary theatre for its ability to summon and reinvest many theatrical genres, as shown by Nurit Yaari (Yaari 2006). Hanoch Levin made a name for himself first by writing political satires, then by developing a modern tragic style imbued with ancient myths and with the rewriting of Greek classics. *The Trojan Women* and *Hecuba* by Euripides inspired him to write *The Lost Women of Troy* (*Nechot Troya*), written in 1982 during the Israeli invasion of Lebanon and staged in 1984. In his last play, sarcastically titled *The Lamenters* (*Habakhyanim*), medical staff perform the sufferings of *Agamemnon* (by Aeschylus) for their dying patients. These two plays have only been staged once in Israel. However, it is probably in the play *Murder* (*Retzakh*) that Levin reinvested the very substance of Greek tragedies, condensed to the extreme. Written after the murder of Yitzhak Rabin, it was staged in 1997 in Israel. Through quoting, rewriting, and employing the *mise en abyme*, Levin has explored Greek tragedy to the point of developing his own kind of modern tragedy. However, the author's introduction to Greek tragedy came late in his career. I propose here to expose the reasons and the consequences of his approach to Greek tragedy by placing the Levinian tragic works in the literary, historical and political context of Israel on the one hand, and in the context of their international reception on the other, particularly in France, where the author's first translations were published.

Levinian theatre is not monolithic at all, as it testifies to a journey in an intercultural society undeniably intertwined with the history of the Jewish diasporas and the colonization of Palestine. Greek tragedies were not reinvested in the theatrical practices of Jewish diasporas. Israeli theatre creates its identity with the sometimes contradictory legacies of the Yiddish and Hebrew languages, but also with the desire to modernize such an identity (Part 1). In this context, Levin began his career as a poet and lyricist, investing in the codes of popular theatrical traditions that have historically been undervalued. He is best known for his political satires and comedies. His late involvment with the genre of Greek tragedy appears to be a new attempt to challenge his fellow citizens on his country's political situation. This journey made him known as a politically engaged playwright and gradually legitimized his work (Part 2). Following his death, the cultural transfer of Levin's work to France was accompanied by analyses that linked it to more hegemonic literary and theatrical genres in Western countries. In addition to their dramaturgical function, the tragic materials that Levin borrows from Greek anticuity participate in a form of legitimization of his work in the institutional field that goes beyond Israeli borders, so much so that the tragic interpretation of his plays is pushed to the absurd, namely depoliticization (Part 3). The analysis proposed here is rooted in my point of view as a French researcher and cannot cover the entire reception of Levin's work in Israel. The mode of publicly financing theatre in Israel and France is, however, similar, as are possibly the processes of theatre legitimation (Thiébot 2019).

From the absence of Greek tragedy in theatre in Yiddish to classical theatrical literature in Hebrew: the birth of Israeli theatre

The 'humanism' dependent on ancient mythology is strictly incommunicable to a Yiddish audience. For example, a classical Greek chorus in Yiddish would produce a high comic effect. On the other hand, it is perfectly conceivable, and in the best style, in Hebrew.

Mandel 1965b: 1072[3]

This is what Arnold Mandel (1913–87) asserts in 1965 in the *Encyclopédie de la Pléiade*, an authoritative work in French theatre historiography: he immediately highlights a deep tension, marked by value judgements, between Yiddish and Hebrew. This French essayist, poet, novelist, and journalist received a traditional Jewish education. He defends the literary quality of theatre. According to Arnold Mandel, the development of a European form of theatre in Hebrew is desirable and indicates a movement of sacralization of language and theatrical literature. In addition to historical events, this process explains the lack of interest in Yiddish theatre until recently (Delaunay, Katuszewski, Lindenberg 2022). However, it is not just a question of language or aesthetics but of a political confrontation prior to the birth of Israel, which has had repercussions on the identity of Israeli theatre. It is necessary to briefly come back to it because Levin composes finely with all these heritages.

Arnold Mandel devotes a chapter to the 'spectacular aspects of Jewish ritual' (Mandel 1965a: 163–9) and another to 'Jewish theatres' and more precisely to modern Yiddish theatre (Mandel 1965b: 1058–78). Arnold Mandel believes that 'theatre arose as a phenomenon of foreign occupation', especially with regard to the Greek theatre and the Roman circus, which were condemned by rabbinism (ibid.: 1058). Theatre has developed heterogeneously among the established Jewish Diaspora around the world. First in the 'Syrian East' (Frezouls 1959), notably in Babylon, where there are the remains of a theatre from the Hellenistic period. The Hellenist theatre did not remain 'the prerogative neither of the city of Athens alone nor of the Dionysia alone' (Le Guen 1995: 61), and dramatic performances continued to increase over 'the whole perimeter of the Mediterranean basin' (id.). The success of this model has been the subject of various reappropriations up until Babylon (Le Guen, 2003).[4] Furthermore, the play *Exagōgē*, attributed to the Jewish author 'Ezekiel of Alexandria (5th century before the Christian era)' (Lipsyc 2012: 473), was written on the Greek model. According to Sonia Sarah Lipsyc, the 'birth of the tragedy in Greece and the narration of the Book of Esther ... [which] is precisely at the origin of the only living theatrical tradition among Jews, namely the Purim spiel or Purim play!' (Lipsyc 2012: 481). It was around the Purim celebration that a theatrical tradition was established in medieval Europe (from northern Italy to Ukraine, Lithuania, England, and the Netherlands). During the Purim games, which 'were freely inspired by passages from the Book of Esther or other episodes of the Bible . . . [and] were punctuated by songs, dances, mimes, and acrobatics', a specifically Jewish theatrical tradition developed in Yiddish from the Middle Ages. Arnold Mandel notes that the tradition of the 'Purim Play also exists in Spanish *Juderia* and in the Judeo-Arabic *Mellah*, [but] never developed enough to enter into 'theatre' phenomenology' (Mandel 1965b: 1060). This author recognizes artistic quality only in modern forms that break with the public address which characterizes popular theatres, therefore in Hebrew theatre, which, according to him, surpasses the 'most deplorable genre of Yiddish operetta' (Mandel 1965b: 1070).

The birth of Yiddish is linked to a linguistic and political schism between Eastern and Western Jews in Europe. Some Jews acculturate to the languages of the countries where they settle, while modern Yiddish develops in Eastern Europe, 'by and large adopting a more Semitic than Germanic morphology' (Mandel: 1064). Yiddish becomes 'an autonomous and properly expressive language of the Jewish multitudes of Eastern Europe' (idem), and it is in this context that a modern Yiddish theatre develops in Yiddishland. This term of recent use 'designates the area of Yiddish language and culture in Central and Eastern Europe, where the majority of the European Jewish population resided' (Bruttmann, Tarricone, C. 2018: 126) between the Middle Ages and the Second World War. Yiddishland brings together diverse Jewish populations: 'religious diversity . . . between liberals, orthodox, conservatives, or assimilated'; political diversity 'faced with the social question as with the national question, there are many parties and currents'; and 'ethnic diversity' (ibid.: 71). Arnold Mandel speaks of 'militant Yiddishism':

> The Yiddishists who promulgate the Jewish national sovereignty of 'Mammé-Lochenn' – 'the mother tongue', are also adversaries of hieratic and scholarly Hebrew . . .
>
> Mandel 1965b: 1064

The practise of Yiddish manifests an ideological war of languages between Hebrew (referring to Zionist values) and Yiddish which claims cultural autonomy or deterritorialization (Brossat, Izrine 2014). In her book *Theater and the Sacred in the Jewish Tradition*, Guila Clara Kessous renews the approach to the Jewish theatrical tradition in which Yiddish theatre finds its place among other currents and authors (Kessous 2012: 140). This work dealing with a Jewish theatrical tradition dates from 2012, hence still recent and little known. It is also subject to caution: the same year, in an article on Israeli theatre, Lily Perlemuter affirmed that 'the theatre ... has never been part of Hebrew civilization' (Perlemuter 2012: 465). The same mechanisms and arguments have been used to affirm the absence of theatrical tradition in the Arab world (Thiébot, 2019). A theatre in Hebrew existed before the twentieth century, according to Guila Clara Kessous. However, the theatre in Hebrew associated with the Zionist movement, which accompanies 'the great Jewish national impulse' (Mandel 1965b: 1073), dates from the beginning of the twentieth century. This political project is thought of by its founders as the creation of a European state in the East (Snir 2015) and therefore requires a national identity, whose primary issue is language. Hebrew was not reborn exclusively in Mandatory Palestine: the Habima (in Hebrew, 'the stage') theatre was created in Russia in 1918, and the troupe was supported by 'Stanislavski and Vakhtangov, two non-Jewish artists' (Mandel 1965b: 1074). Once again, the use of this language raises political and ideological issues.

> Gorki became Habima's tenacious defender, immediately becoming the target of violent attacks from Jewish communists of the Yevssektsia (the Jewish section of the People's Commissariat for Nationalities Affairs), demanding the prohibition of this theatre described as reactionary and capitalist, solely because of its use of Hebrew, which its detractors appear to have considered the language par excellence of heavy industry and high finance (id.).

The clash between the Yiddish anti-Zionists and the Hebrew Zionists took place against a backdrop of rising anti-Semitism throughout Europe, which overtook Yiddishland a few years later. However, the political schism is not limited to the Zionist project: Yiddish is regarded as a popular language depreciated by newly Hebrew scholars, whose defenders also oppose Judeo-Arabic culture. Reuven Snir reports on a controversy surrounding Israeli intellectuals, in particular the national poet Haïm Nachman Bialik (1873–1934), who said: 'I hate the Arabs, since they are like the Sephardim' (Snir 2015: 128). This posture 'reflects the hegemonic and canonical Hebrew attitude of the time towards Sephardic or Arabized Jews considered without distinction under the name of Sephardim – people who had an ancient culture in the past, neglected today' (id.). The use of Hebrew within a desired, dreamed-of, and hoped-for nation-state inscribes the Jews in modernity, which explains why Arnold Mandel wrote an article in 1965 that overvalued theatre in Hebrew and depreciated theatre in Yiddish. Hebrew symbolizes the language that saved the Jews from extermination.

Jewish theatre in Mandatory Palestine has therefore been the object of clashes between two political conceptions of theatre since the 1930s, one defended by the national poet Haïm Nachman Bialik, the other by Martin Buber (1878–1955), a philosopher, storyteller, and libertarian pedagogue of Israeli and Austrian nationality. This professor at the Hebrew University of Jerusalem is a Zionist opposed to the political line of Theodor Herlz and in favour of the creation of a binational state (Wolf 2008; Freddy 1980). On the one hand, 'Bialik affirms that theatre must present Jewish plays centred on Jewish history and tradition, while Buber thinks that Habima must broaden its horizon and strive to treat works belonging to the universal theatrical culture' (Perlemuter 2012: 458). According to his wishes, Bialik translated *The Dybbuk* by Shalom Anski (1863–1920) from Yiddish into Hebrew for the Habima Theatre, which presented this play abroad during the 'Palestinian Fortnight of the Hebrew Theatre' (Quinzaine Palestinienne du Théâtre Hébreu) in Paris in 1937. As for the Caméri theatre, it was founded in 1944 and became Tel Aviv municipal theatre in 1971. Around 1948, he produced *The Barber of Seville* by Beaumarchais, arousing public incomprehension: 'The nation needs to model a collective identity, and the theatre at the time must participate in this creation' (Wexler 2011: 306–7). It is in this historical context and with the weight of these legacies that Levin becomes the most important and the most prolific Israeli playwright (Yaari 2006: 5), playing on these two tables (identity and universalism) throughout his career.

The composite style of Hanoch Levin's theatre, from the comic to the tragic: between effectiveness and misunderstandings

Hanoch Levin was born in 1943 in Mandatory Palestine in a 'religious family from a prestigious line of Hasidic rabbis from Poland. He received a religious education and grew up in a modest neighbourhood in southern Tel Aviv, where his father ran a grocery shop. He was twelve years old when he lost his father and was forced to leave school. He finished high school while working as a delivery boy. Levin came of age in the 1960s, in a society marked by deep divisions between native-born and new immigrants, between rich and poor, between Sephardim and Ashkenazi, between Jews and Arabs. These cleavages only worsen after the Six-Day War, when he makes his debut as a playwright' (Yaari 2006: 6–7). In this intercultural society, his theatre deals with spectacular legacies. He drew inspiration from the most popular shows reminiscent of depreciated Yiddish forms: cabarets, operettas, satirical sketches, grotesque farces, and the noblest forms of theatrical literature: ancient and modern comedy and tragedy. Without means at the beginning, he writes poetry, songs and sketches.

The Queen of the Bathroom (*Malkat Ha'Ambatya*) is the play that 'marks Levin's transition from the margins to the Centre of Tel Aviv theatre creation' (Yaari 2006: 22). In this cabaret alternating between sketches and songs, the author criticizes the consequences of the 1967 war. He places the responsibility for the problems caused by the occupation of the territories on the Israelis. He also points to 'the introduction of religion into the realm of politics and the strengthening of the national and religious myth' (id.). Levin depicts a society divided into 'classes or ethnicities' (ibid.: 23) with Jews of Sephardic origin serving as cannon fodder, and 'the Arabs at the bottom of the ladder ... – barbaric, ignorant, inhuman' (id.). The cabaret is built on a quid pro quo that Levin has already developed in his previous satires: he makes a connection between '"holy places"; and what is euphemistically called in Hebrew the "holy place", i.e., the toilet' (ibid.: 24). Levin undermines the discourse of national unity by developing dramatic situations in a family setting that becomes the site of a political confrontation. In an ordinary family, the Woman decides to chase away the roommate who is her Husband's cousin. Faced with his resistance, all the family members take over the bathroom and proclaim their sovereignty, one and indivisible, over the 'Great kingdom of the toilet' (Yaari 2004: 218). Levin mobilizes the nationalist and unitary discourse and destroys it in song. To keep this show on the bill despite external pressure, Levin is supported by the Tel Aviv Municipal Theatre, the Cameri. But he also worked for other theatres, such as the Habima Theatre, the Haifa City Theatre, and the Khan Theatre in Jerusalem (Yaari 2006: 7). In general, his satirical cabarets are based on ostentation, social satire (triviality of language) and political satire (in the sense that he seeks dissensus). Levin's legitimacy was to be built on a dissension regarding the political dimension of his first plays, which legitimizes his theatre by giving it a valued critical function. Many of the theatrical performances in Israel have led to public disturbances (Nurit Yaari reports fights in the theatre, false bomb threats, stink bombs thrown, etc.), but only one of Levin's plays has been partially censored by the Israeli government. It is a cabaret not translated into French (Le patriote – 1980),

> which tells the story of a settler who moves into the occupied territories and at the same time buys land in California. There is a sketch that shows a fascist Israeli settler calling his Arab servant to burn his fingers on the Shabbat candles. This moment was censored. So, when the show was performed, the lights were turned back on and another actor in the audience stood up and said: 'I will now read to you what was censored'.
>
> Krawczyk 2015: 445

In the Israeli context, Levin thus tends to counter the hegemonic discourse in all its forms. It is less a question of arguing and articulating a clear political discourse than of countering the dominant representations. Thus, Nurit Yaari stresses the importance for Levin of developing a dramaturgy 'that invites us to open our hearts and love what is human, weak, fearful, and illusory' (Yaari 2008). In fact, this dimension of the human condition is not part of the Zionist warrior imagery and governmental policies relay a conquering and glorious image. The translator Laurence Sendrowicz and Levin himself have emphasized how these plays cannot be understood outside their context and time. Laurence Sendrowicz reports Levin's reluctance to translate his entire body of work, saying that he had to 'fight' (Yaari 2008: 111–17) with himself and his friends, and that he did not care about being performed outside the borders of Israel. What mattered to Levin was to write for Israelis, to be read and heard (id.) by them. It was with this concern to appeal to his fellow citizens that he then took on the tragic genre.

Levin wrote *The Lost Women of Troy* in 1982, during the Israeli invasion of Lebanon. It is a rewriting of Euripides' *Trojan Women* that concludes his trilogy on the Trojan War, also including the character and fable of Hecuba. By taking the side of the defeated, the author denounces the futility of war in a succession of tableaux. The violence rises to a crescendo and seems endless. *The Trojan Women* is a linear tragedy, without action, and Euripides' most pathetic, whereas Hecuba depicts the revenge and the end of one of these defeated women. One difference between Euripides' and Levin's texts is the absence of the gods: Poseidon and Athena open the prologue to *The Trojan Women*. In Levin's rewriting, no God can explain anything, and it is even his own gesture that the artist questions in the first place:

Neoptolemus
The great artist up above is calmly sketching the final lines
into the picture of war: a column of smoke rising above a demolished house,
a dress rolling in the dust, a woman, her hair in disarray, being shoved by a
soldier into the town square.
Here too is a dog busying itself with the entrails
of a rotting human corpse.
The picture is perfectly complete.

Levin 2020a: 106

From the very first lines, Levin underlines his own contradictions by questioning the role of the artist who is content to report events from a distance, with an indecent concern for realism. The painting Levin speaks of is the writing through which he seeks to make the horror of war heard. His text is reminiscent of the well-known Greek tragedies, but without the grandiloquence and emphasis characteristic of the genre. Between the dialogues of the famous Greek characters, Levin inserts trivial and vulgar interjections from the chorus of captives, whose more modern language brings it closer to the comic genre with which he is familiar. The chorus sings a lullaby-like text as Astyanax is led to his death.

> PRISONERS
> Your day is over, child, and so is the world,
> night has come and marches on,
> you had a ball to play with but
> it has dropped out of your hands, and gone.
> The world we lost will return in a dream,
> like an old, forgotten toy;
> close your eyes, rest your head on my lap,
> we'll say good night and sleep, sweet boy.
>
> Ibid.: 138

Levin also mocks the sanctimonious speech that the messenger Talthybios delivers to Andromache when he comes to fetch her child for execution, forcing his cynicism:

> TALTHYBIOS
> Accept the sentence, be wise: you are a mother, yours is a mother's heart,
> but in the world there are not only mothers.
>
> Ibid.: 133

The situation of women handed over to conquering males draws a parallel with the asymmetry of power relations in the conflict. The play was written during the Israeli invasion of Lebanon in 1982 and performed in 1984 when the responsibility of the Israeli army was denounced. The Sabra and Shatila massacres took place 'with the so-called silent approval and non-intervention of Israeli army units close to the scene' (Yaari 2008: 32). The Peace Now movement is at its peak: 'some 400,000 Israelis gather in Tel Aviv's City Hall Square to demonstrate against the right-wing government' (id.). During a rally, a peace activist, Emile Greenzweig, is killed in an attack by the Israeli far right, bringing the political divisions between Israelis to the fore. If the play is therefore set in a particularly tense political context, its reception is dependent on it. Levin tries to activate the critical reflexive function of the theatre, with the major difference that, in the

Israeli context, the whole of the city does not attend these performances which no longer disturb public order. The author was certainly aware of this when he wrote *The Lamenters* a few years later (Levin 2011: 145–85).

In this final play, the nursing staff of a Calcutta hospital try to distract their patients from an inevitable death by acting out Agamemnon's suffering: it is a *mise en abyme* of the first part of Aeschylus' *Oresteia*, which relates the return of the conquering hero to his wife Clytemnestra, accompanied by her captive, Cassandra. Cassandra predicts the death of Agamemnon, who will indeed be murdered by his wife. Levin was himself on his deathbed and the play was staged after his death in 2000. He then put into perspective his work as a playwright who is always looking for a style of writing that can touch his audience as well as depict the violent political reality of his country. In *The Lamenters*, the hospital staff announce that they are going to stage a Greek tragedy for hospice patients: the 'longest-term resident' (HP 1), the recently arrived resident'(HP 2), the 'newest arrival' (HP 3) and the Exhausted Old Man who are painfully sharing the same bed.[5] But from the very beginning, after the Orderly has announced the title of the play, none of the three characters understands the choice:

HP1
Why Greek?
HP2
Why old?
ORDERLY
Terrible things happen in it, which will remind you of your condition.
HP2
Why?
ORDERLY
You've been warned – there will be blood!
HP2
Why blood? Don't you have a comedy? A funny sketch? A ditty?
HP1 [*just waking up*]
...A dancing girl with a bare ass?

Levin 2020b: 242–3

This brief exchange already reflects the misunderstandings between Levin and the expectations of his audience, as reported by Laurence Sendrowciz in one of the few interviews with the author: 'for him, the theatre is a boxing ring. All he does is throw punches, so he doesn't understand why the audience laughs. He wants to knock the spectator out, to hit him, like in a boxing match' (Krawczyk

2015: 443). A little further on in *The Lamenters*, Cassandra takes offence at the indifference of her audience (the people):

CASSANDRA. – There will be murder here. Right here. An axe will be swung. Blood will spurt. And everyone stands and watches. No one moves, no one utters a word, no one puts out a hand to stop the blade already raised in the air. And this I do not understand either: that I, too, will not shout, will not protest . . .

Ibid.: 241

While the audience of the three agonists regularly fall asleep during the show, their awakening at the end of the first part reinforces the misunderstandings, as well as Levin's message:

HP1
Didn't make me laugh, that comedy. The one guy said this, then the other guy stood like that, and fell like this.
HP2
And then the one guy said this, and she came in and said that.
HP1
And then she told him this, and he told her that.
HP2
And she answered him this.
HP1
And he told her that.

Ibid.: 242

This comical exchange of about ten lines reflects the characters' inability to understand the play and ends with the eldest patient, the 'Exhausted old man' waking up and the hospice Patient 1 proudly announcing: 'You were asleep, Grandpa. There was a whole comedy here' (ibid.: 243). The second part of *Agamemnon*'s *mise en abyme* again emphasizes the inaction of the people in the face of death and the horrors they witness. *The Lamenters* ends between laughter and tears with the young nurse embracing the senile old man who, at death's door, demands attention and then grotesque sexual favours. The young nurse laughs and tells him that he is a clown and concludes the play with the words: 'We are all clowns' (ibid.: 241). In this testamentary play, tragedy, and comedy rub shoulders and shed light on Levin's path, as he never wanted to be confined to a specific category or genre. The theatre serves his project: he wants to transform it into a boxing ring. But if this mixture of genres and codes has already disconcerted the Israeli public, the reception abroad, and particularly in France, will be in the mode of the absurd and of depoliticization.

From the tragic to the absurd: the depoliticization of Levin's theatre in France

One of Hanoch Levin' plays, *Murder*, built on the model of Greek tragedy, is a good example of how the political dimension of Levin's work is neutralized when it is staged in France. The play is minimalist, Levin seeks a condensed and concise writing style, as he did in *Women of Troy* and *The Lamenters*. The initial situation is that of a teenager, the 'Arab boy' who has been tortured by three soldiers with varying degrees of experience: the Pale Soldier (we guess he is a novice), the Flushed Soldier who is an initiate, and the Tanned Soldier who is indifferent to the violence. The Father appears and observes the wounds of his dead son. Each of his observations is minimized by the soldiers who do not grant him the status of a human being. As the three soldiers set up an ambush to kill this embarrassing father as a traitor, a messenger arrives and proclaims peace.

MESSENGER
The time of murder is over. The time of murder is over.
The furious rage has become to an end, winds of reconciliation are blowing, the time of murder is finished. People look at the bad times and ask: How could we? How was it possible? Our children will not understand, our grandchildren will laugh, and our great-grandchildren will not know what it's about. They will study history with a shrug. With a smile of waking from a deep sleep, people say to one another: Peace. [*Exits.*]

Levin and Harshav 2002: 132

This messenger, worthy of the Greek tragedies, interrupts the action. The soldiers leave. Act II takes place three years later and seems at first to have no link with the first act. A wedding ceremony has taken place. The bride and groom have left the guests on the beach. The father (from Act I) observes the groom and thinks he recognizes him as one of the soldiers who murdered his son. Despite the groom's denials, the father shoots him in the head, rapes the bride and shoots her in turn after she asks:

BRIDE
Why...? Why...?
THE FATHER
'Why'. We're long past the question 'why'. 'Why'. The question 'why' shouldn't be asked. The question 'why' belongs to other times.
[*He shoots her in the head and exits.*]

Ibid: 142

The exchange refers to the situation in Act I, when the Father was questioning the soldiers in vain, as they refused to explain why they had tortured the teenager to death.

Act III takes place five years later, in a 'rich suburb' at night (ibid.: 144) in which two 'old and poor' Arab workers are wandering: there are the 'Wrecked Arab Laborer' and the 'Cracked Arab Laborer'. Both look at the villas of the rich, fantasizing about their way of life and the women who live there, and begin to masturbate, out of frustration. 'Orange Whore' enters. She introduces herself as a 'housewife' (ibid.: 145) from the neighbourhood who does not appreciate seeing those she calls Arab garbagemen. She seduces the cracked worker and, with the help of 'Pink Whore' and 'Purple Whore', takes advantage of his intoxication and weakness to search his pockets, convinced that he has robbed in the neighbourhood villas. While they are kicking him, disappointed at not having found anything on him, an explosion sounds and the panicked 'chorus of neighbours' arrives: an attack has taken place at the end of the street. The orange whore accuses the almost powerless worker. The neighbours lynch him. A man who is passing by ('The Passerby') tries to stop the massacre but the orange whore continues her racist logorrhoea. The little sister of the bride from Act II then arrives and says she recognizes the murderer. He is killed by the whores and then decapitated. The pink whore wants to spit on him and the Passerby who tried to stop the massacre questions her: 'Why? He's dead! Why do you want to spit on him?' (ibid.: 150). He does not get an answer to his question, which echoes what happened in the first acts. The pink whore urinates into the decapitated head. The officer and soldiers enter the scene and notice the body and head. After checking the papers which prove that he is 'not one of [them]', the officer questions the orange whore: 'why did you do that?' (ibid.). It is at this point that the Messenger, very similar to that of Greek tragedies, enters to put an end to the action:

MESSENGER
   The time of calm is over. The time of calm is over. The winds of reconciliation have flown away, war is at the gate. People look at the illusory calm and ask: How could we? How was it possible? Our children will not understand, our grandchildren will laugh, our great-grandchildren will not know what it's above. They will study history with a shrug. With a smile of waking from a deep sleep, people say to one another: To arms.

                                                                            Ibid.

This speech transforms the officer's behaviour who concludes Act III:

THE OFFICER

[*gives the severed head to the Orange Whore*] Straighten your dress and lift up your head. At this moment you have entered history, you are inscribed in the annals of our nation.

Ibid.

Finally, in the play's very short epilogue, the Pale Soldier from Act I returns. He is now old and blind. He speaks to an elderly Arab man and explains that there was no legitimate reason to kill his son.

Murder is an extremely violent play, but Levin keeps his composite writing style: he inserts grotesque trivial situations (often related to sex) between the acts of violence (except in Act I). The structure of Greek tragedy is present and condensed to the extreme with the messenger whose words are repeated almost identically whether he is announcing war or peace; the anonymous characters principally defined by their kinship and their position on one side or the other; the passionate revenge motivated by hubris. Although there is no chorus, small groups of characters act in concert (the soldiers, the whores), especially the bystanders who lynch the worker at the end of the play. The construction of these three acts and the epilogue create a coherent sequence of events and a gradation of violence. The starting point is the impunity of the soldiers who hold the legitimacy of the use of force and do not question it. This is the meaning of the 'why' repeated in the following acts.

Levin denounces the military occupation in the first place. The title of the play, '*Murder*' in the singular, clearly indicates a starting point, an injustice. Here, the Israeli playwright challenges his audience on the need to get out of a mechanism of violence that begins with the military occupation. Let us remember that, since the 1967 war, Levin has never ceased to assert the need to return the occupied territories. In the light of the current political situation in Israel, there is a thin line between tragedy and absurdity in this play: Levin wrote it just after the first Intifada and the assassination of Prime Minister Yitzhak Rabin. Hope follows despair after the Oslo Accords' failure, each new confrontation erasing the reasons for the previous one. We should analyse more closely what the tragic form allows here: it is probably an exercise in style and a diversion used by Levin as part of his political critique at the same time. We should also show that there is a thin line between tragedy and absurdity, which probably has to do with the interpretation of the logic of *fatum* which is at work in *Murder*. Have we reached a point where the conflict and the fate of the Palestinians can no longer be treated solely in the tone of the absurd?

However, Levin's work has circulated in France with a decontextualization that renders the criticism of the Israeli government ineffective. The various stagings and the publishing process have paradoxically depoliticized Levin's plays, whereas it is precisely his sulfurous reputation that has allowed his work to be recognized. The enthusiasm for Levin was accompanied by a reading of his plays as belonging to the genre of the theatre of the absurd (Billard, M., Girard, C. and Hispard, G. 2011: 328). It is Levin's cabarets and comedies that are most frequently staged in France, while plays inspired by the Greek tragedies have been published but never staged. This is a particularity in the field of contemporary French theatre where it is difficult to have a text published that has not been performed or whose production is not planned.

In an article titled 'Mettre en scène les textes de Hanokh Levin' (Jolly, G. 2007), the author and academic Geneviève Jolly begins by pointing out the 'militant', 'historically dated', 'geographically localized' (ibid.: 6) dimension of Levin's work, which is marked by 'the extermination and exile of the Jews', the 'conflicts that followed the foundation of the State of Israel', and the 'difficult cohabitation with the Palestinians' (ibid.); before asserting:

> But as this theatre is decontextualized, in the sense that the author does not necessarily specify the geographical or temporal universe in which the characters move, [it] raises other difficulties, imposes (or not) choices for their staging and the way they are performed today in France . . . Thus, in Stéphane Braunschweig's production of *L'Enfant rêve*, the soldiers who persecute certain characters and ask the child and his mother to leave are dressed in Nazi uniforms, whereas Clément Poiré chooses to represent *Meurtre* [Murder] in a 'neutral' universe . . .
>
> Ibid.[6]

Not all Levin's plays are therefore decontextualized: this does not seem to be the case for those that may evoke – even implicitly – the Shoah, such as *L'Enfant rêve* (The Dream Child) directed by Stéphane Braunschweig (2006). On the other hand *Murder* has been written in a strong context: it was created in 1997 and is set against the backdrop of the first Intifada, the assassination of Prime Minister Yitzhak Rabin, and the announced failure of the Oslo Accords. But Clément Poirée, when he staged the play in France in 2005, neutralized its political contextualization to make it abstract:

> Levin develops the complex subject of violence as a vicious circle: how it animates and submerges beings . . . In a clever role-playing, he shows that the values of justice and responsibility are not enough to distinguish between victim

and executioner: a salutary reminder that strips barbarism of its external justifications in order to better show its profound truth: that of human nature.

Poirée 2005[7]

The position of neutrality in the staging is not one of neutrality: the discourse carried by Clément Poirée appears to be an hegemonic political discourse insofar as it establishes the reversibility of the executioners and the victims (Neveux 2011: 509–30). This approach to Levin's work in the mode of the absurd has become prevalent. Thus, paradoxically, Levin's theatre, initially written to challenge hegemonic representations, has become part of a dominant mode of theatrical representation in France, that of a post-political (Hamidi-Kim 2013) or one-dimensional (Neveux 2013) theatre, which asserts itself as universal precisely because it obliterates the identity dimension of the theatre.

Conclusion

The distance from the Israeli – and Israeli-Palestinian – situation and the neutral interpretation of these texts whose political dimension is erased – except when it comes to the Shoah, which belongs to the past – creates a real paradox in the interpretation of Levin's theatre in France: it seems to be forbidden to speak about the present time even though it is Levin's ability to speak about the present that gave him recognition. The place of tragedies in his work confirms this, since he uses tragic material to make a constant political satire, which becomes audible and acceptable when it passes through the prism of Greek tragedy (well identified as such: *The Lost Women of Troy*, *The Lamentors*) in a strictly Israeli context. Levin's tragedies make sense in the face of a specific political situation, and that is why he reinvested some Greek tragedies: to give them a new meaning. At the same time, Levin permanently seeks to challenge his audience, to make them react. It is probably a reason why he mixes the tragic with the comic and the trivial, refusing to leave the audience in peace. But this mixing of genres can also confuse the subject matter and make the tragic material work differently, leading it towards the absurd and depoliticized.

To conclude, it seems important to remember that, as he was seeking political effectiveness from the stage, Hanoch Levin not wish to see his work translated, because he probably feared a 'ridiculous recuperation' (Billard, Girard and Hispard 2011: 323).

Notes

1   Personal translation from French.
2   All the quotations from Nurit Yaari in this chapter have been translated from French by myself.
3   All the quotations from Arnold Mandel in this chapter have been translated from French by myself.
4   All quotations from Le Guen in this chapter have been translated from French by myself.
5   For the translation of the characters' names, see the following translation from Hebrew: Levin, H. and Harshav, B. (2002). 'MURDER: A Play in Three Acts and an Epilogue', *Hebrew Studies*, 43, 127–51. www.jstor.org/stable/27913597.
6   Personal translation.
7   Personal translation.

References

Delaunay, L., P. Katuszewski and J. Lindenberg (2022), 'Retour sur l'histoire du théâtre yiddish', *Revue d'Histoire du Théâtre*, 294.

Billard, M., C. Girard and G. Hispard (2011), '"La vie est une guerre permanente": entretien avec Laurence Sendrowicz', in D. Lescot and L. Veray (eds), *Les Mises en scène de la guerre au XXe siècle,* 319–29, Paris: Nouveau Monde.

Bruttmann, T. and C. Tarricone (2018), *Les 100 mots de la Shoah*, Paris: Presses Universitaires de France.

Brossat, A. and J.-M. Izrine (2014), 'Le Yiddishland, une déterritorialisation révolutionnaire', *Chimères*, 83: 103–8.

Frezouls E. (1959), 'Recherches sur les théâtres de l'Orient syrien', *Syria*, 36, fascicule 3–4: 202–28.

Hamidi-Kim, B. (2013), *Les Cités du théâtre politique en France depuis 1989*, Montpellier: L'Entretemps, 2013.

Jolly, G. (2007), *Mettre en scène les textes de Hanokh Levin*, Strasbourg: Université Marc Bloch.

Kessous, G. C. (2012), *Théâtre et sacré dans la tradition juive*, Paris: Presses Universitaires de France.

Krawczyk J. (2015), 'Agresser le spectateur: généalogie d'une politique: Edward Bond, Rodrigo Garcia, Hankoh Levin', PhD diss., Université Paris 3, Paris.

Le Guen, B. (1995), 'Théâtre et cités à l'époque hellénistique', *Revue des Études Grecques*, 108: 59–90.

Le Guen, B. (2003), 'Théâtre, cités et royaumes en Anatolie et au Proche-Orient de la mort d'Alexandre le Grand aux conquêtes de Pompée', in F. Prost, *L'Orient méditerranéen de la mort d'Alexandre aux campagnes de Pompée: Cités et royaumes à l'époque hellénistique*, 329–55, Rennes: Presses universitaires de Rennes.

Levin, H. and B. Harshav (2002), 'MURDER: A Play in Three Acts and an Epilogue', *Hebrew Studies*, 43: 127–51.

Levin, H. (2020a), *The Lost Women of Troy*, trans. N. Tammuz, *Selected Plays Two*, London: Bloomsbury, 2020.

Levin Hanoch (2020b), *The Lamenters*, trans. J. Cohen, E. Fallenberg, *Selected Plays Three*, London: Bloomsbury, 2020.

Lipsyc S. S. (2012), 'Talmud et théâtre: Genèse d'une réflexion métaphysique et sociologique sur le théâtre juif', in E. Feuillebois-Pierunek, *Théâtres d'Asie et d'Orient: Traditions, rencontres, métissages*, 469–86, Bruxelles: Peter Lang.

Neveux, O. (2013), *Politiques du spectateur: Les enjeux du théâtre politique aujourd'hui*, Paris: La Découverte.

Neveux, O. (2011), 'Présences critiques de l'impérialisme dans le théâtre contemporain', in D. Lescot and L. Veray (eds), *Les mises en scène de la guerre au XXème siècle: théâtre et cinéma*, 509–30, Paris: Nouveau monde.

Mandel, A. (1965), 'Aspects spectaculaires du rituel juif', in G. Dumur (ed.), *Encyclopédie de la Pléiade: Histoire des spectacles*, 163–9. Paris: Gallimard.

Mandel, A. (1965), 'Les Théâtres juifs', in G. Dumur (ed.), *Encyclopédie de la Pléiade: Histoire des spectacles*, 1058–78, Paris: Gallimard.

Perlemuter, L. (2012), 'Le théâtre israélien', in E. Feuillebois-Pierunek (ed.), *Théâtres d'Asie et d'Orient,* 465–7, Bruxelles: Peter Lang.

Poirée, C. (2005), 'La violence comme cercle [note d'intention]', *Meurtre, dossier pédagogique*, Théâtre de la Tempête. Available online: www.la-tempete.fr/ saison/2005-2006/spectacles/meurtre-352.

Snir, R. (2015), *Who Needs Arab-Jewish Identity? Interpellation, Exclusion, and Inessential Solidarities*, Leiden/Boston: Brill.

Wolf, S. (2008), '"Le vrai lieu de sa réalisation est la communauté": L'amitié intellectuelle entre Landauer et Buber', in A. Bertolo (ed.), *Juifs et anarchistes: Histoire d'une rencontre*, 75–89, Paris: Éditions de l'Éclat.

Raphaël, F. (1980), 'Le sionisme de Martin Buber', *Esprit* 38(2): 76–108.

Thiébot, E. (2019), 'Dramaturg(i)es du conflit israélo-palestinien en France: entre assignations identitaires et résistances', PhD diss., Université Caen Normandie. Available online: https://tel.archives-ouvertes.fr/tel-02864282v2.

Wexler, Z. (2011), 'Israël, le théâtre de la guerre', in D. Lescot and L. Véray (eds), *Les mises en scène de la guerre au XXème siècle: théâtre et cinéma*, 299–310, Paris: Nouveau monde.

Yaari, N. (2004), 'Les pièces politiques: L'occupation, la malédiction des vainqueurs', in H. Levin, *Théâtre Choisi III pièces politiques,* 217–20. Montreuil-sous-bois: Éditions Théâtrales.

Yaari, N. (2006), *Le théâtre de Hanokh Levin*, Montreuil-sous-bois: Éditions Théâtrales.

9

Sophocles' *Antigone* by French Director Adel Hakim (2011)

Using Greek Tragedy to Pay Tribute to Palestinian Resistance

Astrid Chabrat-Kajdan

In 2011 Sophocles' *Antigone* premiered at the Palestinian National Theatre (PNT) in Jerusalem, Palestine. The production was directed by Adel Hakim, author, director and former director of the Théâtre des Quartiers d'Ivry (TQI) in France.[1] *Antigone* is the biggest success of the French institution in terms of the number of representations on European institutional stages, as well as in terms of recognition by peers, journalists and audiences. It also represents a considerable success for the Palestinian theatre, in terms of international touring and programming on institutional stages. In contrast with Hakim's success, Palestinian theatrical productions or those relating to the Palestinian question struggle to find their way onto European institutional stages. They often remain limited to activist and associative networks. Similarly, when, following the tour of *Antigone*, Hakim decided to write a contemporary tragedy about the Israeli-Palestinian conflict from the end of the Second World War until the first *intifada*, entitled *Des Roses et du Jasmin* (Roses and Jasmine), he experienced scheduling difficulties. The success of Hakim's *Antigone* is thus a noticeable fact. This chapter aims to question this success through the study of the different stages of the creative process.

In the first part, I will analyse the production stage of the show in light of the fact that it already fulfils a condition for the success of *Antigone* outside Palestine. As talking about Palestine can be a challenge even within a cultural institution,[2] Sophocles' text and its translation as well as Adel Hakim's staging have established the possibility of the play's touring success. Consequently, Adel Hakim's translation and staging choices have to be questioned in a second part. I shall finally attempt to uncover the kind of narrative *Antigone* delivers on the 'Palestine Question'.[3] To tackle these questions, I will rely on fieldwork carried out at both the TQI and the PNT in 2016 and 2017, including the second French tour of the show in 2017.

(Co)producing *Antigone* between France and Palestine

Adel Hakim was born in Giza, Egypt, close to Cairo (Hakim 2016: 2) in October 1953 and died in Ivry-sur-Seine, France, in August 2017. After his childhood in Egypt and his schooling with the Jesuits in Lebanon, he moved to France in 1972 where he completed a PhD in philosophy and trained in theatre with Ariane Mnouchkine[4] and John Strasberg.[5] With the French actress and director Elisabeth Chailloux, they created the Théâtre de la Balance company in 1994 and then shared the direction of the TQI founded by Antoine Vitez in 1972, from 1992 until Hakim's death in 2017. In 2003, the French Ministry of Culture decided to make the TQI a National Dramatic Centre (CDN). The CDN label is awarded to theatres run by 'artists whose project is selected by an assembly composed of members of the State and members of local authorities'[6] (TQI website). The CDNs are 'structuring tools of the cultural decentralization policy at the service of contemporary creation and theatrical emergence in the regions' (ibid.). In addition to subsidies, they receive various types of support from the State and local authorities to guarantee the material conditions necessary for their artistic missions and responsibilities, such as an operational venue, a work team and technical equipment. However, for thirteen years the municipality did not find a suitable venue for the TQI in Ivry-sur-Seine. So, it was only in 2016, when it moved to the Manufacture des Oeillets, a former metallurgical factory in Ivry-sur-Seine, that the TQI truly became a CDN.

The theatre's structural project is based on two strong lines. The first is part of a legacy and consists of maintaining and assuring the flourishing development of the amateur theatre workshops set up by Catherine Dasté, a French actress and director who directed the TQI from 1985 to 1992. The second is an initiative of Adel Hakim and is entitled 'Théâtre des Quartiers du monde'.[7] The aim of this project is to develop sustainable collaborations – from training workshops to produce creations – with partners in 'peripheral' countries[8] (ibid.: 14). It is largely thanks to this guideline that the theatre has been granted the CDN label by the French Ministry of Culture. Hakim's foreign collaborations were mainly developed in Chile, but in 2011 Hakim opens a partnership with the TNP in East Jerusalem and chooses Sophocles' *Antigone* to inaugurate it.

In Palestine, the PNT located in Jerusalem is, like all the theatres in the Occupied Territories, supported by foreign funding since the Oslo Accords[9] of

1993. The aim of these agreements is to establish a self-governing Palestinian administration, called the Palestinian Authority, which potentially makes the transition to an independent Palestinian state. Since the end of the probationary period, the occupation has continued, as has the establishment of Israeli settlements, and the idea of a Palestinian state is still but a mere shadow. Foreign aid, which was supposed to encourage the creation of a Palestinian state, is becoming unavoidable in the context of an impossible rise of an autonomous Palestinian economy in the conditions of occupation. Since then, international donors have assisted Palestinian society despite the occupation. Theatrical activity is no exception and theatres therefore turn to the foreign donors who are providing financial aid to Palestine, led by the European Union's institutions and European countries. While foreign funds have contributed in developing a 'permanent theatrical industry' (Al-Saber 2021: xi), they are allocated under conditions that may be motivated by political strategies.[10] Moreover, since the Oslo Accords, collaborations between Palestinian and European institutions and artists have multiplied. They can represent an alternative to foreign funding, since they are not, at first sight, conditioned by political criteria, because the collaborations are primarily between one institution and another or even between one artist and another. They can allow for a sustainable partnership for Palestinian theatres, as opposed to requests for funds allocated for a specific project limited by time and subject to criteria. A partnership with a European institution or artist can contribute to the visibility of Palestinian artists on the one hand, and the visibility of Palestinian issues on international institutional stages on the other. It is therefore the combination of obtaining foreign funding and developing collaborations that can ensure the professionalization and development of Palestinian theatres and their inclusion in the international field of performing arts.

The PNT is much more subject to foreign donors because of its location in East Jerusalem. The city is administered by Israel and the Palestinian Authority is prohibited from subsidizing institutions located in the city. The theatre cannot therefore be supported by its own ministry. The Oslo Accords also fragmented the territory, and the city of Jerusalem is only accessible to Palestinians from the Occupied Territories if they obtain a permit from the Israeli authorities. On the eve of the (co)production of *Antigone*, the TNP was going through a particularly difficult period; its very survival was threatened. The co-founder and director of the company behind the PNT, François Abou Salem, died on 1 October 2011 and the theatre was accumulating financial and managerial problems (Chabrat-Kajdan 2017). Adel Hakim and the TQI team were therefore obliged to review their expectations: it was not possible to set up a fair sharing of production costs in view of the PNT's situation.

However, *Antigone*'s contracts reveal that Adel Hakim decided nonetheless to give this partnership the form of a co-production.[11] The choice of co-production is essential, even if the two parties to the contract cannot contribute equal amounts of money. The PNT needs to be able to justify concrete activities. A co-production like this one can consolidate the theatre, protect it from possible closures by the Israeli authorities and give it credibility in the eyes of future foreign donors. The East Jerusalem theatre also needs to prove that it is capable of conducting partnerships with foreign countries. The partnership with the future French CDN is a windfall. Adel Hakim and the administrative team of the TQI decide to opt for a bipartite co-production contract. This arrangement has several advantages. Under it, the PNT provides a lump sum contribution and not a percentage of the overall production cost of the play; it does not engage the Palestinian theatre – designated as the co-producer, when the TQI is the producer – in case of financial losses, since the parties are not jointly responsible. Both parties own the exploitation rights in the geographical areas defined by the contract (partnership and co-production agreement). However, an asymmetry persists: the PNT owns the rights in Israel and the Palestinian Territories only, while the French theatre owns them in Europe and the rest of the world. When touring outside Palestine, the French institution signs individual contracts with each Palestinian actor. Nevertheless, this allows the Palestinian theatre to avoid paying salaries in countries outside of Israel and Palestine, which are often higher due to charges.

Adel Hakim has set himself a mission that goes beyond co-production: to help the PNT by trying to provide the necessary conditions to guarantee its survival and functioning. It turns out that the form of the collaboration is a construction that reflects both the difficulties of the Jerusalem theatre and the strong asymmetry between the material and political contexts of the two theatres. The production step creates an unbalanced power relationship on several levels. This collaboration reveals, in spite of everything, the political commitment of the French director to the Jerusalem theatre and, more broadly, to the Palestinian cause. An artist cannot announce a partnership with Palestine without showing his position on the Israeli-Palestinian conflict. Establishing a partnership with Palestine does not just imply artistic and financial collaboration of the kind of international co-productions that are increasingly common in the globalized performing arts market. On the contrary, they have the effect of helping to maintain and even strengthen Palestinian theatres and artists.

Hence, *Antigone* initiated a partnership comprising three collaborations.[12] At first, the choice of this play surprised the Palestinian partners. In the history of Palestinian theatre, only a few theatrical productions from Jerusalem and the Palestinian territories were Greek tragedies. In each case, the Greek texts are adapted, or used as a reference. In 2014, the play *This Flesh is Mine,* adapted from Homer's *Iliad,* premiered at the Ashtar Theatre in Ramallah.[13] In 2020, a play inspired by Aeschylus' *Suppliants* was staged at Al-Harah Theatre in Beit Jala.[14] It is to be noted that in these three cases, the directors and authors are European, and these productions are part of European-Palestinian partnerships. The use of Greek tragedy is therefore not the choice of Palestinian theatre artists. The play *Antigone* is neither the result of a choice by the Palestinian team, nor a shared Franco-Palestinian choice. In the cast, the Palestinian team is mainly a performer, except for the costumes and sets, which are respectively attributed to the Palestinian actress Shaden Salim who plays the role of Antigone, and to Abd El Salam Abdo. The Palestinian part of the (co)production did not participate in the staging of the play. However, this kind of collaboration is not specific: it is in line with the European collaborations that have multiplied since the Oslo Accords, and which testify to an almost systematically European authorship. Dramaturges, authors and directors are almost systematically European (whether in the case of Greek tragedies or not). Nonetheless, the plays that emerge from these collaborations always deal with the Palestinian situation. In a way, it can be said that the European artist partners express a point of view on the situation and the (Question of) Palestine through the collaborations, such as Adel Hakim with *Antigone.*

Translation and/or adaptation: the complicit relationship between Sophocles and Mahmoud Darwish

In 441 BC, Sophocles wrote *Antigone,* which is one of the author's tragedies about Oedipus and the royal family of Thebes. The play can be summarized as follows: After the death of their mother, Jocasta, and the exile of their father, Oedipus, who ruled Thebes, the two brothers, Eteocles and Polynices kill each other in a struggle for the throne. The first is given an honorary funeral. Because he fought against his country, the second is deprived of a burial. Despite the decree of her uncle, the new king Creon, Antigone, the sister of the deceased, grants Polynices a burial. Because she publicizes her action, Creon sentences her to be walled up alive. Her fiancé, Haemon, who is also Creon's son, joins her in the tomb. Antigone has hanged herself, and Haemon commits suicide at her side. Faced with this news, Eurydice, Creon's wife and the mother of Haemon, commits suicide in turn.

Since the performances took place mainly outside Palestine for an audience of mainly non-Arabic speakers, Sophocles' text was translated twice, from Greek to Arabic, and from Arabic to French for the subtitles. Hakim used the literary Arabic translation made by the Egyptian Abdel Rahman Badawi. From the Arabic version, he realized the French translation used for the subtitles, which is a slightly more concise version of the text. The choice of Egyptian Arabic and not Palestinian Arabic for the translation is explained by the poetic qualities conferred on this dialect (Sanbar et al. 1997). However, it has consequences for Palestinian actors and audiences. Since the early 1970s, Palestinian plays have been performed exclusively in Palestinian dialect in order to reach audiences from towns to villages. It was therefore a challenge for the actors in the cast to learn and understand their parts, as for the audience during the performances held in Palestine. The choice of translation shows that the targeted audience was mainly non-Palestinian and that Adel Hakim anticipated that the tour would take place mainly outside of Palestine: the play mostly targets a French or at least a French-speaking audience. As Nicole Loraux states, there is no 'translation of a Greek tragedy for the theatre or not that does not generate, in one way or another, a gap – in a word, that becomes an adaptation' (Loraux 1999: 24). This is primarily a question of the untranslatable character of the 'literal materiality' (ibid.) of Greek tragedy. Adel Hakim does not accumulate gaps. On the contrary, he reduces them to a minimum: the codification of the genre is respected: 'the tone [and] the metrical structure' (ibid.) as well as 'the respective distribution of the dialogue parts and the lyrical moments' (ibid.) up to the stage directions, are carried out by the text and then by the staging.

Adel Hakim undertakes a single modification to Sophocles' text. The fifth, a recitative song of the chorus, which constitutes its last intervention in the play, is deleted and replaced by a poem by Mahmoud Darwish. The poet was born on 13 March 1941 in Al-Birwa in Galilee, Palestine, and died on 9 August 2008 in Houston, USA.[15] He was the author of nearly twenty collections of poetry as well as prose works and is considered one of the greatest Arab poets. Darwish heads the list of most translated Arab poets, with his work appearing in more than twenty languages, and is thus internationally recognized. The Palestinian poet was also known for his unwavering commitment, both literary and political, to the struggle of his people, which led to his imprisonment. He lived a considerable part of his life in exile and this condition strongly influenced his work. Memories and the lack of the homeland are a recurring theme in his poetic work. Adel Hakim substitutes the fifth stasimon of the Greek play with the Palestinian national poet's poem 'On This Earth' (Darwish 2019). This last stasimon is situated after the soothsayer Teiresias' visit to Creon, and Creon's discussion with the chorus. Because Teiresias predicts great evils for the new king who has just sentenced Antigone to death, the chorus convinces him to release Antigone and thus to grant Polynices burial. Creon sets out with this purpose and the chorus intervenes at this point to sing the praises of Dionysus and Thebes.

CHORUS
(Str. 1)
Thou by many names adored,
    Child of Zeus the God of thunder,
    Of a Theban bride the wonder,
Fair Italia's guardian lord;

In the deep-embosomed glades
    Of the Eleusinian Queen
Haunt of revelers, men and maids,
    Dionysus, thou art seen.

Where Ismenus rolls his waters,
    Where the Dragon's teeth were sown,
Where the Bacchanals thy daughters
    Round thee roam,
    There thy home;
Thebes, O Bacchus, is thine own.

(Ant. 1)
Thee on the two-crested rock
    Lurid-flaming torches see;
Where Corisian maidens flock,
    Thee the springs of Castaly.

By Nysa's bastion ivy-clad,
By shores with clustered vineyards glad,
There to thee the hymn rings out,
And through our streets we Thebans shout,

All hail to thee
Evoe, Evoe!

(Str. 2)
Oh, as thou lov'st this city best of all,
To thee, and to thy Mother levin-stricken,
In our dire need we call;
Thou see'st with what a plague our townsfolk sicken.
  Thy ready help we crave,
Whether adown Parnassian heights descending,
Or o'er the roaring straits thy swift ways wending,
  Save us, O save!

(Ant. 2)
Brightest of all the orbs that breathe forth light,
  Authentic son of Zeus, immortal king,
Leader of all the voices of the night,
  Come, and thy train of Thyiads with thee bring,
  Thy maddened rout
Who dance before thee all night long, and shout,
Thy handmaids we,
Evoe, Evoe!

Sophocles 2011:123-4

The chorus implores the god 'of many names' (Loraux 1999: 24) to give thanks to Thebes. This moment is special and 'intense' (ibid.: 135) because, according to Nicole Loraux, it manages to 'isolate an element of the performance for the sole purpose of better suggesting the whole tragedy' (ibid.). The chorus is deluding itself, 'against all likelihood, [it believes] in the possibility of a happy ending' (ibid.). In other words, it regains confidence and hope:

> The chorus gives to see and hear with a 'metatheatrical' way the self-forgetfulness as a tragic chorus, and this forgetfulness is accompanied by a momentary disregard of the dramatic situation: the chorus dances and sings its joy at the very moment when the irremediable is about to happen, and thus behaves as if it were engaged in a cultic or dithyrambic celebration; this discrepancy, this gap provokes in the spectator the reminder of the true nature of the performance ...
>
> Alaux 2002: 205

This stasimon expresses 'the purely theatrical form of the Kàtharsis' (Loraux 1999: 135), which Loraux defines as 'the purification of the spectator's relationship to the theatre as tragedy' (ibid.) since 'metatheatricality and reflexivity bring the spectator back to the specifically tragic nature of the spectacle . . .' (Alaux 2002: 206). Creon will first grant burial to Polynices, then free Antigone from the tomb. He then reversely accomplishes the two actions he announced, and thus 'the drama of his son's and then his wife's suicide is tied up' (Loraux 1999: 135) and 'everything returns to the order of the tragic genre' (ibid.). The audience is in a way an accomplice of the tragedy. This moment of complicity between the play – and thus the author – and the audience is the same in Darwish's poem:

'On this earth'
On this earth what makes life worth living:
the hesitance of April
the scent of bread at dawn
an amulet made by a woman for men
Aeschylus' works
the beginnings of love
moss on a stone
the mothers standing on the thinness of a flute
and the fear of invaders of memories.
On this earth what makes life worth living:
September's end
a lady moving beyond her fortieth year without losing any of her grace
a sun clock in a prison
clouds imitating a flock of creatures
chants of a crowd for those meeting their end smiling
and the fear of tyrants of the songs.
On this earth what makes life worth living:
on this earth stands the mistress of the earth
mother of beginnings
mother of endings
it used to be known as Palestine
it became known as Palestine
my mistress:
I deserve, because you're my mistress
I deserve life.

Darwish 2019

Mahmoud Darwish's speech takes the place of the chorus and, at the same time, of the Theban people in the play. His voice is broadcast and the verses of the poem are projected in French and Arabic on the wall at the back of the stage. The moment when the chorus of Sophocles' *Antigone*, for a brief moment, is fooled into hoping for a happy resolution, is replaced by an ode – literally, as a lyrical poem accompanied by music – to Palestine, the Palestinians born on this earth and who 'deserves life' (Darwish 2019: 320). Palestine is substituted for Thebes. As it is the only modification in Sophocles' text, it is then around that moment the complicity between the tragedy and the audience is articulated. The audience is prompted to guess the new intrusion of Darwish's poem and of Palestine in *Antigone*, and is moved by these Palestinian words.[16]

This change is, however, in accordance with the tragedy. The concordance between Sophocles' chorus and Darwish's poem occurs on several levels. First, there is a formal match, since the poem in music matches the stasimon. Both are almost of similar size. Above all, the stasimon and the poem advocate for the same values. Both the stasimon and the poem describe a land and its inhabitants. The poem itself talks about the Palestinian people born on this earth. In both cases, the chorus and Darwish remember why their earth is beautiful and for these reasons they believe, for the one, that Thebes deserves the visit and help of Dionysus and, for the other, that the Palestinian people 'deserves life' (ibid.). Both are caught up in hope. It is within this only change in Sophocles' text that the entire *palestianity* of *Antigone*'s tragedy is poetically woven. Because of the 'thematic and structural kinship' (Alaux 2002: 207) between Sophocles' text and Adel Hakim's version, we can limit Hakim's gesture to a translation. Even if the replacement of the fifth stasimon by Darwish's poem blends into the original work, it is still modified. Occurrences intrinsic to Sophocles *Antigone* are also understood in the light of the Palestinian issue. In this sense, Adel Hakim's version is between a translation and an adaptation.

The staging of *Antigone* or the obvious propaedeutic to the Israeli-Palestinian conflict

Adel Hakim's production begins with music: Ismene and Antigone weep and mourn over the bodies of Polynices and Eteocles, their brothers who have killed each other. Apart from this opening scene, added by the director as a prologue to Sophocles' prologue, music is used mainly for the interventions of the chorus.[17] The Trio Joubran, a Palestinian instrumental group of three oud-playing brothers from Nazareth composed the music of the show. For their 2009 album *À l'ombre des mots* (In the shadow of words), the group called on Mahmoud Darwish to put some of his poems into voice. Adel Hakim uses the instrumental tracks from the album for the show, with the exception of 'On This Earth', which is put into voice by Darwish. The music comes in when the tone of the chorus members is more recitative and singing. The musical additions also meet the requirements of the ancient material.

The costumes are very sober and of only three colours: black, white and grey. The chorus members all wear black trousers and shirts. In addition to this ensemble, the new king Creon, his son Haemon and Antigone's fiancé, the Guard and the Messenger wear a suit jacket. The soothsayer Teiresias also wears a jacket that is white and reminiscent of a medical coat. The jackets reveal the place of the characters on the social ladder. Antigone, Ismene, the sisters, then Eurydice, Creon's wife and mother of Haemon wear skirts, or dresses and jumpers or trench coats with boots, in white, black or grey. As she is led to the tomb, Antigone changes her costume. She is barefoot, wearing a white dress. The costumes are modern but carry no connotation.

Yves Collet's stage design is simple: a wall is erected in front of the audience from the stage to the ceiling and is used as a projection screen. The wall is pierced by a door in the middle – the lair of Creon's palace – and by several squares distributed like tiny windows and can evoke mashrabiya, or the single face of a photophore. Light squares often subtly illuminate the scene. On the floor, a slightly raised rectangle forms a proscenium. The characters who tell the story are placed on the proscenium, while those who listen and/or comment on the action stand outside of it. The space is orderly, symmetrical, geometric, very clean, as if under strict control. Creon is equipped with a lectern and a microphone when he speaks, which remind us of the modalities of politician speech. As the costumes, all the set design and scenery are modern but do not participate in the inscription in a specific context. The incursions of Palestine into the play are therefore limited to the replacement of the fifth stasimon of Sophocles' *Antigone*, the setting in voice of Darwish's poem and the instrumental music of the Trio Joubran. We can add the Arabic language of the show, even if it is Egyptian Arabic, and potentially the evocation of the mashrabiya. In fact, the presence of the Palestinian actors on stage, announced in the programme of the show distributed before the performance, constitutes the heart of the *palestianization* of *Antigone*.

Adel Hakim's staging provides Sophocles' tragedy and the presence of the Palestinian actors enough material. He does not (re)historicize or (re)sociologize *Antigone* in the Palestinian context. Thus, the press review of the play shows different passages that shed light on the obvious aspect of *Antigone* interpretation by Palestinians.

The burial, the native land, Mahmoud Darwish: there is no mistaking it, we are still in *Antigone* as Sophocles imagined it a few centuries ago. The show directed by Adel Hakim will also pay tribute and do justice to him [Sophocles], without it seeming out of place, as it seems so right. There is no need to force the issue in his staging, it is enough – since it is probably the most difficult thing in the world to be in this kind of humble evidence – to follow the course of things, that of the poet's words. And the word works, clear and luminous, through the voice and the body of the performers who assume it almost naturally, without embellishment, without 'acting', one might be tempted to say.

Han 2012

The French drama critic Jean-Pierre Han has already noted the thematic concordance between Sophocles' play and Adel Hakim's version in the light of the Palestinian question. The 'humble evidence' (ibid.) that he attributes to the French director's artistic gesture is also based on the quasi-mechanical precision implemented in the adaptation of Sophocles' text by the poetic fusion between the chorus and Darwish/Thebes and Palestine. The staging continues this mechanics with the diffusion of Darwish's voice and the music of the Joubran Trio. Both the poet and the Palestinian group are monuments of Palestinian culture – internationally known and legitimized – and the poet has even reached posterity. This adaptation finds its power in the symbolic changes it offers: an ode for another one, a word for its more modern equivalent, and even more importantly, a monumental cultural reference – Sophocles – for another culturally important work of art – Darwish and the Trio Joubran. Sophocles' play is not distorted. The relationship with the public in Hakim's play echoes with the context in which Sophocles' *Antigone* was played. It was not a Theban spectator who witnessed the struggle between Creon and Antigone, but an Athenian spectator. The performance takes place in another time and place. The same is true for the *Antigone* directed by Adel Hakim, since most of the performances took place outside Palestine. It is the Palestinian people who express themselves in front of a foreign audience. A collective message is presented to them from within their own culture and thus reactivates the same relationship between Sophocles' *Antigone* and its contemporary audience.

Another statement can also be made based on the consideration of Greek tragedy, and *Antigone* specifically, as 'propaedeutic [comparison] to the Israeli-Palestinian conflict' (Alterman 2015). The comparison of the Israeli-Palestinian conflict to a Greek tragedy is explained according to Aline Alterman because 'in Greek tragedy, if there is tragedy it is because men speaking of legitimate rights cannot give recognition to the legitimate rights of the other' (ibid.). Israeli author, Amos Oz,[18] and Leila Shahid, former Ambassador of Palestine to the European Union, also lend themselves to the comparison, arguing that both the Greek tragedy and the Israeli-Palestinian conflict lie in a clash between law and law, between justice and justice (Planche 2003). *Antigone*, among the Greek tragedies, is probably the most likely to meet the comparison made by Alterman, Oz and Shadid, because it 'offers a very large place to the rivalry of the heroes [since] the conflict between Antigone and Creon opens up, for the spectator, a reflection concerning the values of the city, and gives rise to an ethical questioning on human behaviour' (Gaudé et al. 2010: 250–1). Above all, Laurent Gaudé, Hélène Kuntz and David Lescot define the conflict set up by Sophocles 'as a competition between two individuals, opposed to each other by their system of thought or their state, but where each adopts a justifiable point of view. It is difficult to separate the opponents, difficult not to hear each of their arguments, and the tragedy feeds precisely on this difficulty' (ibid.).

Antigone, a socially acceptable narrative of Palestinians?

For the premiere of *Antigone* at the PNT, the TQI organized a professional trip, gathering directors and programmers of different French cultural institutions. However, Estelle Delorme, the TQI's production administrator, had to make sure the programmers would buy the show before inviting them to the premiere, and thus offering them the trip. In other words, they had to buy it before even having seen it. The theatre directors' gamble was only made on the basis of the production file. Sophocles' text is translated, so they all know the play in advance. Estelle Delorme obtained seventeen pre-purchase dates and twelve directors participated in the trip. As for the journalists, if the theatre wanted them to come to the preview, their trip had to be fully paid for, apart from meals. The press articles were very positive about the show and *Antigone* was assured to be scheduled widely. Since 2011, the show has been performed almost one hundred and fifty times in Palestine as well as in France, Belgium and Cyprus. Two tours took place, the first between 2011 and 2013 and the second in 2017. The press kit for this show is nearly one hundred pages long and the articles in it are unanimous. The enthusiasm generated by *Antigone* went beyond the borders and the success hoped for. The mayors of the towns hosting the play were very keen to have workshops led by the actors in theatres and schools. The show has received unwavering support from municipalities, theatres, the press and critics. *Antigone* won the 2011/12 Syndicat de la Critique award in France for best foreign show. It should also be noted that the availability of the show in its entirety on YouTube is the greatest success in terms of views of the Théâtre des Quartiers d'Ivry.

The Palestinian-American intellectual Edward Said, writer and theorist of post-colonialism, reminds us that 'effective, and especially narrative, renderings of the Palestine-Israel contest are either attacked with near-unanimous force or ignored' (Said 1983–4: 31). Performed mostly outside Palestine, the performances of *Antigone* have neither been ignored nor attacked. Two hypotheses therefore arise. The first: Because *Antigone* is 'less historical and sociological than mythical and metaphorical' (Prin 1996: 8) and because it speaks to a 'generic man' (ibid.) and not specific man, it is not an effective narrative representation of the Israeli-Palestinian conflict. The second: Because Antigone may have been considered in Europe as 'the greatest of Greek tragedies' (Steiner 1986: 360–1) or even as a work of art bordering on perfection (ibid.) to the extent that 'Sophocles' text and the figure of Antigone have become talismans of the European mind' (ibid.: 7), Adel Hakim's play constitutes 'a socially acceptable narrative' (Said 1983–4: 34) of the Palestinians, in Said's words. Palestinian otherness has been made presentable (Jawad 2014) by the masterpiece model of *Antigone*. By not touching Sophocles' *Antigone*, Palestine can be heard and made to be listened to. It can tour and find a place on institutional stages,

Figure 7 *Antigone*, Sophocles, directed by Adel Hakim, 2017. Credit: Nabil Boutros.

without any kind of obstacles. In *Antigone*, the *palestianity* of the actors, the music and Darwish merge with Sophocles' tragedy, and it is precisely this (con)fusion that ensures and reassures the play's success. Sophocles' *Antigone* is a tribute, a 'donation that expresses respect [and] admiration' (Larousse online, n.d.) from the French director to the Palestinian part of the cast and to the PNT. Adel Hakim considers the play and the figure of Antigone to be a way of expressing the admiration he feels towards the Palestinian resistance, resilience, and struggle for freedom and the dignity of both the dead and the living.

Notes

1   Adel Hakim co-directed the TQI from 1992 until his death in August 2017. See the section '(Co)producing *Antigone* between France and Palestine'.

2   *Des Roses et du Jasmin* (2015) is a three-hour play based on the dramaturgical model of Greek tragedy with a chorus and messengers. As a direct representation of the events of the Israeli-Palestinian conflict, the play has not toured as widely as *Antigone*. Nevertheless, it was welcomed by audiences and critics with as much enthusiasm as with *Antigone*. However, many programmers – mostly directors of CDNs like Hakim – did not want to take up the challenge of a contemporary tragedy about the Israeli-Palestinian conflict. The same goes for the project's partner-producers, who were fewer in number and committed less money than for *Antigone*. From one tragedy to another, Greek and then contemporary, the difficulty of dealing with the Palestinian question became apparent.

3   *The Question of Palestine* is the title of a book by Edward Said, published in 1979, which aims to raise awareness of the Palestinian question among the American public. Said is a Palestinian-American intellectual, writer and theorist of post-colonialism. The book focuses on the period between the end of the nineteenth century and the first half of the twentieth century. Said explains that the use of the words 'the question of' serves to formalize an ancient problem that generates complex and unresolved issues. He points out that 'the question of' can also suggest that the status of the thing is undetermined and debated. Palestine is arguably one of the most debated notions at the international level since the post-war period. At the United Nations, Palestine is also called 'the question of Palestine'. This is the name given to the whole range of issues on the subject, including the question of Palestinian refugees, resolutions relating to the territories and the inalienable rights of Palestinians.

4   Ariane Mnouchkine is a French director who has run the Théâtre du Soleil at the Cartoucherie de Vincennes since 1964.

5   John Strasberg is an American actor and director who has set up theatre schools, one of which is based in Paris.

6   All translations from Arabic and French into English are mine, unless otherwise indicated.

7   'Freedom of expression is only given to Franco-French people. I was thinking of leaving France. Maybe going to Brazil. I had some acquaintances there from Lebanon. But I didn't leave. From 1997 onwards, I regularly fled France, invited by peripheral countries that honoured me. With the support of the French embassies in these countries. Quite surprising. This allowed me to develop the concept of Théâtre des Quartiers du Monde.' (Hakim 2016: 14) Personal translation.

8   Ibid. Peripheral countries are seen as dependent on other countries for their development.

9   They were signed in Washington by Yitzhak Rabin, Prime Minister of Israel, Yasser Arafat, Chairman of the Palestine Liberation Organization (PLO) and US President Bill Clinton.

10   For example, the EU makes the distribution of funds conditional on the fight against terrorism. However, Palestinian political parties can be included in the EU's list of terrorist organizations, just as the Palestinian resistance can be classified as such.

11   The financial contributions come mainly from the TQI, which has managed to obtain numerous grants, notably from the French Consulate General in Jerusalem, the Chateaubriand French Cultural Centre, the Italian cooperation department of the Ministry of Foreign Affairs, the TAM and the 'Groupe des 20 théâtres en Île-de-France'.

12   *Antigone* (2011); *Zone 6, Chroniques de la vie palestinienne* (2012); *Des Roses et du Jasmin* (2015).

13   *This Flesh Is Mine* (2014) written by British playwright Brian Woolland and directed by British director Michael Walling in partnership with the Ashtar Theatre in Ramallah.

14   *The Suppliant Women* (2020) directed by the Swedish artist Dretro Kasabi.

15   After three days of national mourning announced by the Palestinian Authority and a national funeral ceremony organized in Ramallah in the Palestinian Territories, he was buried in the same city near the Palace of Culture.

16   The modification of Sophocles' text is not announced by Adel Hakim in the publicity and information given to the public. The audience does not know in advance that the fifth stasimon has been deleted and replaced by Darwish's poem.

17   In most editions, the sung moments are in italics.

18   Amos Oz notably spoke about this in a 2012 lecture in Washington at a plenary session of J. Street, an American Jewish peace organization.

References

Alaux, J. (2002), 'Catharsis et réflexivité tragiques', *GAIA: Revue interdisciplinaire sur la Grèce ancienne*, 6: 201–25.

Alshaer, A. (2019), *A Map of Absence: An Anthology of Palestinian Writing on the Nakba*, London: Saqi Books.

Al-Saber, S. and G. M. English, eds (2021), *Stories under Occupation and Other Plays from Palestine*, Calcutta: Seagull Books.

Alterman, A. (2015), 'De la tragédie', *Lignes*, 46: 11–22. Available online: www.cairn. info/revue-lignes-2015-1-page-11.htm (accessed 13 August 2021).

Chabrat-Kajdan, A. (2017), 'L'épopée d'une création théâtrale: *Des Roses et du Jasmin*, d'Ivry à Jérusalem', MA diss., UFR LESLA, Université Lumière Lyon 2, Lyon.

Darwish, M. (2019), 'On This Earth', in, A. Alshaer (ed.), *A Map of Absence: An Anthology of Palestinian Writing on the Nakba*, London: Saqi Books.

Gaudé, L., H. Kuntz and D. Lescot (2010), 'Conflit', in J. P. Sarrazac (ed.), *Lexique du drame moderne et contemporain,* 49–50. Belval: Éditions Circé.

Hakim, A. (2016), 'Autobiographie', unpublished document provided by the author.

Han, J. P. (2012), 'Voyage en Palestine', *L'Humanité*, 1 March 2012: 3.

Jawad, R. (2014), 'Aren't We Human? Normalizing Palestinian Performances', *The Arab Studies Journal*, 22: 28–45.

Larousse, (s.d.), 'Hommage' in *Dictionary online*. Available online: www.larousse.fr/ dictionnaires/francais/hommage/40237 (accessed 6 August 2022).

Loraux, N. (1999), *La Voix endeuillée: Essai sur la tragédie grecque,* Paris: Gallimard.

Partnership and co-production agreement between the Théâtre des Quartiers d'Ivry and the Palestinian National Theatre, *Antigone* and *Des Roses et du Jasmin*, unpublished document provided by Estelle Delorme, Théâtre des Quartiers d'Ivry, 2016.

Press review of *Antigone*, Théâtre des Quartiers d'Ivry, available on the theatre's website until the change of director in January 2019.

Prin, C. (1996), 'Le personnage tragique, aujourd'hui', *Théâtre/Public,* 130/1: 8–9.

Production file of *Antigone*, Théâtre des Quartiers d'Ivry, available on the theatre's website until the change of director in January 2019.

Production file of *Des Roses et du Jasmin*, Théâtre des Quartiers d'Ivry, available on the theatre's website until the change of director in January 2019.

Planche, J. C. (2003), 'La résistance du quotidien: Entretien avec Leila Shahid', *Les Cahiers du Channel*, 4 February. Available online: http://lechannel.fr/wp-content/ uploads/2015/11/Cahier04.pdf (accessed 23 August 2021).

Said, E. (1979), *The Question of Palestine*, New York: Times Books.

Said, E. (1983–4), 'Permission to Narrate', *Journal of Palestine Studies*, 13(3): 27–48.

Sanbar, E., S. Hadidi and J. C. Pons (1997), *Palestine: l'enjeu culturel*, Belval: Éditions Circé.

Sophocles (2011), *Antigone,* in *The Oedipus Plays of Sophocles*, trans. F. Storr. 90–129, New York: Pacific Publishing Studio.

Sophocle (2013), *Antigone,* trans. P. Mazon, Paris: Folioplus classiques, Gallimard.

Steiner, G. (1986), *Les Antigones*, trans. P. Blanchard, Paris: Gallimard.

Le TQI, Le CDN, website of the Théâtre des Quartiers d'Ivry- CDN du Val-De-Marne, Available online: https://www.theatre-quartiers-ivry.com/TQI/cdn-manufacture/, (accessed 8 August 2022).

10

Looking at Iraq from Afar

Two *Oresteia* on European Stages

Pauline Donizeau

During the 2018–19 theatre season, two performances, created and presented in major theatrical national institutions, tackled the issue of contemporary Iraq and its political troubles. *Looking for Oresteia*, directed by French director Célie Pauthe in collaboration with Iraqi director Haythem Abderrazak (Hay̱tam ʿAbd al-Razzāq), premiered at the Dramatic National Center of Besançon (France) in September 2018. *Orestes in Mosul*, directed by Swiss director Milo Rau, premiered in April 2019 at the National Theatre of Ghent (Belgium).

The two projects share multiple features. Both belong to an intercultural theatrical tradition. There are many definitions of the word 'interculturality', which have been discussed at length (Pavis 1996). In this case, we stick to a simple fact: the two European directors seized a topic related to an extra-European actuality and thus chose to confront their own cultural and social background with the foreign. The interculturality on the European stages, which we can trace back to the turn of the twentieth century, necessarily overlaps with – and particularly in the case of Iraq – the issue of Orientalism as Edward Said defined it, as the East invented and conceptualized as 'Orient' by the West (Said [1995] 1978). Moreover, in the present day, the issue requires a documentary perspective: not necessarily aesthetically, but because the performance will have to provide information about a context alien to the audience. Furthermore, there is a mixed cast in the two shows, in which we find European and Iraqi performers. During the creative process, the two projects' participants travelled to Iraq (Mosul for the Belgian team, Baghdad for the French team). The notion of interculturality thus here takes another dimension linked to the internationalization of exchanges that allows for the development of cultural projects on a global scale. But, above all, in these two projects the directors tackle the issue of contemporary Iraqi conflicts through the lens of Greek tragedy – where the Anglo-Saxons, who had been much quicker to display the Iraqi issue on stage, had favoured documentary forms and verbatim theatre (we think in particular of Richard Norton Taylor's *Tribunal plays* on the Iraqi file in 2003, 2007, 2011 and 2016).

This is not the first time a Western director has confronted the political situation in Iraq – and in the Middle East in general – through Greek classical texts. Notably, we might recall the great adaptation of Aeschylus' *The Persians* by American director Peter Sellars in 1993. More recently, in 2019, Christiane Jatahy directed a show titled *Notre Odyssée II – Le présent qui déborde* (Our Odyssey II – the present that overflows) in the Festival d'Avignon in France. For this production, she has brought together the exile stories of Palestinian, Lebanese and Amazonian refugees and juxtaposed them with Homer's *Odyssey*. Here, she explained her choice of classical Greek material to tackle this political issue:

> It is interesting to see how people react to the *Odyssey*. In Lebanon we worked with Druzes who knew Greek mythology very well. In Palestine, the actors immediately related it to other stories from their own culture. In Amazonia, we worked with Indians forced to flee their lands because of the deforestation encouraged by Jair Bolsonaro. They recognized in Homer images of their own mythology. The strength of these great stories is that all cultures find parallels in them.
>
> Le Tanneur 2019a[1]

Christiane Jatahy is from Brazil, so she is not from this Europe that has to be 'provincialized' according to Chakrabarty (Chakrabarty 2000). However this show was produced and created in France, in the heart of a Europe that claims its Greek origins and considers Greek heritage a main part of its founding culture.[2] Then, several questions might arise. In what measure are texts inspired by the Greek tragedy suited to tackling Middle Eastern issues? Is their use in an intercultural context justified, and by what? What could be universal in these texts, beyond the parables that the stories allow? Why mobilize these narratives when working in an extra-European context? In a nutshell, these different experiences question the presupposition of the classical texts' universalism and in particular those of Greek heritage. This issue becomes even more delicate when the artists are looking from Europe to former colonized regions whose cultural practices and heritage are often considered as subaltern and/or folkloric.

To a certain degree, we can consider Greek heritage as a common heritage, and even as an Eastern heritage. As the Tunisian islamologist Youssef Seddik, who collaborated on the *Looking for Oresteia* project, has shown, the Greek myths and the proto-Islamic myths share common Mesopotamian sources, which passed on to Arab culture and to Greek and Latin culture (Seddik 2018). Myths, in their symbolic dimension, are therefore a common heritage, but the structuration of the narratives is not the same in the two cultures. They passed to Western culture via tragedy and epic, in structured and codified forms integrating the notion of theatricality, which did not take hold in Arab-Muslim countries. Thus, even if one can find common myths in European and Arab-Muslim cultures, the genre of tragedy does not belong to Arab-Muslim culture. Rather, it constitutes a rational reading of the world, a codified structuring that has no place in the spectacular or poetic practices of Middle Eastern countries. The choice of tragedy to address the current situation in Iraq constitutes a reverse trajectory. It reads the Iraqi chaos through the structured form of tragedy, aiming at a rationalization whose limits must be examined.

Regarding the object of our study, the *Oresteia* appears to be a relevant parable to address the contemporary situation of Iraq at war(s). Aeschylus' trilogy, presented in Athens in 458 BC, depicts the murder of Agamemnon by his wife Clytemnestra and her lover Aegisthus upon his return from the Trojan War, to avenge his sacrificing of their daughter to achieve victory (*Agamemnon*); then the murder of Clytemnestra desired by Electra who seeks revenge for her father's death, a matricide finally carried out by her son Orestes on Apollo's order (*The Libation Bearers*); and finally Orestes' trial organized by Athena and which sees him being acquitted and puts an end to his pursuit by the Erinyes (*The Eumenides*). Often referred to as a tragedy of revenge, the *Oresteia* speaks of the endless cycle of violence. From that perspective, the story itself seems to provide a good example to allude to the situation of an Iraq in which the destruction of evil has always led to worse: the removal of Saddam Hussein by the West in 2003 led to the social and political disorder that contributed to the surge of the 'Islamic State' (ISIS). The fight against ISIS, which the weakened Iraqi state was unable to carry on its own, strengthened the already existing Shia militias, which gained legitimacy and power. This led to factional struggles across the country and prevented the Iraqi state from achieving control over its own territory. The war in Iraq clearly shares common features with the tragic fable of *Oresteia*. First and foremost, there is the *hubris* that characterizes its protagonists. The political Iraqi situation also meets the *fatum* logic. We may recall that some researchers and international actors issued warnings about the probable tragic outcome of the war launched by the United States in 2003.[3] The *Oresteia* is also known to be a tragedy about justice, featuring the first democratic court in history. However, the allegory shows its limits when it comes to the conclusion of the play. The tragedy ends with a return to order after chaos, through the establishment of democratic bodies in the city. This appears to be a fundamental difference between the outcome of Aeschylus' tragedy and the reality of Iraq where conflicts persist.

This chapter seeks to analyse Rau's version of the *Oresteia* as well as Pauthe and Abderrazak's version, in order to see how the artists place Aeschylus' tragedy in a dialogue with the Iraqi context, namely their own cultural heritage and an 'elsewhere' to be comprehended and represented within international teams. I will focus specifically on these elements: the way in which the artists explain their choices of topic and the Greek material, the place this creation occupies in their personal work in general, the dramaturgical and aesthetical choices (and the part played by cultural exchanges) and the treatment of the play's denouement. I intend to present them as two very different results of intercultural theatrical experiences and shows.

Milo Rau's *Orestes in Mosul*: a mise en abyme of the Western gaze

Milo Rau is a Swiss stage director and filmmaker. He also studied journalism and sociology. His theatre can be described as politically engaged and he always tackles historical topics or news items in his plays. He wants to stick to reality – a notion that he keeps challenging at the same time. When it comes to his aesthetic choices, he never stops probing how art can transform the world we live in, and following that perspective he works on the dialectic between reality and fiction to reach what he calls a 'global realism' (Rau 2018a). Since 2018, he has been the director of the National Theatre of Ghent, Belgium. When he took office, he wrote and published the *Ghent Manifesto*: a sort of commandment in ten points that he prescribed for himself in his theatre practice.

Milo Rau rarely adapts existing theatrical texts. His work on the *Oresteia* is almost an exception. In an interview for the presentation of *Orestes in Mosul* at the Theatre of Nanterre Amandiers (France), he said:

> My logic . . . is not to stage adaptations of classical or other texts, but to rewrite the works through a context where reality has a real influence.
>
> Le Tanneur and Rau 2019b[4]

In the case of *Orestes in Mosul*, the classical material meets the context of Iraq at war. The tragedy is a useful tool to make Iraq's chaos comprehensible – unless, on the contrary, the Iraqi case brings out other meanings in the tragedy. It also meets Rau's specific and complex personal poetics. All these elements announce a theatrical challenge.

An important dramaturgical work was thus necessary. Rau and his dramaturge Stefan Bläske cut and transformed the original text, then mixed it with other materials. This work meets the fourth requirement of the *Ghent Manifesto*:

> Four: The literal adaptation of classics on stage is forbidden. If a source text – whether book, film or play – is used at the outset of the project, it may only represent up to 20 percent of the final performance time.
>
> Rau 2018b

Thus, if the performance's dramatic progression follows that of Aeschylus' play, many changes have been made. In Rau's *Oresteia*, Electra's character disappears, as do those of the gods: Apollo's text is taken over by Pylades, Athena is absent and does not participate in the Orestes' trial at the end of the play. The relationship with the divine is removed: vengeance and justice become the business of men, and therefore a matter of politics.

Along with the dramatic elements from Aeschylus' play, the documentary material is prominent in the performance. During the creative process, the team travelled to Iraq to discover Mosul and meet Iraqi artists. This experience fulfils another demand from Rau's *Manifesto*:

> Nine: At least one production per season must be rehearsed or performed in a conflict or war zone, without any cultural infrastructure.
>
> Rau 2018

The show then appears more as the result of a creative process than as an adaptation of the Greek tragedy. The associations of the different elements that make the performance create multiple layers of reading, depending on how they relate to reality. First, the actors and actresses play on stage different key scenes of the *Oresteia*. In addition, some elliptical passages of the text are developed. For instance, a quite long scene shows a family dinner during which Agamemnon presents his Trojan captive Cassandra to his wife. The actors and actresses play all these scenes from the fiction in shimmering and deliberately Orientalist costumes, and they embody their characters without any distance. All these elements exacerbate the theatricality, as does the fake blood covering Cassandra and Agamemnon's corpses after they die. Secondly, the actors and actresses sometimes talk directly to the audience as themselves. They share their memories and feelings about the trip to Mosul and reflect on their personal relationship to the so-called 'Orient'. They also talk about their personal relationship with the characters of Aeschylus' play. These moments distance the fiction, allowing for commentary and mise en abyme. Finally, the images that the documentary maker Daniel Demoustier shot in Iraq during the team's trip are projected onto a screen placed at the back of the stage, in an overhanging position. These images have different status in their relationship to reality. We thus find images that show scenes of the *Oresteia*, played in Iraq by the actors and actresses of the Belgian team, accompanied by an amateur Iraqi choir. Most of the time, these images overlap with the same scenes performed on stage. We also find documentary shots that Demoustier filmed in Mosul. On these, we can see the play's actors and actresses discovering Mosul or talking with Iraqi people about their personal situations, and shots of the city in ruins. There are also more complex images, as they are filmed as documentary footage, but deviate from reality: the Belgian actors and actresses are seen being taken hostage and executed by fake ISIS militants. The fictive representation of violence is confronted to the real violence in Iraq. The use of fake blood creates a distance from the crime but, at the same time, it activates the emotional impulses specific

Figure 8 *Orestes in Mosul*, directed by Milo Rau, 2019. Credit: Fred Debrock.

to the theatre. The conjunction of these layers allows for a meta-discourse on violence and theatre.

The setting and scenography also contribute to this reflection on reality and theatre. At the back of the stage stands a transparent cube. Inside, we can see a table and some chairs. Above, a neon light reads 'Cafeteria and restaurant', written in Arabic. The actors and actresses use this space during Agamemnon's return dinner scene. As the show progresses and we discover the images shot in Iraq, we notice that this element of the set reproduces identically and transposes into the regime of fiction the dining room of the hotel complex in which the actors stayed in Iraq – a complex whose history, linked to the economic policies of Saddam Hussein, will be explained. A doubt remains: is it a fictional or a real space? Rau permanently plays on this ambiguity.

The encounter between Greek tragedy, the situation in Iraq and Rau's personal poetics brings the risk of a blurring of meaning. Regarding the dialogue between the tragedy and the political situation of Iraq, the parable is exploited to the fullest. Agamemnon is at the heart of the play. He represents the belligerent Western figure. His dramatic trajectory is different on stage from what is told on screen, as if we were witnessing two different consequences of his ambitions. In the video, he is murdered by Orestes. During his execution, he is dressed in an orange suit reminiscent of ISIS victims' clothing. We suppose that he was killed in Iraq/Troy before his return to Europe/Greece. Orestes here would then embody ISIS as evil begotten by evil and plagued by a desire for revenge. On stage, Agamemnon comes back home and brings Cassandra (played by the Belgian-Iraqi actress Susana Abdulmajid) hostage. At first presented as a war trophy, she ends up being too troublesome and is eliminated. Perhaps she represents a refugee figure, a collateral victim of the Western wars in the East – here, Iraq seems to be merging with Syria or any other country in the Middle East where war forces inhabitants to leave. Milo Rau explores two consequences of the Western intervention in Iraq.

In the final scene of Orestes' trial, the parable shows its limits. If we follow the proposed parable, a question arises: should we pardon ISIS/Orestes? In today's Iraq, political and sectarian conflicts are perpetuated on the ruins of the American invasion and the ISIS dictatorship, which means that there is no trial by Athena to provide forgiveness. But Rau is not only talking about Iraq. Instead, he also talks about the role played by the West in the conflict. Rau seems to be aware of this limit and mentions the contradiction between Aeschylus' fable and the political situation in Iraq: the former 'describes the birth of civilization through forgiveness' (Le Tanneur and Rau 2019b) when the latter is 'the story of the impossibility of forgiveness' (ibid.). In the show, he seems to avoid the denouement. The final scene of Orestes' trial is not played on stage – as it is both a fictional space and a concrete location in the European cities where the show is performed. This question is impossible to address from a Western perspective and the scene was performed in Iraq and filmed. Rau gathered the choir of Iraqi people in a bombed building, then asked them the question: should ISIS be convicted? After a brief moment of debate, the video – and the performance – ends with an Iraqi woman looking at the camera and declaring in Arabic: ''*Intahat al-ḥarb*' (The war is over).

The use of tragedy thus finds its limits as it seems to reveal a semi-failure while confronting the situation of Iraq at war, but the most interesting thing in the performance is probably that Milo Rau's interest has shifted from Iraq itself to the relationship between Europe and Iraq. Through the dramaturgic choices, it becomes clear that the Iraqi situation is captured from the outside and that it necessarily provides the audience with a partial point of view. Then, the different layers of relationship to reality allow the shedding of new light on our relation – as a Western audience is the show's main target – to Iraq, between reality and fiction/myth, between the tangible and the unreachable.

From this perspective, it is to be noted that the actors and actresses are watching the videos shot in Iraq at the same time as the audience. When they do not embody the characters of the *Oresteia*, they become mere witnesses of the situation in Iraq, unable to do more than be spectators. As such, the opening scene of the play can be considered as programmatic. In this scene, the actor Johan Leysen, who will later play Agamemnon's part, talks directly to the audience. He speaks of the admiration he had as a child for Heinrich Schliemann, the nineteenth-century German adventurer and archaeologist who claimed to have discovered the ruins of Troy and the tomb of Agamemnon based on his reading of Homer's texts. Schliemann kept the myth alive until his discovery was disproved. He was later convicted in Turkey as a tomb raider. This historical character thus embodies the relationship of Europeans to the myth of the East as the Orient: fascinating, dreamy, built on lies and an imperialist agenda (Said [1995] 1978). By placing his show under the sign of an admitted lie, Milo Rau justifies his position as a Westerner taking on a complex Iraqi issue for which his peers are partly responsible, and offers a mise en abyme of the European gaze.

Figure 9 *Orestes in Mosul*, directed by Milo Rau, 2019. Credit: Fred Debrock.

Célie Pauthe and Haythem Abderrazak's *Looking for Oresteia*: experiencing the uncommon

Célie Pauthe is a French theatre director. She has been the director of the Dramatic National Center of Besançon (France) since 2013. She met Haythem Abderrazak during a stay in Iraq with Siwa platform, a cultural association that was founded in 2007 by Yagoutha Belgacem and organizes cultural encounters and workshops between artists in Europe, Tunisia and Iraq. For his part, Abderrazak is an emblematic figure of Iraqi theatre.[5] Then, a French team led by Pauthe and an Iraqi team led by Abderrazak met and took part in theatre workshops over a period of five years through the intermediation of Siwa. From these work sessions emerged a collective performance project. Aeschylus' *Oresteia* was chosen as work material. Thus, in this project, the collaborative process appears to be as important as the finished result. The work that was performed in Besançon in September 2018 is presented as a work in progress whose very title testifies to its heuristic dimension. *Looking for Oresteia* is a four-handed production: Haythem Abderrazak directed the first part of the tragedy, *Agamemnon*, Célie Pauthe the second, *The Libation Bearers*, and they co-directed the third, *The Eumenides*, around a common dramaturgical project. The two

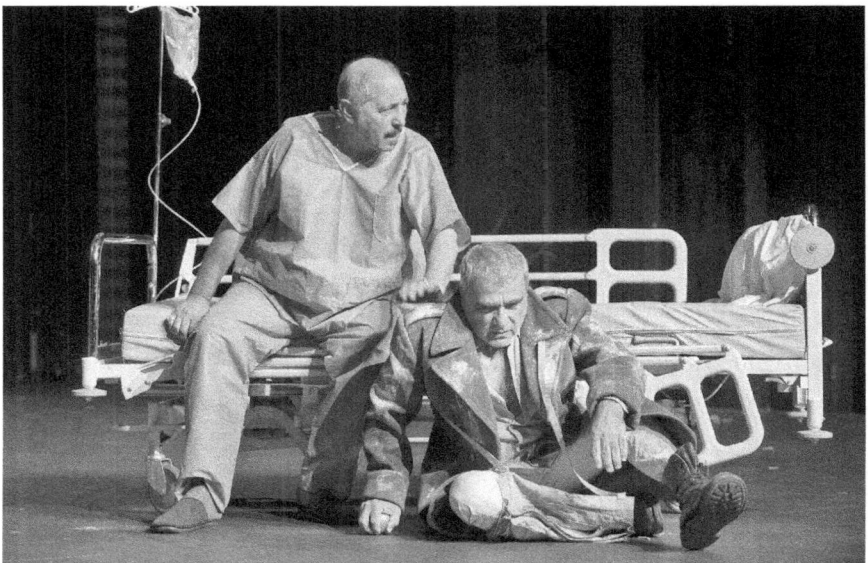

Figure 10 *Looking for Oresteia* (part 1 *Agammemnon*), directed by Célie Pauthe and Haythem Abderrazak, 2018. Credit: Elisabeth Carecchio.

directors chose to remain very close to Aeschylus' text and preserved the play's structure and dialogues. The French text, in Florence Dupont's translation, was then translated and adapted into Arabic by the Tunisian anthropologist, philosopher and islamologist Youssef Seddik.

French director Célie Pauthe was the one to propose the *Oresteia* as work material. Yagoutha Belgacem, the head of Siwa platform, who closely accompanied the creation explained:

> When Celie proposed the *Oresteia*, it was a text that the Iraqi team members knew and that was important to them: they could identify with it because it is a monument of the theatre but also because it resonated with today's Iraqi society.
>
> Donizeau and Dumont-Lewi 2019: 96[6]

As in Rau's case, the team explains this choice by the relevance of the parable. But Belgacem also presents Aeschylus' text as a cultural 'monument': this looks like an argument of authority asserting the universality of the Greek text. Nevertheless, things appear to be more complex. Indeed, if we consider Pauthe's previous works, this *Oresteia* is the first Greek tragedy she stages. Even if Aeschylus' tragedy is a major text in her European theatrical culture, this is the first time she deals with the play, and with a Greek tragedy in general – she was at that point of her career more interested in staging contemporary plays. As regards Abderrazak's career, it appears that he has only staged foreign plays.[7] He explains that he does so 'by choice' because 'all Arab works are or were written in contexts of censorship: if not state censorship, at least self-censorship' (Donizeau and Dumont-Lewi 2019). This radical statement – which would need to be debated but is not the subject of this chapter – testifies to his involvement in the choice of a text that is most often associated with the Western theatrical heritage. The work on Aeschylus' text, as the two artists presented it during the interview they gave us, allowed the proximity between the Greek and Islamic cultural heritage and a 'porosity between East and West' (ibid.) to be highlighted.

However, even if these statements insist on the research of the common, the creative process such as the work in progress presented in Besançon shows a research of the uncommon as dramaturgical material. Through the intercultural experience, several cultural gaps appear and the directors seem to play with them, or deliberately maintain them. The show is thus performed in three languages (French, classical Arabic and Iraqi colloquial Arabic). The French team performs in French, the Iraqi one in Arabic and the dialogues are never subtitled. This choice postulates that one can understand the meaning even without speaking both languages – unless, on the contrary, this choice values the uncommon without underlining it as a problem but as a fact that does not prevent coexistence.

When she staged *The Libation Bearers*, Célie Pauthe confronted what could have been a problematic misunderstanding. She first chose to take inspiration in the Shia rituals in order to represent the *kommos* (the Libation Bearers' mourning song). Such a choice belongs completely to the tradition of interculturality that implies 'the imitation and borrowing elements from outside its own culture' (Pavis 1996). But the Iraqi team prevented Pauthe from making this choice. Pauthe narrates:

> Haythem told me that it was impossible to integrate these rituals on stage if we wanted to present the play in Baghdad one day. Because if we use these rituals, then our show will become community oriented, which is not what we want to do.
>
> Donizeau and Dumont-Lewi 2019: 99[8]

So she finally chose a more neutral mourning performance, but still accompanied by musicians and an Iraqi singer.

It is actually in the third part of the trilogy, the *Eumenides*, which Pauthe and Abderrazak staged jointly, that the intercultural dialogue is most at stake. This is the moment of Orestes' trial, which is undoubtedly, as we have already noted, the most complicated part of the trilogy to treat in a parabolic way. It is also the crux of the intercultural process. The directors decided to show two versions of the trial, which follow each other in the play. The first remains very close to Aeschylus' play, and Athena leads the trial between Orestes and the Erinyes. As noted above, this trial is famous because it is presented as the first democratic trial in history. At its end, Athena acquits Orestes. On stage, we can hear the goddess' entire final tirade. She is embodied by a male Iraqi actor. This choice is important for many reasons. First, the choice of a man underlines the misogynistic dimension of the verdict:

ATHENA
With me it rests to give the casting vote,
And to Orestes I my suffrage pledge.
For to no mother do I owe my birth;
In all, save wedlock, I approve the male,
And am, with all my soul, my father's child.
Nor care I to avenge a woman's death
Who slew her husband, guardian of the house.

Aeschylus 1986: 704-10[9]

At the same time, this choice highlights the phallocratic and patriarchal dimension of this first democratic court in history, and thus questions the foundation of this institution which Europeans have made their point of reference: Athena defends Orestes because he killed his mother, and not his father. The question of gender thus takes a central place in the dramaturgy – when, on the contrary, Rau chooses to suppress the female character of Electra. Secondly, the actor lies on a sofa during the whole scene of the trial. He is dressed in a precious colourful and shimmering robe. These elements assertively recall an Orientalist imagery. But he listens to Edith Piaf's *La Vie en Rose*, and he finally seems to be the spokesman and representative of Western democracy through its judiciary institution. The Iraqi Athena here appears as a strong supporter of the West and its so-called universal principles. He is implementing them in an Eastern context; so does Athena in the play, who organizes this trial to put an end to the Erinyes' ancestral justice. In this stage proposal, gender issues intersect with postcolonial issues and demonstrate an intercultural dialogue. During the interview with the creation team, Pauthe explained that the misogynistic dimension of Athena's verdict was the most problematic point of the play; when Abderrazak insisted on the very nature of the democratic institutions in Iraq as they have been imported by the Americans, presented as universal, and unable to put an end to the political troubles in the country.

This first trial scene must be read in relation to the second, which ends the performance. This second treatment of the trial looks more specifically into the Iraqi situation. On a screen on the stage background, images shot in Iraq in 2018 during the last workshop are projected. This is the first time in the show that the audience is confronted with filmed images that reveal the creative process. Pauthe first proposed documentary images shot in Baghdad in 2018, but the Iraqi team refused. She explained:

> We asked ourselves a lot about the end of the show. I had proposed to show images shot in Baghdad in the spring of 2018 during the legislative elections ... But the Iraqi team refused. Either we showed footage of elections in all the democracies of the world, to talk about the state of our democracies today (including Trump's in the United States, Bolsonaro's in Brazil, those in Eastern Europe), or we showed nothing. So we chose to delete these plans.
>
> Donizeau and Dumont-Lewi 2019: 99[10]

So, the last images of the performance show an assembly of Iraqi teenagers debating the responsibilities of the different entities that are fighting for power in the country. They are questioning who should be regarded as culpable for the

Iraqi tragedy: Saddam Hussein? The Americans? The militias? Sectarianism? The question remains unsolved and the show ends without giving any definitive answer.

The two treatments of the trial are in fact complementary and should be read in conjunction with one another. Their aim is to question the democratic principle and its flaws. The first treatment through fiction engages the idea that democracy always excludes a part of the population (and here in particular women) and is done to their detriment, and that its imposition results from an arbitrary and authoritarian decision:

> Athena, supported by Apollo, by instituting the first human democratic tribunal which will acquit Orestes of the murder of his mother, is in fact nothing more than a democratic, violent, cynical coup d'état led by the new masters of Olympus, against the Erinyes, guarantors of an ancient order, of a justice that makes blood pay with blood.
>
> Han 2018[11]

This first observation is confronted with the documentary treatment through the projection of images shot in Baghdad, and allows us to establish a problematic link between this democratic order, designated as fallible and incomplete, and its implementation in Iraq by foreign authorities, as Haythem Abderrazak explains:

> The problems of democracy that we address in our work do not come from within Iraq, but come to us from outside, from abroad. The extremists were brought to Iraq by outside forces. The foreign powers, the British and the French in particular, imposed a political system and leaders on us not in the interest of Iraq but in their interest. They are the ones who brought the political problems to Iraq.
>
> Ibid.

As the democracy imposed in Iraq by the West gave power to Saddam Hussein, there is a doubt here about the final decision imposed by Athena, which breaks the precarious but ancestral law of retaliation. Therefore, the end of the tragedy does not mark a return to order, or if it does, it is only a temporary order. The return to a balanced society through the establishment of justice and democracy is thus denounced here as ambiguous and potentially foreshadowing another cycle of conflict. The end of the trilogy echoes its beginning: the order imposed from above, from outside, by powers that understand nothing of human social organization (the Olympean gods in the tragedy, or Western imperialism in the real Iraq) could give rise to a new autocrat supported by external powers and reignite the cycle of violence.

Thus, as they question the political and institutional deadlock set up by the Europeans and their imperialist aim in Iraq, the directors also question the relevance of the European cultural material transferred to an Iraqi context. The *Oresteia* is not a parable that works entirely. The analogy is thus made between political and cultural domination in a constant to and fro that leaves the field of interpretations open. The show brings questions of domination linked to a postcolonial world structure. The meeting of tragedy and Iraq is never arbitrary or anecdotal, but constantly challenged, even in the dramaturgy. This way, the performance leaves space for a part of *uncommon*, of *unshared* cultural elements. This space allows the unpredictable to emerge, and thus it becomes possible to make theatre out of it.

The two projects can be described as belonging to the intercultural performance. Both projects intend to provoke an encounter between a Greek material that is a priori considered to belong to European culture on the one hand and a non-European context on the other. But the results were different, in particular as regards the treatment of tragedy as a culturally based material.

In Milo Rau's case, the director and his team seem to have realized their inability, as Europeans, to seize all the Iraqi stakes. The use of tragedy did not help; neither did the documentary images. But this admitted position gave its specificity to the project: it is not an *Oresteia* about Iraq, but about the relationship Europe and Europeans have with Iraq. The gap between the fable and the Iraqi situation led to the performance, in which the creation and research project appears as important as its result. Thus, the tragic material is not displaced; it remains on the European side, as a tool to observe a foreign context.

In Célie Pauthe's case, she tried to view the *Oresteia* as an unfamiliar foreign text; as unfamiliar as the Iraqi situation was to her at the start of the creative process. Moreover, the reality of a bicultural team imposed choices and compromises that have been kept as dramaturgical material. Working with the Iraqi director Haythem Abderrazak does not appear as a means to reduce the cultural and political gaps between the different interpretations of the text, but to reveal and even assert them.

These two analyses show that the notion of intercultural theatre has evolved significantly since its emergence in the 1970s. In 1990, Erika Fischer-Lichte warned:

These two analyses show that the notion of intercultural theatre has evolved significantly since its emergence in the 1970s. In 1990, Erika Fischer-Lichte warned: The starting point of intercultural staging is thus not primarily an interest in the foreign – the foreign theatre or the foreign culture from which it is taken – but rather a situation completely specific within its own culture or a completely specific problem having its origin within its own culture.

Fischer-Lichte 1990: 283

She was pointing out a kind of hypocrisy of intercultural theatre, especially in a postcolonial context. As for Patrice Pavis, a few years later, he highlighted with a touch of cynicism the link between intercultural performance and the depoliticization of exchanges on a global scale in favour of a liberal logic: 'the world is in the process of moving from its nationalistic phase to its cultural phase, and it's preferable to distinguish cultural areas rather than nations' (Pavis 1996: 6). Interculturality would thus be 'naturally involved with the internationalization of exchange, and tied to the concept of a cultural pilgrimage, while still recognizing the hard laws of marketing' (ibid.). The two experiences studied in this chapter seem to avoid these problems. The directors do not neglect the cultural gaps. Thus, intercultural performance becomes the crucible for new questions: it is also not about questioning/discovering a foreign culture in order to enrich our own, but in order to rethink the position of Europe, its culture and its imperialism on the international stage. Interculturality does not neutralize the conflict, but displaces it.

Notes

1   Personal translation from French.
2   Her preceding show, *Ithaque* (Ithaca), adapted from Homer's *Odyssey* as well, was created in 2018 in the Odeon Theatre in Paris, France.
3   We think, for instance, about the speech that the French Ministry of Foreign Affairs Dominique de Villepin made at the United Nations on 14 February 2003 to convince his counterparts to abandon military intervention in Iraq against Saddam Hussein: 'Such intervention could have incalculable consequences for the stability of this scarred and fragile region. It would compound the sense of injustice, increase tension and risk paving the way to other conflicts ... we must assess the impact that disputed military action would have on this level. Would such intervention today not be liable to exacerbate divisions between societies, cultures, peoples; divisions that nurture terrorism?' Available online: www.nytimes.com/2003/02/14/ international/middleeast/statement-by-france-to-security-council.html.
4   Personal translation from French.

5 For more detail regarding Abderrazak's career in Iraq and abroad, see Chapter 7 of this book.
6 Personal translation from French.
7 During the same 2018–19 season at the CDN de Besançon, as part of the 'Focus Irak', he presents *The East Disease* (*Maraḍ al-šarq*), based on Heiner Müller's *Hamlet/Machine*.
8 Personal translation from French.
9 This translation in English is Anna Swanwick's translation (London: George Bells and Sons, 1886). In the show, this tirade is in classical Arabic, in a translation by Yousef Seddik from the French version by Florence Dupont (L'Arche, 2013).
10 Personal translation from French.
11 Personal translation from French.

References

Chakrabarty, D. (2000 [2007]), *Provincializing Europe*, Princeton: Princeton University Press.

Donizeau, P. and L. Dumont-Lewi (2019), 'Une *Orestie* franco-irakienne: Autour du projet *Looking for Oresteia*. Entretien avec Haythem Abderrazak, Yagoutha Belgacem et Célie Pauthe', *Théâtre/Public*, 233: 96–9.

Fischer-Lichte E. (1990), 'Staging the Foreign as Cultural Transformation', in E. Fischer-Lichte, J. Riley and M. Gissenwehrer (eds), *The Dramatic Touch of Difference: Theatre, Own and Foreign*, Tübingen: Narr.

Han, J.-P. (2018), 'Décentrer, bousculer, casser, réinventer: Entretien avec Célie Pauthe et Haythem Abderrazak', *Looking for Oresteia* programme for the CDN of Besançon.

Le Tanneur, H. (2019a), 'Au festival d'Avignon, périples et périls des épopées antiques', *La Vie*, 3 July. Available online: www.lavie.fr/ma-vie/culture/au-festival-davignon-periples-et-perils-des-epopees-antiques-4810.php (accessed 30 October 2022).

Le Tanneur, H. (2019b), 'La naissance de la civilisation à travers le pardon'. Interview with Milo Rau. *Orestes in Mosul* programme for the CDN Nanterre-Amandiers.

Pavis, P. (1996), *The Intercultural Performance Reader*, London, New York: Routledge.

Rau, M. (2018a), *The Ghent Manifesto*. Available online: www.ntgent.be/nl/manifest.

Rau, M. (2018b), *Globaler Realismus/Global Realism*, Berlin: Verbrecher Verlag.

Said, E. (1978 [1995]), *Orientalism: Western Conceptions of the Orient*, London: Penguin Books.

Seddik, Y. (2018), Conference held in Besançon, 20 September 2018.

11

Tingitanos by Zoubeir Ben Bouchta

A Moroccan Tragedy

Omar Fertat

Hercules is a familiar figure to the people of Tangier, you can ask anyone, everyone here knows Hercules.

Fertat and Ben Bouchta 2021

Neither Athens nor then Rome is the centre of Hellenism and culture . . . Syrians, Lebanese, Maghrebians can claim Greek and Roman heritage just as much, if not more, than the French, Italians or even Greeks of today.

Fertat and Dupont 2022

The Roman past of Morocco: a forgotten heritage

During the Mauretanian period, from the seventh century BC, Morocco experienced the settlement of Phoenician populations on the Mediterranean and Atlantic coasts. Subsequently, while the context was marked by the confrontation between Rome and Carthage, a local kingdom was born: the Moorish kingdom, which lasted from the third century BC to 33 BC. Rome ended up gradually imposing itself on the whole Mediterranean and Morocco, like other regions, did not escape its domination. It was one of the last provinces to join the sphere of the Empire, which it integrated in AD 40 and became the province of Mauretania. Roman domination did not end until the beginning of the fifth century.

After its annexation, under the reign of the Roman emperor Claudius (AD 41–54), Mauretania was subdivided into two entities, Caesarian Mauretania and Tingitanean Mauretania, with Iol-Caesarea (Cherchel) and Tingi as capitals. Tingitanean Mauritania corresponds to the north-western part of present-day

Morocco. It had the shape of a triangle whose vertex coincides with the Strait of Gibraltar and whose base is constituted by the line connecting the cities of Rabat and Meknes. Remains such as Volubulis, Sala or Lixus, which had the status of *municipe* (cities under Roman law, but whose inhabitants were not all Roman citizens), still testify to a past marked by this Latin civilization. These ancient Moorish cities, some of which date back to the Phoenician period, were endowed with public monuments that show that the Tingitano cities, like the other cities of the Empire, were aligned with the model of the city of Rome. These monuments include several theatres and amphitheatres that can be found at the site of Lixus (near Larache). Moreover, according to some historians, a large part of the population of Mauritania, under Roman domination, enjoyed games and spectacles and assiduously frequented these places:

> The monuments of the games are indeed markers of the assimilation of the populations to the Roman culture. Initially, it was the foreign elite who brought their cultural baggage, like Juba II who revived the games of his Roman childhood within the walls of his Mauretanian capital. This way of life was quickly taken over by the local elite and then by the urban populations. The Mauretans were as enthusiastic as the rest of the Empire about ludi, munera and venationes. The Roman government could not but encourage this movement, as the ceremonies made it possible to religiously bind the people to their leader and to calm the spirits tempted by revolt by giving them bread and games. Theatres were built later, and efforts were made to continue to maintain or transform them to suit public taste. Testimonies such as that of St Augustine show that theatres were always full in Africa at the beginning of the fourth century AD.
>
> Pinchot 2014

More than that, Mauretania gave birth to several local dramatists who marked their time. Among these we can mention Terence Publius Terentines (195–159 BC), writer and poet who left six comedies; Apuleius, (AD 125–70), writer and philosopher, author of *The Golden Anne*; Minucius Felix (second century) poet and man of letters; Martianus Capella, (fifth century), author of the oldest 'encyclopaedia' of antiquity; and even King Juba II (50 BC–AD 23) who, being very interested in theatre, wrote an important work on the history of the theatre in seventeen books.

However, the various sultans who succeeded each other on the Moroccan throne, whether they were Idrissid (789–974), Almoravid (1073–1147), Almohad (1147–1269), Marinid, Wattasid (1269–1554), Saadian (1554–1659) or Alouite (1659 to the present day), paid no attention to the Roman remains that were to be found in the lands they were ruling. On the contrary, they had no problem with the local population using these memorial sites as quarries to extract stones for building their houses. In fact, the first archaeological excavations of Roman sites in Morocco were carried out by French archaeologists during the Protectorate period. The historian of Archeology Salima Naji (2011) thus explains:

> Archaeology in Morocco was established under the French protectorate (1912–1956) through the first excavations of monuments from Roman antiquity, uncovered by the handful of archaeologists who first formed around the figure of Marshal Lyautey (1854–1934), in the wake of Jérôme Carcopino (1881–1970) and the École française de Rome. These men, who came from the Public Education or Saint-Cyr schools, felt invested with the mission of saving a little-known culture from oblivion, threatened by the spread of 'progress'. Louis Châtelain (1883–1950), the first director of Antiquities in Morocco, set up his department in 1918 on a major Roman site, Volubilis, before transferring it ten years later to Rabat, the capital, in the archaeological museum that would bear his name.

In spite of the work of rehabilitation of these archaeological sites by the French, we have the impression that the Roman past of Morocco, still today, does not arouse the interest of either Moroccans or their intellectual elites. Rarely are Latin-speaking Maghrebi authors quoted or inspired by the stories or personalities who lived in Maghrebi lands during this period. It is as if there is some kind of break with this past and that the history of Morocco only begins with the arrival of Islam. It must be said that the promoters of this new monotheistic religion, whose armies began to flock to the Maghreb as early as the seventh century, did not encourage the new converts, who moreover put up fierce resistance to them, to take an interest in a pagan past that was partly dominated by yesterday's enemies (i.e. the Byzantines).

If we look at Moroccan theatre, for example, except for a few plays by certain playwrights such as Mohamed Kaghat, who directed Sophocles' *Electra* (1977) or *Prometheus 91* (1991), Graeco-Roman mythology is completely absent from Moroccan dramatic writings and, I would even say, from the Moroccan popular imagination in general.

From Graeco-Roman hero to local hero: Heracles in Tangier

However, there is one exception, that of Hercules or Heracles. This famous hero of Graeco-Roman mythology is an omnipresent figure in Tangier, where many places are linked to the memory of this Greek hero. The most famous of these sites is the Cave of Hercules, located south of Cape Spartel on the Atlantic coast, which has become one of the highlights of local tourism.

If Hercules is also present in this part of the world, it is because, according to Greek mythology, he passed through to accomplish one of the twelve tasks ordered by Eurysthe, which consisted in stealing the golden apples from the Hesperides' gardens, once offered by Zeus to Hera, but stolen by the Hesperides, daughters of the Titan Atlas. The Hesperides were nymphs from the West who watched over the wonderful garden full of golden fruits with the help of Ladon, the hundred-headed dragon. Hercules managed to take the coveted fruit by sending Atlas to fight Ladon instead. However, before completing the eleventh of his labours, Hercules was forced to fight the giant Antaeus, who ruled over the domain where the Hesperides gardens were located. It was a tough battle. Each time Hercules defeated him, Antaeus drew his strength from contact with the earth, in other words, Gaia, his mother. In the end, the Greek hero had to lift Antaeus off the ground while choking him. During this titanic battle, one stroke of Hercules' sword opened the Straits of Gibraltar. Then the son of Zeus and Alcmene raised two columns on either side of the strait. Another version of the legend attributes the opening of the strait to a shoulder blow from Heracles. The columns of Hercules were to symbolize the limits of the known world for many centuries. It should be noted that during the Phoenician period (the Phoenicians established themselves in the Maghreb at the beginning of the eleventh century BC), the god Melqart was celebrated, and a temple was erected at Lixus, which, through the *Interpretatio graeca*, was assimilated by the Graeco-Romans to Heracles.

The Garden of the Hesperides, in which Hera planted her apple tree with golden fruits, is said to be located, according to some versions, on the slopes of Mount Atlas, where the horses of the Sun's chariot end their journey when they set down west of the Atlantic Ocean. According to Latin sources, the gardens of the Hesperides are located off the ocean shores of Spain or Morocco, near the city of Lixus between Tangier and Larache in Morocco. In addition to the fact that this mythological episode takes place on Maghrebian soil, it also involves local heroes from Berber legends: Antaeus and Tingi.

According to Plato, the region of Tangier, as well as the rest of 'Libya',[1] was the domain of the giant Antaeus[2] who was the son of Poseidon and the Earth (Gaia). According to some legends, Antaeus was a Mauretanian king. The latter, a perfect illustration of the barbarian in the eyes of the Greeks, was, according to some historians, only integrated into the story of Hercules at a later date. According to G. Camps (1988):

Mythographers usually locate Antaeus in Libya, but like the Garden of the Hesperides, the Triton and Atlantis, his place of residence was gradually pushed westwards to settle in the region of Tingi (Tangiers) ... Tangier is the safest residence, the one where the legend is most firmly anchored. This location in a region particularly charged with sacredness, where the Ocean, the Mediterranean, Europe and Africa converge, is particularly appropriate for this giant son of the Earth and the master of the waters; the intervention of Hercules can be explained by the importance of the cult of Melqart in the region, particularly in Gades and in Tingi itself. Indeed, it is known that the Phoenician Melqart was generally assimilated to Heracles.

According to other historical sources,[3] the city of Lixus had a temple dedicated to Antaeus.

As for the goddess Tinga or Tingé, she is the wife of Antaeus and the mother of Sophax:

According to Plutarch (Sertorius, IX) 'The Tingites tell us that after the death of Antaeus, his wife Tinga had an affair with Hercules and that Sophax, their son, reigned over the country and founded a city to which he gave the name of his mother.'

Ibid.

According to another version, Antaeus himself founded a city to which he gave the name of his wife. This is how the city of Tangier or Tingi was born, which gave its name to the north-western part of present-day Morocco, which for centuries was known as Tingitanean Mauritania:

This foundation myth refers to a context linked to the Phoenician expansion in Morocco and it is not known whether King Sophax, whose name recalls that of the Masaesyl king Syfax, was a historical figure forgotten by literary sources and whether he had any connection with the Moorish dynasty.

Kably 2011

It is this tale of origins or founding myth, in which local Berber legend and Greek-Roman mythology intersect, that will serve as the fable for the play *Tingitanos* by Zoueir ben Bouchta.

When local Berber legend and Graeco-Roman mythology intersect: the play of *Tingitanos*

Zoubeir Ben Bouchta (born in 1964 in Tangier) is a Moroccan playwright in Arabic (classical and dialect), scriptwriter and director of the 'Bab Bhar Ciné Masrah'

company. He wrote a dozen plays, some of which have won awards: his first play
The Octopus (_al-'uḫtubūṭ_) won the 1992 Union of Moroccan Writers' Prize for
Young Authors, _Lalla J'mila_ (_Lāla Ǧmīla_)[4] and White Feet (_Aqdām bayḍāʾ_) won in
2004 and 2008 respectively the prize for the best dramatic text at the Moroccan
National Theatre Festival. Some of his plays, such as _White Feet_,[5] _The Man of the
Naked Bread_ (_RaǦul al-ḫubz al-ḥāfī_),[6] _The Red Light_ (_al-nār al-ḥamra_)[7] or
Shakespeare's Lane (_Zenkat Sheksbīr_)[8] have been translated into English and
French. Zoubeir Ben Bouchta's works differ from other Moroccan playwrights
because of its total anchorage in the author's native city, Tangier, whose history,
spaces, figures and legends constitute an inexhaustible source of inspiration from
which he weaves the fables of his plays. For many years he has patiently sculpted an
original work in which he celebrates this mythical city. Nevertheless, his work
Tingitanos (2015) marks, to use Hasan Mniaï's expression, a turning point in his
dramatic writing 'because its style differs from that of the previous texts and
because it deals with a theme that is part of the mythology' (Ben Bouchta 2015).[9]

Indeed, as we have already noted above, it is very rare for Moroccan
playwrights to be inspired by Greek myths and even rarer that they update a
myth whose events take place on their own soil.

To build his fable, Zoubeir Ben Bouchta has updated the myth of Hercules by
adapting it to his own vision and by passing it through the filter of his own
sensitivity. He chose to make the confrontation of the Greek hero with Antaeus
the main event of his play – when it is only a secondary episode in the story of
the Labours of Hercules.

Tingintanos is the story of Hercules who invades the kingdom of Antaeus and
imprisons him for ten years in a cave, so that he can make a weapon that will
allow him to kill Ladon, the hundred-headed dragon. For only Antaeus, gifted
with an extraordinary intelligence, could kill Ladon. By confining him, Hercules
separates Antaeus from his wife Tangis, whom he also reduces to slavery, by
making her the servant of Dejanira, his wife. Attracted by her, he rapes her. When
Dejanira learns that Tangis has become pregnant by Hercules, she becomes mad
with rage. A rage that Antaeus, dying after being mortally wounded by Hercules,
takes advantage of to convince her to give her husband his favourite costume,
the skin of the Nemean lion soaked in his poisoned blood, for the celebration of
his marriage to Tangis, which he plans to celebrate with great pomp. He makes
her believe that his blood will act as a love potion that will return her to her
husband. Dejanira carries out the plan and causes Hercules' death.

To build his fable, the Moroccan playwright does not hesitate to make changes
and modifications to the story of the Labours of Hercules. In the first scene, 'his

tresses are a story', the story told by Dejanira, who tells Tangis about her husband's exploits, the tenth task during which Hercules defeats the three-bodied giant Geryon and steals his herd of oxen, is replaced by 'the eternal story of Hercules who built the columns on the frontiers of Kadesh and Achaqar' (Ben Bouchta 2015: 25). Thus Zoubeir Ben Bouchta transforms a secondary episode, that of Hercules' construction of the two columns on both sides of the European and African continents, into a major fact that becomes the tenth work of Hercules. Consequently, the tenth labour of the original story, that of the theft of the herd of oxen Geryon, becomes, in the Moroccan play, the twelfth and last of the labours. Whereas the episode of the Descent into Hell and the capture of the Cerberus, which is the twelfth of the labours in the original story, has simply been deleted. Thus, in order to accomplish his last mission, the theft of Geryon's oxen, Hercules needs the help of Antaeus, who must make him a powerful weapon capable of striking down Geryon, referred to in the text as *al-Mārid* (the genius) and the Cerberus, referred to in the text as 'the two-headed dog guarding the bulls' (ibid.), who becomes the guardian of the herd of oxen.

Another episode of the Herculean myth, this time towards the end of the play, has been modified. It concerns his death. Indeed, after being mortally wounded by Hercules, Antaeus succeeds in deceiving Dejanira by convincing her to give Hercules, on the day of his marriage to Tangis, the skin of the Nemean lion, soaked in his own poisoned blood, making her believe that his blood will work as a filter of love that will make Hercules fall in love with her again. Thus Antaeus' post-mortem revenge is accomplished and he succeeds in killing his enemy. In this sequence the Moroccan playwright adapts the story of the death of Hercules by making two changes: he replaces Iolè, daughter of Eurytos, king of Oecaly, whom the latter has asked to marry him, with Tangis, and Nessus the centaur, who, mortally wounded by Hercules, persuades Dejanira that the blood flowing from his wounds will be a powerful charm to keep her husband's love, with Antaeus.

Thanks to these changes, Zoubeir Ben Bouchta succeeds in incorporating the two Maghrebi figures into his fable and into the Graeco-Roman mythological narrative to make them heroes on a par with the Greek characters. This desire to anchor the myth in a local *terroir* is shown by the use of other intertexts from the oral tradition of Tangiers. Among these, the Moroccan playwright has chosen the one that would explain the origin of the name of Tangier. According to a local legend, the name of the city comes from the Arabic expression '*al-ṭīn ǧā*', which can be translated as 'the clay has arrived', which is the phrase spoken by Noah when, after weeks of sailing on board his Ark following the flood, he saw a dove with a bit of clay in its beak and realized that he was not far from land and therefore from deliverance. Other local toponymic references, such as the hill of Charf, are also used. According to this local legend, this is the place where Antaeus was buried.

Inverting the points of view: the Greek/western barbarian and the Berber/Arab hero

The aim of these changes and adaptations by the Moroccan playwright, which give rise to a fable composed of Graeco-Roman mythological stories and local legends, is, in our opinion, to highlight and perhaps rehabilitate Antaeus and Tangis, local heroes. These local deities become, under the pen of Zoubeir Ben Bouchta, living beings who express human feelings that make them almost contemporary.

Indeed, *Tingitanos* is the story of love, sacrifice and injustice experienced by the couple at the centre of the play. One of the strongest and most beautiful scenes is that between Antaeus and Tangis. To underline the power of their love, the lines exchanged between the two desperate lovers, who know that they cannot escape their fate, take the form of very beautiful and lyrical verses, taken from the poem *Two Souls in One Body* by the Arab mystic Mansur al-Hallag (dead in 922).

In *Tingitanos*, Zoubeir Ben Bouchta deconstructs the Graeco-Roman myth of Hercules by reversing the roles usually assigned to the Greek hero and the Libyan giant. Thus, Hercules is no longer the Greek hero famous for his courage, strength, compassion and generous character, as great in his benefits as in his excesses, the one who is often invoked under the name of Alexikakos, the one who deflects evils, embodies the being who acts for the good of mankind. He becomes the violent oppressor who does not hesitate to invade the country of others by enslaving its inhabitants and desecrating their most sacred places. Tangis does not hesitate to describe him in one of his lines as 'the myth of a giant who has desecrated a civilisation' (Ben Bouchta 2015: 18). As for Antaeus, he is originally the bloodthirsty giant who does not hesitate to attack travellers in order to build a hotel with their skulls to the glory of his father Poseidon, which is supposed to convey the image of the barbarian that the Greeks had of the uncivilized inhabitants of this extreme West. In the Moroccan play, however, he takes on the features of a cerebral man, a master of the sciences, 'a prisoner of his science, of his genius' (Ben Bouchta 2015: 45). This 'man' is too proud, and ready to sacrifice himself for his honour. He also appears as a delicate being who loves his wife passionately, a victim of the delusions of grandeur and the violent instinct of a Hercules, who consequently becomes the very representation of barbarism. Thus Hercules, the symbol of the civilized world, becomes the barbarian and Antaeus, the representative of the bloodthirsty and savage Libyan people, becomes the civilized being.

If the events of *Tingitanos* are set in a distant legendary and mythological past, they are also of burning relevance today. For it is an allegory of the Gulf War (2003), which saw an American giant invade an Arab land with no other justification than economic and geopolitical interest, whose motivation was a thirst for domination. Indeed, *Tingitanos was* written by the author in reaction to the American invasion of Iraq. He told us in an interview that it was when he saw Gorges Bush on TV one day saying: 'We liberated Iraq from the Iraqis' that he got the idea for the play (Fertat and Ben Bouchta 2021).

Tingitanos is a tragic story that reflects the current situation of the Arab peoples, oppressed by various modern avatars of Hercules: dictatorships, multinationals, unbridled capitalism, merchants of war . . . Some see in this play a denunciation of the condition of the Arab peoples and their stubbornness in stagnating and not moving forward. Abdelmajid Elhouasse, who directed *Tingitanos* in 2015, writes in this regard:

> The text is unstable and it is in this instability that its importance lies. It asks you more questions than it answers. You are at the same time inside and outside a myth. While inscribing his city Tangier in the myth of Tingitanos, Zoubeir opens the doors of the Sufi universe to you through the story of the banished love that links Antaeus, exhausted and imprisoned, to Tangis, enslaved. A form of tragedy that does not bet on catharsis more than it opens the reader's own wounds. And as we go through the text we come closer to the now. Outside the myth, the present appears in broad daylight: Antaeus, the imprisoned god, the inventor in love, instead of freeing his kingdom from the grip of Hercules and taking back his wife, remains a prisoner of his narcissism and the illusion of his genius, like any Arab power that believes itself to be all-powerful when it is in the depths of distress.
>
> Ben Bouchta 2015: 106

As part of an overall work that is a celebration of Tangier, this play updates the myth of its foundation. 'It is from the bowels of the myth that Tangier has emerged' (Ben Bouchta 2015: 5), as Tangis says in the play.

By updating the myth of Hercules while appropriating it and anchoring it in local culture, Zoubeir Ben Bouchta demonstrates that it is possible to revive a part of Moroccan history, its Graeco-Roman past, and make it a subject suitable for dramatic expression. As Florence Dupont points out, the Graeco-Roman heritage is not exclusive to Westerners:

> There is a persistent prejudice that Greece and Rome are the cradle of Western civilisation, the roots of the West or the origins of European culture. However, if we look closely, the Greek world extended, for the most part, over a non-European territory: Pergamon, Antioch and Alexandria were, after Athens, the main intellectual centres. The Roman Empire did not only unite Italians, Iberians, Gauls and Bretons: the provinces of Syria, Arabia, Egypt and Africa were among the most prosperous and dynamic. Can we seriously consider the Greeks and Romans as Westerners or Europeans? Did the Greco-Roman heritage stop at the borders of the Western world? This is the first question that can be asked of this discourse on origins. From a more contemporary point of view, references to the Greeks and Romans have spread to all continents, in scholarly and popular culture. Decentralising ancient studies by de-Europeanising them thus implies listening to the way in which we speak of this antiquity today from Africa, India, China or Japan. What images do they have of the Greeks and Romans and what uses do they make of them? Have these others rejected this heritage as a legacy of the colonial past? Or how have they adapted and transformed it in their own culture?
>
> Fertat and Dupont 2022

Notes

1 Ancient Libya is a name by which the ancient Greeks referred to an ancient region west of the Nile River corresponding to northwest Africa (present-day Maghreb).

2 Mythographers usually locate Antaeus in Libya, but like the Garden of the Hesperides, the Triton and Atlantis, his place of residence was gradually pushed westwards to the region of Tingi (Tangier).

3 See Kably (2011).

4 The play has been translated into French by Saïd Benjelloun: *Lalla J'mila: Le rocher des filles* (2017), Toulouse: Presses universitaires du Midi. It has also been translated into English: Mustapha Hilal al Soussi, *Lalla Jmila*, Publications de l'Institut des études des arts du spectacle, Tanger, 2007.

5 *Pieds blancs*, trans. S. Benjelloun, Toulouse: Presses universitaires du Midi, 2021. This play was also translated by Zohra Makach and published in the Publications de l'université Ibn Zohr, Agadir (Morocco) in 2013.

6 *L'homme du pain nu,* trans. S. Hammoud, series 'Horizons/Créations', Pessac: Presses universitaires de Bordeaux, 2019.

7 *The Red Fire,* trans. M. H. al Soussi, Tangiers: Publications of the Institute of Performing Arts Studies, 2008.
8 *Shakespeare's Lane*, trans. R. al Khaloufi, Tangiers: Publications of the Institute of Performing Arts Studies, 2008.
9 My translation.

References

Ben Bouchta, Z. (2015), 'Introduction', in *Tingitanos*, Tangier: The International Institute of Entertainment Studies.

Camps, G. (1988), 'Antaeus', *Encyclopédie berbère*. Available online: http://journals. openedition.org/encyclopedieberbere/2519.

Fertat, O. and F. Dupont (2022), '"Decentring, De-Europeanising, De-ethnicising and De-racialising Greco-Roman history": Interview with Florence Dupont', *Expressions Maghrébines*, 21(1): 193–220.

Fertat, O. and Z. Ben Bouchta (2021), Interview with Zoubeir Ben Bouchta.

Kably, M. (2011), *Histoire du Maroc: réactualisation et synthèse,* Rabat: Edition of the Royal Institute for Research on the History of Morocco.

Naji, S. (2011), 'Archéologie coloniale au Maroc, 1920–1956: civiliser l'archaïque', *Les nouvelles de l'archéologie,* 126: 23–8.

Pinchot, A. (2011), 'Theatres and amphitheatres: tools of Romanisation in Mauretania?', *Études de lettres,* 1–2, available online: http://journals.openedition.org/edl/113.

Afterword

Writing this book was challenging. The deep thematic complexity of Greek myth as interpreted by Middle Eastern theatrical actors in different times and states allows us to engage with a myriad of concerns. We had to develop a methodology that was appropriate for this study, deal with the issue of selecting our corpus and organizing it according to our purpose and constraints, support alternative readings and approaches, and, last but not least, be cautious of Orientalist and neo-Orientalist approaches.

First, we would like to stress that understanding the methodology and even the results of research in the MENA region must be adapted to the conditions of research in this region. Access to the field is still not straightforward. This complexity arises differently for the foreign and/or Western researcher, and the indigenous researcher. Each is subject to various difficulties in gaining access to data and the field. We can mention a few factors: the importance of oral culture in relation to the written word, the lack of a complete archiving system, the absence of public access to certain data, the difference between the organization of events and shows in the West, the delayed relationship with time and the notion of programming, and the question of freedom of speech in the transmission of information.

It is because of these and other factors that it is sometimes difficult to fully grasp the issues at stake in shows and their organization for a reader who is not very familiar with the socio-political, economic and artistic context of MENA. This is not a problem in itself, but it does need to be taken into consideration in order to better understand certain works in this region.

Moreover, as this is the first volume on the Greek myth and the Middle East, we had to select a first corpus to study and could not include all the cases of Middle Eastern Greek myth that are deserving of attention. For instance, as we mentioned in our Introduction, it would be interesting to study the Greek classics in Egypt, those produced in the late 1990s and early 2000s, as well as Munira Karawan's translations of Greek myths, Abo El Seoud's *Antīgūn fī*

Ramallāh, Antīgūn fī Bayrūt (*Antigone in Ramallah, Antigone in Beirut*) and the more recent *Antigone's Law* (Dina Amin, 2022). A focus on the character of Antigone – especially related to the Arab Revolutions – would also include *Tsunami* (2013), by the acclaimed couple al-Jaʿāybī-Bakkār and *The Last Day of Spring* (*Akhir yawm fī 'l-rabīʿ*, 2018) directed by the Palestinian Fidaa Zidan. Scholars could also focus on *The Trojan War* (*Ḥarb ṭarwāda*) by the Lebanese playwright Roger Assaf and its relevance to the present.

For the same reason, as this is a primary study, we have decided to adopt a linear approach, which gives an idea of the temporal trajectories of Greek myth in Middle East, with a focus on three main topics underlying three main steps of this evolution – adaptations and translations in colonial contexts, the Greek myth to tackle political issues and the question as to whether it can be considered a common heritage. However, this book can also be read in a transversal way. For instance, the reader will find two contributions with a gender approach, namely a discussion about contemporary Lebanese and Iranian Medeas and a study about contemporary Iranian Antigones (Chapters 5 and 6), Chapter 4 suggests a gender approach to the Arab Iphigenias and Medeas defying the state of emergency imposed on them. A transversal reading of the characters of Medea, Antigone and Iphigenia through the different contributions allows for more considerations on the power of the Greek heroines in the contemporary MENA interpretations. We have just touched upon the matter to recognize that Greek myth and the Middle East in the lens of gender studies deserves further study and attention.

We can also refer to other alternatives to discover other aspects of our research in MENA. In 2021, following the project *The poetry of taʾzieh*[1] Y. Khajehi, together with N. Shahrokhi, staged Sophocles' *Antigone* using the aesthetic of taʾzieh (traditional Shiite religious theatre).[2] This research-creation process led to a public presentation in the amphitheatre of the archaeological site of the ancient city of Dion in Greece at the north-east foot of Mount Olympus. The performance of *Antigone*/taʾzieh gave the artists and researchers the opportunity to explore new avenues of research into the circulation of theatrical traditions between the ancient worlds and between East and West such as the relationship with the audience and the role of song and choir. This project is still in progress.

Finally, we would like to address a more delicate question, that of the Orientalist remnants that always threaten a work like ours, in the same way as the reception of the artists of our corpus in Western contexts.

Regarding the title of the present volume, we preferred the formula 'Greek Tragedy *and* the Middle East' rather than 'Greek Tragedy *in* the Middle East', which was a possible choice. By choosing the conjunction 'and', we wanted to show that our study was not that of tragedy imported as exogenous material to the Middle East, but that our approach was intended to be dynamic. As the reader will have understood, our aim is to study the adaptation of Greek material – as shaped by the West – in the MENA countries, as well as the traces of the founding myths at the very heart of these countries. We have also examined the treatment of Greek tragedies in the European area after their passage to the East. Thus, we have also considered Greek tragedy as a means of bridging East and West. Apart from the case of Milo Rau (Chapter 10), a European director who stages Iraq through the prism of tragedy, many examples in the corpus also show MENA artists invited to stage Greek tragedies in Europe (in collaboration, or with European funding), or whose stagings of tragedy are programmed especially in Europe. Finally, many Arab, Iranian and Turkish artists living in Europe today are in a diaspora situation, and their integration into new cultural markets must always be questioned, since there is a risk of neo-Orientalism, understood as 'consisting largely of the representation of indigenous populations in an exotic discourse by an indigenous artist supported and financed from abroad' (Mouawad, 2012).[3]

While editing this book we had the great pleasure of discovering the richness of the matter through the words of our precious writers, and we also had to confront some complexities. A controversy about the use of 'nice wordings' that were actually giving a generalizing judgement on the Islamic religion using what we felt to be offensive words, brought us to reconsider the presence of neo-Orientalism in the Middle Eastern Studies. The menace of slipping in the traps of Orientalism, especially for such a topic that interweaves East and West in periods of colonialism, always lurks around the corner. Moreover, the sources some of us examined were often Orientalists, so we had to maintain a distance from them. Besides that, the fact of expressing ourselves in a language that is not our mother tongue (for ten contributors out of eleven) puts us at a higher risk of not really understanding the implications of the words used. Patient dialogue solved clashes. Indeed, we were inflexible on that front. We hope that future research will take the same perspective and investigate the materials that exist, particularly in MENA university libraries, but are difficult to find due to a shortage of access and classification.[4]

Notes

1   See https://phase2.hermapartprojects.org/the-poetry-of-tazieh Project financed by HerMap, Bozar Brussels, the Goethe Institute and European Union funds.

2   See also TDR (1988–), Vol. 49, No. 4, Special Issue on Taʿziyeh (Winter, 2005).

3 Mouawad, W. (2012), 'Petite réflexion sur le néo-orientalisme: Le cas Nadine Labaki', *Les Cahiers de l'Orient*, Vol. 106, No. 2, 99–104. Personal translation from French.

4 Archiving initiatives are on the increase. As an example, we can point to Arturo Monaco's Marie Skłodowska-Curie Postdoctoral project on 'Digital Mythology and Arabic Literature: A Digital Archive to Study the Dynamics of the Reception of Greek Myths in Modern Arabic Literature'.

Index of Subjects

Index of Names

Index of Places

www.ingramcontent.com/pod-product-compliance
Lightning Source LLC
Chambersburg PA
CBHW070528100726
47907CB00004B/1032